representing black britain

Culture, Representation and Identities is dedicated to a particular understanding of 'cultural studies' as an inherently interdisciplinary project critically concerned with the analysis of meaning. The series focuses attention on the importance of the contemporary 'cultural turn' in forging a radical re-think of the centrality of 'the cultural' and the articulation between the material and the symbolic in social analysis. One aspect of this shift is the expansion of 'culture' to a much wider, more inclusive range of institutions and practices, including those conventionally termed 'economic' and 'political'.

Paul du Gay is at the Faculty of Social Sciences at The Open University. **Stuart Hall**, is Emeritus Professor at the Open University and Visiting Professor at Goldsmiths College, the University of London.

representing black britain

a history of black and asian images
on british television

sarita malik

SAGE Publications

London • Thousand Oaks • New Delhi

First published 2002

Apart from any fair dealing for the purposes of research or
private study, or criticism or review, as permitted under the
Copyright, Designs and Patents Act, 1988, this publication
may be reproduced, stored or transmitted in any form or by
any means, only with the prior permission in writing of the
publishers, or in the case of reprographic reproduction, in
accordance with the terms of licences issued by the Copyright
Licensing Agency. Inquiries concerning reproduction outside
those terms should be sent to the publishers.

 SAGE Publications Ltd
6 Bonhill Street London EC2A 4PU

SAGE Publications Inc.
2455 Teller Road
Thousand Oaks, California 91320

SAGE Publications India Pvt Ltd
32, M-Block Market
Greater Kailash - I
New Delhi 110 048

British Library Cataloguing in Publication data
A catalogue record for this book is available from the British
Library

ISBN 0 7619 7027 4
ISBN 0 7619 7028 2 (pbk)

Library of Congress Control Number available

Typeset by Photoprint Typesetters, Torquay
Printed and bound in Great Britain by Athenaeum Press, Gateshead

contents

foreword

How the 'Black British' experience has been constructed and made sense of on British TV over the years since World War II is a topic of recurring public interest. It has provided an object of policy debate and institutional reform; it has emerged as a topic of critical discussion and scholarly research; it has become a focus of political struggle, popular criticism and campaigning. Critics, academics, researchers and students in different fields have frequently made studies of its different aspects and will have much that is new and insightful to learn from this new study. What we may call 'the race question' – whether in the form of colour and biological, or cultural and ethnic difference – entered the mainstream political agenda with the rise of post-war migration and has never left the headlines.

It would therefore be unthinkable for television – the mass medium of social interpretation, which 'came of age' during this same period – not to have played a critical role in how that issue came to be defined, understood and interpreted. At a certain moment, the question of how the issue was represented became a front-line issue in the new forms of cultural politics around race – the issue of 'recognition' and 'the politics of representation' coming to take their rightful place alongside, and without substituting, the politics of equality and social justice. During the 1970s and 1980s, when the question of 'access' to TV by neglected or marginalized social groups was pushed up the agenda by an active campaign, the question perforce became central to the institutional agendas of TV organizations, and to policy-makers in a broader sense. From the beginning, it has been debated in the wider context of the recurring tensions which, over the years, have marked and disfigured racialized relationships between mainstream society and the so-called 'ethnic minority communities' within Britain.

This study is therefore a timely and impressive contribution to that on-going contestation. It is wide ranging in scope and ambition. It offers one of the very few over-arching 'mappings' of this field across what we may call the 'high period' of terrestrial TV broad-casting which – with the onset of narrow-casting and the digital age' – is rapidly coming to assume the shape of a distinct 'era'. Of course, as Sarita Malik acknowledges in her introduction, her study cannot be comprehensive in the full sense. The subject is too wide to be easily encompassed by a single study; and the archives from which such a comprehensive history could be written are quite inadequate to the task – patchy, variable in quality and often, inexplicably, selective. That said, a very wide pathway has been carved here through the tangled mass of materials, in an attempt to establish significant patterns – of presences and absences, gaps and distortions – in the coverage. A very wide range of programming is referenced. This 'survey' aspect of the study – invaluable in itself – is complemented in each chapter by detailed, in-depth, case-studies of particular programmes so that the emerging generalizations about 'patterns' and the discussion of their causes and conditions of existence, are substantiated by concrete analysis. The result of combining these breadth-and-depth approaches is to enable us to understand more critically not only *what* was shown and seen, but *how* its meanings were actually constructed.

What is more, this broader analysis of recurring and divergent patterns in the programming and significant moments of rupture and shift, are cross-cut by a powerful understanding of the way the visual discourse of TV shapes 'what is said', and of the critical role which the television *genres* play in this practice of constructing meaning. In the case studies, the text mobilizes a number of critical concepts and engages a number of strategic debates in contemporary media studies and cultural studies fields, bringing them to bear on the main subject of the argument. As the study clearly shows, the 'play' of *genre* conventions (form) fundamentally reshapes and redistributes the meaning of what the programmes claim to represent (content). This approach has the added value of interrupting any temptation the critical narrative may otherwise have had to relapse into a 'reflective' or mimetic model of how television works.

This rich analysis of programme materials and forms, which constitutes the analytic core and heart of the project, is solidly buttressed by two further pillars. On the one hand, it is set in the context of the shifting institutional framework of the television providers and of media policy more broadly, which throughout this period were adjusting both to the concrete demands for more, more adequate, and more complex coverage of 'black experience' (leading, for example, to the rise of 'access television', and later, to the minority interest brief for Channel 4), and to wider demands for access to the opportunities to work in television, and thus to influence from behind the screen what was (and was not) being shown on it (leading to a modest level of professional recruitment). This whole institutional and policy aspect demands a detailed institutional and political history of its own – but it is widely documented and integrated into the general story here. It is enriched and sustained by a series of interviews with key players which constitute a valuable cache of 'primary materials' lodged at the centre of the book.

On the other hand the study provides a route-map for how we may set about 'mapping' the shifts within television and the television institutions against the broader socio-political history of race as it evolves in British society over the period. This is not only a reminder of how the climaterics of this tumultuous history made their impact within and on television. It also reminds that the medium is always located within a broader system of socio-political relations and forces – always part of a wider structure of cultural power. Television has been, throughout, attuned, in many indirect and often unconscious ways, to the changing cultural and political currents around race within which it operates. What is critical here is not simply the particular climaterics which have recurred, with predictable frequency and disturbing regularity, across the period – from Notting Hill and Southall, the 'sus' laws, policing and urban resistance, through the first wave of Paki-bashing, to the uprisings of the early 80's, the murder of Stephen Lawrence the high drama of the Inquiry and its historic report, Oldham and Bradford – but also the broader currents of the political response to racialized disadvantage and social injustice: from assimilation, black power and anti-racism to multiculturalism to cultural diversity.

What emerges from this study is the outline of what Sarita Malik calls the distinctive shape of 'a racialized regime of representation'. This phrase is bound to be picked out and selectively 'read' by some critics; not least because, even after 400 years as a colonizing and imperial nation, the British still find it difficult, if not impossible, to tell the difference between 'racial' and 'racist'. The subtlety of Sarita Malik's analysis eschews at every point any such vulgar and simplistic judgements as could be interpreted as suggesting all British television has been and is for evermore destined to be 'racist' – a phrase calculated to set alarm bells ringing deep in the collective unconscious of the British psyche. What the phrase means is that the Black British experience has been represented by British TV in very distinctive ways: ways which are different in certain critical respects (though not, of course, *absolutely* different), from the way other social groups and other cultural differences are represented. This 'difference' – itself changing in form over time – has something to do with a racialized nature of the way these people are collectively seen and their behaviour and experiences understood, signified and interpreted. What is distinctive – different – about this 'regime of representation' is the question at the centre of this challenging book.

Stuart Hall

acknowledgements

I would like to thank Stuart Hall and June Givanni for their tireless support and guidance throughout the project, from PhD to publication. It is a real luxury to have such positive, attentive and knowledgeable mentors.

Thank you very much to BFI Stills, Jason Baron at Channel 4 Picture Publicity, Carl Daniels at the Black Film Bulletin and to Richard Paterson and all those at the British Film Institute and Open University who helped the foundation research progress. To Julia Hall, Rosie Maynard and Seth Edwards at Sage Publications for their continuous patience and professionalism. To my PhD examiners, Jim Pines and Ken Thompson, for their positive response to my doctoral thesis which led to the book. Thank you to all those whom I interviewed whilst at the BFI, including Imruh Bakari, Colin Prescod, Henry Martin, Parminder Vir, Trevor Phillips, Treva Etienne, Terry Jervis, Samir Shah, Narendhra Morar, Farrukh Dhondy, Ruhul Amin and Yasmin Anwar. Their testimonies proved to be an important part of the book.

To Katie Epstein, Andy Medhurst, Charlotte Brunsdon, Richard Dyer and Reece Augusite who all, in ways they may not have realised at the time, have helped and encouraged me and my work along the way. Special thanks to my friends for their support (they know who they are), to my parents, Saroj and Inder Malik, for their constant love and assurance, and to all my family. To my dearest Bob, who without pause or end, gives me support, motivation, time and love.

Figure 1: The SS Empire Windrush, courtesy of Camera Press Ltd.

Figure 2: *Eastern Eye*, London Weekend Television for Channel 4, Presenters Aziz Kurta & Shyama Perera, courtesy of Channel 4 Picture Publicity

Figure 3: *Mind Your Language*, a picture of the cast, courtesy of London Weekend Television/Rex Features

Figure 4: Sacha Baron Cohen as Ali G for Channel 4's '*The 11 o'clock Show*' courtesy of Channel 4 Picture Publicity

Figure 5: Linford Christie holding the Union Jack at the 1992 Barcelona Olympic Games © Mark Sherman

Figure 6: Pressure ©1974 British Film Institute. All Rights Reserved. Image supplied by BFI Collections

Figure 7: *Bhaji on the Beach* with Asha (Lalita Ahmed) and Ambrose (Peter Cellier) courtesy of Channel 4 Picture Publicity

Figure 8: *East is East*, a shot of the cast, courtesy of Channel 4 Picture Publicity

introduction

Britain is constantly engaged in debates about race, racism and national identity. The identification in Sir William Macpherson's Report (following the unprovoked murder of Black British teenager, Stephen Lawrence, in 1993) of 'institutional racism', triggered a new set of discussions around British race relations, and helped many to belatedly recognize that racist processes are at work within the deep-seated culture of institutions such as the police, the media, education and the government (Macpherson, 1999).[1] Although the British media might not have seen itself as directly implicated in the findings of the report, it has always been located as a key site of contestation and cultural negotiation in matters of race and ethnicity, where we, as the viewing nation, both publicly and privately struggle to make meanings around Blackness.

Britain, in general, has been perceived to have a 'good multicultural record', and its television is often held up as a mark of success with respect to this. In response to this supposition, the media has, in general, been averse to criticism in relation to its treatment of Black and Asian people on a representational and personnel level. Such resistance was perfectly exemplified in the disturbingly hostile but predictably parochial public and media response to the findings in *The Future of Multi-Ethnic Britain: The Parekh Report* (Runnymede Trust, 2000), a report drawn by the Commission established by the Runnymede Trust, Britain's leading independent think-tank on ethnicity and cultural diversity. The Commission's much-misreported altercation with the word 'British' was taken by a large section of the British public as unpatriotic, dissentient and divisive rather than being seen as opening up a timely and critical debate about the 'racial' (not 'racist') connotations of the term: that is, that the term 'Britishness' is still essentially assumed to belong to the White English. Amongst its many findings, the Commission rightly cited the British media as a critical area in need of change with respect to its definitions of 'in' and 'out' groups (Runnymede Trust, 2000: 159–72). As if to prove the point, large sections of the media (who led the furore over the report) used the report to inaugurate a Macpherson backlash, suggesting that it is 'institutional anti-racism' which is preventing 'good race relations' in Britain rather than notions of 'institutional racism' (see *Runnymede's Quarterly Bulletin*, No. 324, December 2000 for analysis of media coverage of the report). This is a common scenario in the British media: it gives with one hand what it takes with another; leaving the question of 'race', and more specifically signs of Blackness, at a point of uncertainty and contestation. In any case, the Commission had much more to say about the symbiosis between the seemingly incongruous drives towards an inclusive 'One Nation' *working alongside* exclusionary strategies of resistance. It is perhaps a little early in the discussion to throw this next suggestion into the proverbial 'melting-pot', but I want to contend that as much as modern Britain embraces multicultural and anti-racist strategies, it continues, in varying degrees and fashions, to resist them. Television is at the heart of this confusion.

This book draws on and is an extension of earlier research conducted as part of the British Film Institute's 'Black and White in Colour' project in the early 1990s. Professor Stuart Hall (formerly of the Open University's Sociology Department) and June Givanni (former Head of the African-Caribbean Unit at the British Film Institute) were supervisors of the PhD thesis on which the book is based, which laid out, in a loosely chronological way, the history of a Black on-screen presence. The book takes on a more discursive dimension, identifying and exploring key ways in which those representations have been organized, produced and communicated. It is a conceptual survey with an institutional, historical and political focus and aims to identify a 'racialized regime of representation' (Hall, 1997: 245), rather than to serve as an absolute catalogue, encyclopaedia or celebration of Black images on British television.[2] In what follows, I want to examine how traditional television broadcasting, the primary site where the nation is imagined and imagines itself, has contributed to what we understand 'race' to be. These contexts work hand in hand, because cultural meanings cannot be disassociated from 'real life', and representations, as Stuart Hall reminds us, 'organize and regulate social practices, influence our conduct and consequently have real, practical effects' (Hall, 1997: 3). The genres discussed include documentary, news, comedy, sport, variety, drama and film, and are almost totally based on Britain's five major terrestrial, networked channels (BBC1, est. 1936; BBC2, est. 1964; ITV, est. 1955; Channel 4, est. 1982; and Channel 5, est. 1997.[3] Whilst we cannot ignore the impact and pathways opened by multi-channel systems and the pressures they have placed on free-to-air systems (*The Guardian*, 23.12.95), at the end of 2000 there were only about 6 million digital homes in Britain (about one in four homes, out of a population of just under 60 million).[4] The current scenario suggests that everyone is being served in different ways: those who pay for access to extensive tiers and packages of programming (in Pay-TV and pay-per-view for example), and those who stick with basic media resources such as terrestrial television (Barwise and Gordon in Briggs and Cobley, 1998: 192–209). Traditional broadcasting channels still dominate the viewing practices of people in Britain, even those who are connected to alternative delivery systems[5] and they remain an important point of municipal contact, public debate and private domestic rituals.

There are, roughly speaking, three main trajectories which I hope to have 'knitted together' in the book. These are: (1) the sociopolitical context of Black Britain; (2) textual matters in terms of how Black people have been represented on-screen; and (3) off-screen matters in relation to the institutional context, broadcasting policy, regulation and specialist programming. The overall focus is on questions of representation. The project draws, in part, on a number of original interviews that I conducted between 1995 and 1998 with a range of Black people who have had direct experience, knowledge and involvement in the British television industry (actors, commissioning editors, producers, academics, filmmakers). Interviewees included Imruh Bakari, Colin Prescod, Henry Martin, Parminder Vir, Trevor Phillips, Treva Etienne, Terry Jervis, Samir Shah, Narendhra Morar, Farrukh Dhondy, Ruhul Amin and Yasmin Anwar – and I would like to thank them all for their time and contribution, which provided essential background information for the book. We felt that these selected oral testimonies were important for the project, partly as a continuum of Pines' *Black and White in Colour* (1992), the book of interviews collated with key players in this history, but also because many of these people have not been asked in any great detail about a history that they themselves have been a critical part of. History after all, is not of its own making; it needs real human agents to make things happen. If there was one dominant thread that came out of the interviews it was that, far from being passively resistant to various exclusionary political and cultural processes in Britain, many Black people have been involved in a series of individual and collective campaigns to gain (media) access and recognition.

I don't want to get too preoccupied with explaining (the reasons for) my usage of various terms in this book, but some explanation might be helpful. 'Black' is used as a collective political working term to refer to those of African, Caribbean and South Asian descent, although I accept its limitations two decades on from the original anti-racist struggles that gave rise to it within a British political context, and am finding it increasingly necessary to use the phrase 'Black and Asian'. When it does not suffice, I do use 'Black and Asian', or 'Asian' when referring to those specifically from the Indian sub-continent (again, I take on board that 'Asian' is used in other contexts to include the people and cultures from other Asian countries). 'Race' (often found cased in inverted commas) does not simply refer to the 'new communities', but is used as an analytical concept referring to the social construction of ideas related to different ethnic and cultural groups and formations. I recognize that race in general and Blackness in particular, exist and are represented through a range of variables such as class, religion, gender and sexuality. 'Blackness' or 'Whiteness' are terms that cannot be simply or conclusively defined, and consequently phrases such as 'White/Black-produced', 'Black programme', 'Black production' are loose terms which are not meant to imply that any production or audience is ever simply or exclusively 'White' or 'Black', or that production input is accordingly 'raced' in any inevitable way. In short, none of these are intrinsic or homogeneous categories or are expected to be taken too literally.

Because of the obvious problems of knowing, in a first-hand way, what many of the early programmes contained, the testimonies of those involved in the productions at the time (such as those laid out in Jim Pines' *Black and White in Colour*) are of critical importance as 'social documents'.[6] This is partly a practical issue because of the paucity of early archive material given the live situation of most output prior to the 1970s, but also because of the popular assumption that Black representations on British television are only a recent phenomenon (i.e. late 1970s onwards). In fact, Black people appeared on British television on the first day of transmission when the African-American performer, Josephine Baker, participated in one of John Logie Baird's experimental television broadcasts from his London studio in October 1933.[7] Three days later (2 November 1936) saw the opening of the BBC's television service in which the African-American piano and tap dance duo, Buck and Bubbles, put on a show for a predominantly White audience. Black people have been on-screen, in one way or another, ever since. British television was installed on a wide-scale basis in the 1950s, after the Second World War – at the same time as the mass migration of people from Africa, the Caribbean and South Asia, and it is roughly there where our retrospective starts.

The impression of an easily accessible, comprehensive and lovingly cultivated television archive on which a critical history could be solidly based is, therefore, largely a myth (see Bryant, 1989; Houston, 1994; Scannell and Cardiff, 1991). The National Film and Television Archives, the largest collection of film and television material in Europe which is overseen by the British Film Institute, stores a vast amount of material, but there are many absences in its collections. There is a further, more specific problem for our concerns; a lot of material which has featured Black people or been filmed by Black people is not in the archives. There are various reasons for this: in some cases, the material has simply not been transferred because people could not afford it or did not realize the importance of getting it professionally stored. But discriminatory approaches within archiving policy and collections departments have also indisputably been a factor, (that is, certain work (particularly television) has not been considered 'classic', important or worthy enough for preservation, reflecting the broader problem (particularly pre-Cultural Studies/the 1970s) of not taking the marginal and the popular seriously). There are shocking stories about rare material featuring Black people, shot on film, being discovered on dusty shelves (including one about a filmed personal interview given by music legend Michael Jackson to a Liverpool youth club in 1972, which was recently found in a cupboard, and subsequently recovered and added to the BFI Collections). Such material is a critical part of our heritage and this cultural amnesia highlights just one of the broader ways in which the Black presence in Britain has been sketchily historicized. Our focus here is on a certain process of recovery in order to forge a heightened sense of permanence and cultural contribution, because Black people are now all too familiar with seeing themselves written out of British history, and the way these public memories emerge is a central part of how our cultural knowledge is situated. It is precisely the speed and capacity of today's cultural turnover that intensifies the educational and political value of looking back.

notes

1   Macpherson defined 'institutional racism' as 'unwitting prejudice, ignorance, thoughtlessness and racist stereotyping which disadvantage minority people'. Note here the important distinction between *institutional* and *institutionalized* – no organization is going to admit that they have institutionalized racism because this would involve a conscious and deliberate inscription of such policy.

2   See Givanni (1987), Pines (1992) and Vahimagi (1994). See www.bfi.org.uk for an excellent bibliography on Black-British film and television related articles.

3   When discussing specific programmes, I have listed the channel and the year. Exact transmission dates have only been given for certain news items and one-off productions.

4   Non-terrestrial television, including digital television took an audience share of 16.7 per cent in 2000. This had the biggest impact on BBC and ITV (www.barb.co.uk).

5   ITC, *Public Service Broadcasting: What Viewers Want*, January 2001; www.itc.org.uk.

6   Pines' book *Black and White in Colour* accompanied a season of archive and specially made programmes on BBC2 (27 June and 3 July 1992), which celebrated the history of Black representation on British and American television. The 'Black and White in Colour: Prospects for Black Intervention in Television' conference was held at London's Institute of Contemporary Arts in November 1992.

7   The BBC began as the British Broadcasting Company, receiving its licence to broadcast on 18 January 1922. In December 1922, John Reith became the BBC's first Director-General (until 1938). He firmly believed that the BBC should function as an impartial, quality, publicly responsible cultural institution (see Asa Briggs, 1995).

representation, history and 'black britain': questions of context

This is an appropriate moment in which to look back at the history of Black representation on British television. 1998 marked the fiftieth anniversary of the arrival of *SS Empire Windrush* (22 June 1948) which symbolized the inauguration of postwar, permanent, mass migration and the 'coming to the homeland' (or in the case of those who had served Britain during the Second World War, the 'return to the homeland') for Black colonial people to Britain (see Figure 1). 1997 had also seen the fiftieth anniversary of the independence of India and Pakistan. One year after the Windrush anniversary, the British nation was once again confronted with the memory of a Black presence: that of Stephen Lawrence, the victim of an ugly and brutal form of British racism. These two distinct iconic moments in British history – the arrival of Windrush and the official inquiry into the murder of Stephen Lawrence – signalled that within and despite the context of a now broad Black presence in the United Kingdom, stubborn forms of racism persist, and that there are still many battles to be won around the contested terrains of 'race', racisms and Britishness both on Britain's streets and within the fabric of its institutions. There was in fact a brief mood of hopefulness, a sigh of collective relief and probably guilt, for a short time following Macpherson's report and the Windrush celebrations; a sense that by both recognizing our failures and celebrating our achievements, we were somehow better equipped for the future. But then came the Euroscepticism, the intensified rhetoric against asylum seekers, renewed claims about 'Black crime', a rise in racial violence, critiques of the Left's apparent lack of patriotism; deepening social exclusion, resulting, for example, in the 2001 Oldham, Burnley and Bradford race riots, this time alongside a cluster of apologetic cultural diversity strategies, 'One Nation' proclamations and official campaigns and legislation to tackle institutional racism in the public sector. And so, once again, things appear to have settled back into these paradoxical, yet collaborative strategies of 'managing race' in the public sphere.

This moment also calls for reflection because it is one in which 'the age of traditional television' is reaching an important juncture, due to the emergence of new and revolutionary information and communication technologies. What is being hailed in Britain as the 'third broadcasting

Figure 1

The SS Empire Windrush

Source: Copyright Camera Press

revolution' (with the combined impact of broadband and wireless technology) is having important effects on the traditional framework of established legislation based around 'public service broadcasting', and on the ways in which we are each located in the new communication world.

Television's time-honoured modes of policy and address are currently under intense review and subject to further change, as interactivity, accessibility, diversity and convergence (the coming together of telecommunication, broadcast, software, computing and internet services) are becoming *the* characteristics of the postmodern media age. Through the 1990s, three distinct but related forces – deregulation, principally inaugurated by the 1990 Broadcasting Act; technological developments (cable, satellite, digital compression, internet broadcasting, pay-per-view, etc.); and increased market competition amongst the terrestrial broadcasters and between alternative delivery systems, both locally and globally – began to have a profound impact on the structural imperatives of British television, and on the simultaneously expanded options and deeper limitations for various television audiences. In the light of these shifts, television itself – its programmes, its role, its value, its past, its future, its economics, its duopoly stronghold, its relation to nationhood, citizenship and the public – is being re-evaluated and strategically modified. Television-specific policy is losing ground as the digital revolution, convergence and multimedia homogenize the distinct regulatory practices between various electronic media. The 2000 Communications White Paper, the Government's response to the new communications environment, inadvertently raises further questions about whether and how British broadcasters can provide an all-encompassing regulatory framework in the convergent media world whilst ensuring that the multiple interests of British society are vigorously upheld in the future (that is, how will they orchestrate a programming structure that is diverse, profitable, governable, locally relevant, public service-providing, and which also has commercial mass appeal)?

The BBC (British Broadcasting Corporation), the cornerstone of Britain's television history (a monopoly until the 1954 Television Act and the arrival of the more commercial Independent Television in 1955), was traditionally founded on Reithian ideals which claimed to hold in place core ideals – such as access, independence of thought, diversity of expression and programming, universality and accountability – in order to cement the corporation's status as a 'public service institution' and to justify the licence-fee.[1] This discussion takes as its starting-point, the straightforward acceptance that the duopoly of public and private which has since dominated British broadcasting, has more or less worked in line with the 'public service' ideal by aspiring to make 'popular programmes good' and 'good programmes popular' (Broadcasting Research Unit, 1985: 3). But it is this 'more or less' that we are concerned with here, specifically in relation to television's alleged impartiality, cultural sensitivity and moral responsibility when it touches on racial lines. The prevailing discourse of post-Reithian public service today pertains most obviously to the BBC (which has always been funded through the sale of television licences) and, to an extent, Channel 4 (funded by advertising and sponsorship but obliged to be a public service, not-for-profit broadcaster and to suport original UK production) and then to ITV and Channel 5 (both funded through advertising and sponsorship). Despite the escalating commercial impulses across the channels, they are generalist, mixed-genre broadcasters with an all-purpose mission to inform, educate and entertain all the people at least some of the time; they share a liberal ideology of universalism, professionalism and moderation which prevents outright commercialism and cross-media ownership. But apart from Channel 4's targeted minority mandate (see Chapter 3), the other channels merely have clauses in their policy documents indicating a 'common-sense', 'responsible freedom' and 'taste and decency' approach to the treatment of race on screen. Although all broadcasters are covered by certain ethical codes of conduct – the commercial sector by the relevant licensing authorities and through the Independent Television Commission (ITC) and the BBC in a more 'in-house' way and through its own Board of Governors – these arguably allow them to operate within similarly subjective parameters. Media policy, regulation and management culture within the institutional context of British television does, however, play an integral part in the way expressions of Blackness are negotiated, produced and reproduced, and in how environments which either nourish or constrain certain kinds of production are formed. For example, British television's founding ethos of 'public service' is important for how it generates and circulates meanings about nationhood, community and society and for the ways in which it marks, excludes and addresses aspects of identity and difference within the construction of the imagined community of the nation. If it weren't such a paradox, I would want to argue, using a more abstract point of view, that 'public service' is based on the generous principle that what 'we' like watching is not always all that 'we' (should) expect television to offer, but its definition of that 'we' is also part of a restrictive and unifying project. As I will go on to argue, this touches at the very heart of how television struggles over cultural difference (or *all* that is not 'we'). In fact, this struggle over formal equality and racialized difference is a key feature of British race relations and has been aptly borne out in the discourses of liberal pluralism and social Whiteness which have characterized the history of Black representations on British television.

Despite television's broad, equality-driven ideals and corporate manifestos, patterns of racism have persisted on and off screen, and the beginning of the third millennium saw nearly all the major terrestrial British broadcasters and arts organizations pledge an improvement in their approaches to cultural diversity; a response triggered both by the loss of disillusioned Black 'customers' to alternative viewing systems, and by the broader impact of the post-Macpherson climate. The need to be seen to register the report's key findings has now become an important part of the competition amongst terrestrial broadcasters and public arts organizations. The year 2000 alone saw the launch of the British Film Institute's three-year Cultural Diversity strategy ('Towards Visibility'), the BBC's public efforts to boost diversity through its 'Diversity Tsars' and diversity database, Channel 4's Black history crusade (with Untold 2000 and the on-line Black and Asian History Map), the newly-established Film Council's Black-targeted development funds and the introduction in October of a Cultural Diversity Network. This last initiative, a cross-industry action-plan established 'to change the face of television' (hence its 'Changing the Face of Television' Manifesto 2000), is supported by all the leading media houses including the BBC, Channel 4, Channel 5, BskyB (satellite) and ITV-linked companies such as GMTV, Carlton and ITN. They plan to set targets for ethnic minority employment (senior level included), establish an on-line talent diversity database, modernize cast and portrayal, share non-commercially sensitive research on cultural diversity and allow the government's Department of Culture, Media and Sport to monitor progress. Such moves towards 'good race relations practice' deserve support, even if many of them are driven by commercial imperatives. Of course, the way in which these visions of diversity are delivered and valued will ultimately determine their efficacy and meaningfulness.[2]

It is this 'pull' between the past (Britain's post-imperial history and the institutional history of British television in relation to a Black presence), and the future (of Black Britain at the turn of the century and of British television in the context of wider technological change), which forms the basis of this book. I want to point to the necessary connections between historical tradition, the unstable present and what will inevitably be a dramatic future in terms of how Black people are located and locate themselves in cultural (and specifically television) representation. These incarnations of Blackness in the cultural field – and, for that matter, new modalities of racism – are inextricably connected to issues of memory, history and race and disrupt notions of a distinct 'now' and 'then'. I want to treat 'history' here as dialogue, a never-ending story, a fluid interaction between facts and opinion, and between primary and secondary sources. Besides, new attitudes towards 'race' – while they emerge in the present – are often tied to older conceptions of 'race' and ideologies of racism from the past. It is important for us to look back, not least because one of the very facets of racist ideology is dependent on actively forgetting. It assumes that 'race' or racism is a new problem which only arrived here when 'the Blacks' did; that Britain was inherently homogeneous and conflict-free before 'the Blacks' came; that Britain's colonial and imperial past has nothing to do with newer forms of racism; and that 'race' and 'racism' operate on the margins of British society and can be made extricable from the internal dynamics of British social and political life (see Hall, 1978). Since images don't simply operate in a social or political vacuum, the context in which they are seen and the timing of their production is just as important as the types of images which are produced. I will use this preparatory chapter to 'set the scene' as it were and to provide some important context to the rest of the book, both in terms of the sociopolitical background and of the related representational questions that define the field of (Black) British Cultural Studies, because this helps us to historicize the discursive roots of *Representing Black Britain*, and to provide a historical genealogy of critical discourse on issues of race and representation.

mapping black britain: the sociopolitical context

Although we can trace the presence of Black people in Britain back to the sixteenth century (Fryer, 1984), the mass migration of those from Africa, the Caribbean and the South-Asian sub-continent (India, Bangladesh and Pakistan) to Europe and North America in the immediate post Second World War years, was a key historical period in which 'the West' interfaced with Black people. Many were 'invited' to Britain in order to provide semi- and unskilled work because of the postwar labour shortage and, under the terms of the 1948 Nationality Act, were entitled to UK citizenship since they were members of Britain's colonies or former colonies. But not all immigrants had come to the UK to face hard labour; many were curious, had come to study, wanted the adventure or aspired towards the creation of new opportunities for themselves and their families. The 1950s saw further requests by the Conservative Government for those from the Caribbean to come to Britain to relieve its acute labour shortage in the public services (transport, health), and this resulted in a second wave of immigration from the West Indies. But Black people's largely poor employment and social status (low-paid work, multiple-occupancy in inner-city slum houses, competing for jobs with the Irish and the Poles, etc.), together with the colonial legacy and biologically and culturally essentialist racist notions of what it meant to be African, Caribbean or Asian, encouraged a specific form of hostility (or, at the very least, a confused response) towards New Commonwealth Black colonial immigrants, compared to White 'newcomers'. Black people were more likely to be the subjects of curiosity, having largely only been seen in imaginary or pictorial form. The legacy of imperialism and subjugation faced by colonial migrants, together with the fact that in Britain, 'much more than in countries more accustomed to immigration, an expectation of social conformity and a rejection of claims of distinct ethnic identity' (Donald and Rattansi, 1992: 2) existed, prompted the divide between who/what was seen as central, normal and universal versus what was perceived as marginal, alien and specific. Britain was also experiencing a turbulent period in home affairs, with immigration and decolonization as key issues in a postwar, welfare state society. The Suez Crisis in April 1956 was particularly significant for un-hinging Britain's world standing. In that year, Christopher Mayhew, the producer of a BBC series entitled *We The British*, summed up the general national mood when he complained that, 'everyone thinks today that Britain can be pushed around' (*Radio Times*, 20.4.56: 5). An awareness of 'race' in new forms of consciousness occurred alongside Britain's postcolonial crisis, and, in time, many saw the modality of 'race' as symptomatic of that decline (Gilroy, 1993b: 22).

Early indications of racial tension were most obviously witnessed in the Liverpool-based anti-Black riots of 1948, which were specifically targeted at Black seamen (it is estimated that there were about 8,000 Black people living in Liverpool in 1948, 30 per cent of whom were seafarers). But there was also a more general 'colour bar' (in housing, hotels and restaurants, in 'no go' areas, specifically targeted at Black students and seamen) epitomized in the slogan 'No Dogs, No Blacks, No Irish'. By the mid-1950s, more blatant and violent forms of racial hostility directed at a Black-British presence emerged. These included: the White riots in Camden (London, 1954), Nottingham and North Kensington (or what was generally referred to as 'Notting Hill') (London, 1958) in which racists attacked immigrant groups; the emergence of organized racism in the form of fascist groups such as the White Defence League, the British National Party, and the League of Empire Loyalists (led by Colin Jordan, Andrew Fountaine and A.K. Chesterton respectively); the general abuse of Black workers, particularly by Teddy Boys (spurred on by the White Defence League) which fed into new moral panics around teen hooligans and troubled youth (rather than about British racism); and the first acknowledged racially-motivated murder (that of Kelso Cochrane, a Black carpenter in Notting Hill (May 1959)). This was also a time characterized by developments within the Black community such as the 'Keep Britain Tolerant' group, the growing activism of Black people in student bodies, trade unions, political parties and churches, the energies put into the organization of the first 'Caribbean Carnival' in Notting Hill (January 1959), and the work of the Association for the Advancement of Coloured People.

As Ambalavaner Sivanandan, who went on to head the Institute of Race Relations, explains in his excellent class analysis of the Black presence in Britain, *A Different Hunger*, 'the economic profit from immigration had gone to capital, the social cost had gone to labour, but the resulting conflict between the two had been mediated by a common 'ideology' of racism' (Sivanandan, 1982: 105). Asians and African-Caribbeans did not all simultaneously recognize that this 'ideology of racism' (based around fears of cultural difference, miscegenation, sharing resources, personal habits) was a process that directly implicated them; many Asians for example, saw themselves as quite separate from the events in Notting Hill. A united (African-Caribbean and Asian) conception of 'Blackness' was yet to develop in any consistent way, and many of the various religious, cultural, class and ethnic migrant communities involved here, had not interfaced with each other until they had stepped foot on British soil. Besides, popular attitudes towards 'Asians' and 'African-Caribbeans' were generally based on and circulated around racially specific 'moral panics'. Paul Gilroy summarizes the distinction between these racist ideologies as, '[West Indians] may not be as different or as foreign as Asians who are, by comparison, handicapped by the strength and resilience of their culture. . . . Where West Indian culture is weak, Asian communities suffer from a surfeit of culture which is too strong' (Gilroy, 1983: 131). Of course, there were important differences: for example, many Asians were traditionally rural people and customarily (extended) family-oriented; and many West Indians came from a working-class background and were experienced craftsmen (Sivanandan 1982: 4–5). What they both shared, was a strong sense of determination to make their lives in Britain as comfortable and successful as quickly as possible, to work hard and invest in education.

Despite the obvious signs of racist hostility, the 1950s continued to see an apparently *laissez-faire* approach towards British racism, both from the British government and the police (Rose, 1969; Patterson, 1969), although there is plenty of evidence to suggest that the Conservative Government between 1951 and 1955 were deliberately inscribing racially discriminatory practice within internal policy and administration (Carter et al. in Owusu, 2000: 21–36). The reality of widespread racist attacks and racialized exclusion was generally glossed over in favour of a seemingly more liberal[3] and complacent rationale which assumed that the best was being done in a 'difficult situation', and that these early signs of racism were just a temporary phase. A more publicly proactive, if misguided, approach to harnessing 'good race relations' began to emerge by the late-1950s and early-1960s during Britain's looming economic crisis. The spate of governmental anti-immigration legislation between 1958 and 1968, marked a critical shift towards a sanctioned and 'official racism', so that, as Peter Fryer put it, 'black settlers in Britain watched the racist tail wag the parliamentary dog' (Fryer, 1984: 381). The obsession with numbers and anti (Black) immigration legislation also contradicted the myth of equality (as inscribed in the 1965 Race Relations Bill[4]) and worked around the exclusionary logic that too many Black settlers were a problem and, more than that, posed a threat to 'good race relations'. In 1964, the Conservative politician, Peter Griffiths, successfully fought an openly racist campaign for his Smethwick (Birmingham) seat in the General Election, marking the first time that racism was used as an official reason for electoral support by a main political party.[5] It was also by the mid-1960s that the wives and children of those from the

West Indies and India began to arrive, so that there was a more obvious sense that Black people were beginning to *settle* in Britain. (The wives of those men who had emigrated from Pakistan and Bangladesh in the 1950s mostly began to join their husbands in the late-1960s and 1970s respectively.)

There were various efforts to tackle institutional discrimination (in relation to access, immigration rights, housing, employment and welfare services). The first was by those individual luminaries who had spearheaded an anti-racist movement since the 1930s. Most notable amongst these, were pan-African figures such as Cyril Lionel Robert James,[6] George Padmore, Ras Makonnen, Jomo Kenyatta, Wallace-Johnson and W.E.B. Du Bois, and Asian radicals such as Udham Singh,[7] Shapurji Saklatvala and V.K. Krishna Menon (see Fryer, 1984). The second was through Black-led organizations such as the International African Service Bureau, the West Indian Standing Conference, the Pakistani Workers' Association (1961), the Conference of Afro-Asian-Caribbean Organizations (CAACO) and the Committee Against Racial Discrimination (CARD) (which was set up in 1965 as a British civil rights coalition following Martin Luther King's visit, but had broken up by 1967) (see Solomos, 1989: 140–59). Finally, radical activity was also emerging on an individual 'grass roots' level, mainly in the form of strikes, by those (often Asian) who had directly faced racism in the workplace usually in terms of inferior pay and conditions (Rockware Glass, Southall (1965), Courtauld's Red Scar Mill, Preston (1965), Woolf Rubber Company (1965), Coneygre Foundry, Tipton (1967)) but also in terms of 'cultural rights' (for Sikhs to wear turbans in the workplace, for time off for religious festivals, etc.) (see Sivanandan, 1982). By the late-1960s, a more strident and coherent political ideology and 'counter-culture' had begun to develop amongst those who were now fighting along class and humanity lines.[8] This was partially influenced by the awareness of the durability and extent of British racist processes, but also emerged within the broader context of the globalization of protest (largely anti-capitalist and anti-imperialist); for example, those in relation to the Vietnam War, American imperialism, US Black Power politics, and Martin Luther King's assassination in 1968.

As the new politics of Black resistance strengthened, so did the popularity of 'Powellism', a new discourse of official and popular nationalism which predicted crisis if Black people were not systematically excluded or recognized as one of the 'Enemies Within' (see pp. 44–7). In February 1967, the National Front was formed (out of the League of Empire Loyalists, the British National Party and sections of the Racial Preservation Society) and proceeded to whip up considerable anti-Black sentiment during the 1970s. By the early 1970s, anti-Black sentiment had become less specific and sporadic and more extensively inscribed and naturalized as a structured and official topic of political debate, with racial discrimination, as Sivanandan puts it, taken 'out of the market-place' (Sivanandan 1982: 18) and institutionalized. Black people were now being popularly associated with notions of crisis, and interpreted through an accompanying language of racism, most obviously in relation to immigration, law and order, and specifically in the moral panics around 'Black crime' ('mugging', see Hall et al., 1978). Throughout the 1970s, the early assumption that racism was a relatively harmless, natural and temporary response to the difference of the Black and Asian 'Other' and that, in time (once the project of 'integration' was under way), the 'melting pot' *would* melt, was now being condemned out of its own liberal mouth. Young Black Britons – with their unique experience and hybrid (their parents' and their own, Black and British) cultural insight – were now beginning to lead the struggle against British racism, partly as a response to vehement extreme Right campaigns. Black women also played an important role. For example, Black and Asian women were active on the Grunwick picket line in 1977, in disputes around Child Benefit provisions in the late-1970s, and in response to the ESN (Educationally Sub-Normal) schools of the 1960s, and subsequent education 'banding' and 'special adjustment units' which led to the creation of the Black Parents Movement.

By the late-1970s, there were various anti-racist interventions to harness 'good race relations', including race-specific public policies, training initiatives and institutional directives (see Anthias and Yuval-Davis 1992: 157–98). Meanwhile, the so-called 'Race Relations Industry' gradually began to work with the US-inspired ideological principle of 'multiculturalism'; an admission that our plural identities make us all different, and that we should aspire towards celebrating this cultural and ethnic diversity. Some of these multicultural approaches came under criticism, particularly by anti-racists, for providing little more than a sugary façade (a 'saris, samosas and steel-bands syndrome', Donald and Rattansi, 1992: 2) to a very discriminatory reality. It was argued that multiculturalism served to re-emphasize the purity and homogeneity of 'White culture' when not interfaced with exotic 'multicultures', and that many of those who had been part of the earlier Black radical struggles to tackle active racism had now been co-opted to 'manage racism' in inconsequential ways under the official banner of 'multiculturalism'. New public spheres and 'ideological spaces', such as the media were identified as playing a crucial role in Black struggle against the state. 'Getting access' to the media was now recognized as a key bridge to cross in order to achieve genuine civic equity and change prevailing attitudes towards 'race'. Besides, African-Caribbean and Asian communities both had a deep-rooted and organic tradition in the arts that many of them now felt was excluded from dominant expressions of British culture.

In January 1978, the soon-to-be-elected Prime Minister, Margaret Thatcher, echoed the sentiments of Enoch Powell's infamous 1968 'Rivers of Blood' speech, when she spoke on British television of the threat of being 'swamped by people with a different culture' (*World in Action*, ITV, 1978; cited in *The Daily Mail*, 31.1.78). The jingoistic bandwagon which Thatcher invited the 'authentic' members of the British population to jump onto and her appointment as leader of the Conservative government in 1979, shifted the party increasingly to the Right, and gave rise to a new voice of popular authoritarianism (mirrored in 1980s America with Reaganism). With its broad class appeal that tapped into persuasive, long-standing ideologies of deterioration, Thatcherism depended highly on producing and mobilizing discourses of difference in order to remodel Britain's domestic and social policy, so that calls for racial purity became a central device in reshaping British social, political and cultural life. 1979 also witnessed the Southall riot, which followed the National Front's direct provocation of Black people by conducting their racist campaign in the densely populated Asian suburb. On 23 April 1979, 2,756 police (and Special Patrol Groups) turned up to apparently ensure that trouble did not incur from the National Front's public anti-Black campaign (5,000 people had turned up the previous day to protest against the fact that the NF had been granted a public space (Ealing Town Hall) to state their case) (Institute of Race Relations, 1981). In fact, many of the anti-Nazi demonstrators were dealt with violently by the police, and Blair Peach, a teacher, was killed. In the same year, the research and education-orientated Institute of Race Relations (through which Sivanandan launched the seminal journal *Race and Class*) submitted *Police against Black People*, a report to the Royal Commission on Criminal Procedure that documented police harassment of Black people. It concluded that the police, rather than reinforcing morality, 're-create it – through stereotyping the black section of society as muggers and criminals and illegal immigrants' (IRR, 1979).

The 1980s can, for a number of reasons, be identified as a 'critical decade' in this history (Bailey and Hall, 1992: 7), not just because of the cultural renaissance that was to take place, but also because it was the moment when the public debate about race relations opened up, and unprecedented degrees of pressure began to be placed on state institutions to alleviate racial discrimination and 'disadvantage'. A series of events during 1981 foregrounded the discontent. These included: the New Cross (Deptford, London) fire attack in January in which 13 Black teenagers died – and the subsequent indifference with which the case was dealt (both by the police and the media); the Black People's Day of Action (or the 'New Cross March') organized by the Race Today Collective on 2 March (approximately 15,000 of whom were Black); and the intensive programmes for policing introduced in Lambeth in early April (see Mercer, 1994: 6–9, and Fryer, 1984: 398). This last 'initiative', 'Operation Swamp 1981' (as part of the London-wide exercise, 'Operation Star'), further encouraged 'stop and search' procedures which had materialized as a legitimized form of discriminatory policing with inordinate numbers of Black people being stopped for no good reason. These can be identified as the key episodes leading up to the uprisings, which were to follow later that year.[9] Those (Black and White people) involved in the civil uprisings in Britain's urban centres during 1980 (Bristol's St Paul's) and 1981 (Brixton, Southall, Toxteth and most major cities) (see Fryer, 1984), as well as responding to the unusually high proportion of Black arrests, were also more generally frustrated with: the rise of neoconservative hegemony in the form of Thatcherism; with the limitations of a liberal multicultural consensus and its notions of textbook integration; and with various anti-racist strategies which, in real terms, appeared to be doing very little to eradicate extensive racial inequality produced by the state and its institutional agencies. The government's official response to the 1980s riots manifested itself in Lord Scarman's 1983 Report. Although some felt that the Scarman report reasserted the pathologies of racial disadvantage amongst Britain's Black communities, it did break with the established compliance towards law and order procedures by prescribing – although not all recommendations were acted upon – race-awareness training for police, community liaison communities and joint efforts to reduce the social and economic dimensions of racial disadvantage. This early official identification of 'institutional racism' was to serve as a precursor to many of the 'remedies' prescribed in subsequent anti-racist policies (such as special funds to be injected into regeneration programmes in rundown areas). But as the death of Colin Roach in Stoke Newington police station in 1983 was to highlight, racist processes were ongoing. 1985 saw further Black-led riots in Broadwater Farm (London) after the death of a black woman, Cynthia Jarrett, following a police-raid in her home.

These moments revealed an important shift in the way 'race relations' in Britain was now being interpreted, framed and contested. As Kobena Mercer put it, 'What was a "riot" in one discourse, was a "rebellion" in another' (Mercer 1994: 7), highlighting both an emerging 'dissensus' (Mercer, 1994: 54) from a singular language of British 'race relations' and a unifying moment between different non-White ethnic communities. Many Black people now began to identify 'inferential' as well as 'overt' racism (see Hall, 1981) and outline how discriminatory practice was not something that only occurred in state institutions (police, government, law, education), but also within welfare services (health, social-work, adoption) and the arts and media. Local government's emphasis on cultural diversity and central government's increasing investment in 'community' related programmes, and initiatives such as the Arts Council's Ethnic Minorities Action Plan, emerged out of this post-1980s riots context. The role of the Greater London Council (GLC) under the Labour Left administration between 1981 and 1986, was hugely significant not only in terms of moving the political debate from 'multiculturalism' to 'anti-racism', but also in boosting Black cultural activities through training, development, education, funding and 'popular planning' strategies. As well as specific research projects on media, policy, race and access, the GLC, with its Ethnic Minority Arts Committee, also provided an important source of funding for the Black arts sector. To this degree, many of those who were to push 'race' onto the agendas of British television channels at this time, largely came from *outside* the broadcasting institutions themselves. The shift towards strategies of 'anti-racism' (positive action, ethnic monitoring, and contract compliance) was generally considered as a tougher and more direct intervention than the ideological struggle for 'multiculturalism'. An increasing number of Black people began to move into public administration, trade unions, business and local government, and many of them were employed as 'race advisers'. In the 1987 General Election, four Black (Labour Party) Members of Parliament (Keith Vaz, Diane Abbott, Bernie Grant and Paul Boateng) were, for the first time, elected to the House of Commons. This was more than doubled to nine (all Labour) in the 1997 election, but Black people still remain massively under-represented in Parliament.

The politically stifling atmosphere prior to the 1980s had acted as a catalyst, not only in terms of the 'riots', but also in activating creativity and a strong desire to express and find a cohesive public voice, and so the imposed labels of 'Negroes', 'Immigrant' and 'Coloured', were transformed into a new Afro-Asian public and political 'working' collectivity called 'Black' (echoing the US Black Power movement of the 1960s). This 'political Blackness', an umbrella organizational category came into usage not only to trample on a history of negation and marginalization, but also to find a unified voice in order to fight collectively for political rights and better representation. It was the shared experiences of both colonialism, racism and, for many, a post-migration history that prompted 'Blackness', in Mercer's words, to be 'de-biologized' (Mercer, 1992: 430) and helped to develop new and strong forms of identification between different ethnic minorities. The rearticulation of Black-British identity, 'showed that identities are not found but *made*; that they are not just there, waiting to be discovered in a vocabulary of Nature, but that they have to be culturally and politically *constructed* through political antagonism and cultural struggle' (Mercer, 1992: 427). For some, however, 'Black' was also an imposed identity which was not culturally specific enough (this was a complaint mostly registered by Asians, many of whom did not identify with the term 'Black') and more than that, only seemed necessary because of the ways in which 'Whiteness' functioned in British society. This was true in so far as African-Caribbeans and Asians essentially became 'Black' in Britain (or as filmmaker Ian Rashid said in relation to the term 'South Asian', 'We do require it – if for no other reason than as an antidote for "Paki" ' (Ghani and Rashid, 1994)). Besides, not all Black and Asian people were consciously involved in anti-racist struggle, so the self-identification with 'Blackness' (or not) did not mean that all Black people were dissenting, either politically or economically, from the same position. Towards the end of the decade, many also began to use the term 'Black and Asian', signalling a general break-up of the term 'Black' into more specific and 'pure' categorical ethnicities, and the increasing difficulty of speaking, thinking and campaigning from a unified Black perspective. The end of the Black parliamentary Caucus, the more obvious economic divide between Asians and African-Caribbeans, and the cultural variations in terms of Black and Asian patterns of family life, popular culture and lifestyles all signalled this fragmentation.

'Official' liberalism in the form of top-down, institutionalized anti-racist strategies had brought its own sets of problems such as an extreme (and often misfired) orthodoxy, tokenism, ethnic absolutism, lip-service and perfunctory corporate manifestos. It had also triggered a popular backlash, a legacy that continues today in the form of anti 'political correctness' (used for example to refute equality-based gestures such as the CRE's pre 2001 General Election pledge for parliamentary ministers to refuse to 'play the race card' in the election campaign, as well as the recommendations outlined in the 2000 Runnymede Trust Report and 1999 Macpherson Inquiry). During the 1980s, popular mythologies around excessive 'political correct-ness' (for example, banning the nursery-rhyme 'Baa Baa Black Sheep', words such as 'blackboard', milk in coffee, and golliwogs), settled in such a way as to undermine the serious work which was being done around issues of equal-ity – making way for 'anti-anti-racism', or the 'PC backlash' (Dunant, 1994). The new 'anti-racist, anti-sexist' climate of cultural sensitivity which had begun to make itself known during the 1980s, was now being lamented (albeit mockingly) for 'hijacking' a more honest and forgiving era and for 'driving racism underground'. Liberal thought, in its 'PC' incarnation, whilst not without its problems, was systematically trivialized, undermined and blamed for repositioning 'the majority' as victim, while itself having largely been invented by those of the Right. Now it was those who supported anti-racist campaigns rather than those who were opposed or indifferent to them, who were widely being seen as the ones 'stirring up' racial tension and ulti-mately obstructing Britain's 'right' to be Great again. Complaints about 'quotas', 'special treatment' and 'the new conformism' began to be voiced (most notably in the British press) and provided a substitute for cogent crit- ical analysis about the deeper politics of 'race' and community.

The political events of the 1980s saw a number of Black people now also beginning to insist and struggle over the definition of 'British'.[10] By the end of the decade, a number of material changes (such as funding cuts for local authorities and the abolition of the GLC in 1986), and the widespread closing up of 'minority' spaces, was a sign of the times, reflecting a more individualistic, competitive and uncompromising code of cultural practice, a new market-oriented language around public issues. This echoed a broader paradigmatic shift from collective and politically-motivated strategies to ones based more on individualism and culture (often with a religious emphasis). But the gains of the 1980s were also apparent: there were signs of greater integration between Black and White Britons; there were more Black figures in strategic, political positions; one impact of Thatcher's entrepreneurial success culture meant that some Black people were doing exceptionally well, with some ethnic groups (and notably the Chinese and East-African Asians) thriving on the economic front. At the same time, racism persisted and equality of opportunity – although inscribed in various policies – was still not a reality for many Black Britons who remained confined to the margins of the national debate and disadvantaged in respect to education, employment, the judicial system, immigration, housing, etc. Certain ethnic groups in certain areas (Pakistanis, Bangladeshis and African-Caribbean males in particular) were suffering educationally and economically.

The 1990s continued these imbricating threads around the state and status of Black Britain. The new uncertainty, partly demographic in origin, and its accompanying nationalisms, shifted the racist emphasis from racial inferiority to the threat which new hyphenated identities ('Black-British', 'Anglo-Asian', etc.) were seen to pose to a 'pure' and 'legitimate' sense of national cohesion (amongst the older hyphenated identity, 'Anglo-Saxon'). Other recent examples which point to this resurgence in social Whiteness and national anxiety have included: the Right's persistent derision of 'multiculturalism'; the resurgence of new acts of violent racism and neo-nationalism across Europe (Harris, 1990; Ramdin, 1999; Gabriel in Cottle, 2000: 67–82); the xenophobic attitudes which continue to surface, particularly in the context of sport (for example, during Euro '96 and Euro 2000 a spate of far-right marches (2001) designed to provoke British-Asians); a depressingly large and persistent racist contingent dominating certain web forums (www.independent.co.uk/argument); the imprisonment of David Copeland for his murderous minority-targeted nail bomb attacks (2000); and the ongoing reactionary populism and race card opportunism which thrives within an increasingly Right-leaning British political environment, particularly and tellingly in the period leading up to the 2001 General Election (which saw the leading parties simultaneously play up to time-honoured conceptions of nationalism and modern ideas of diversity).

The defensive responses to the threat of the loss of national identity posed by globalization, changes in Europe and the supra-nation state developments, have exhibited assertions of singular national identity that are as absolutist and tenacious as early assimilationist models of integration and as vehement in registering cultural sameness for the supposed maintenance of social cohesion and unity. The alterations in European nation-states (development of the single market within the European Community, alterations in border controls, a more cohesive sense of 'European law', the continuation of migration into Europe), and the new processes of devolution and globalization, have given rise to a new pan-European state authoritarianism, a renewed possessiveness over national borders and in reclaiming an 'untouched' and exclusive sense of 'Englishness', despite and perhaps because of, the increasingly 'multi-ethnic' and 'multi-religious' actuality of Britain, and the move towards 'becoming European'. This 'ethnic cleansing' and splitting between those who 'belong' and those who do not, as reinscribed in a spate of moral panics around certain political refugees and asylum-seekers to Britain since the late 1990s (and specifically since the 1996 Immigration and Asylum Act and in the Race Relations [Amendment] Act 2000), have characterized new public xenophobic responses to 'the newcomers', spurred on by the alarmist British media (endless stories on Britain as a 'soft touch', 'bogus' claims and 'welfare scroungers', particularly in relation to Czech Roma and Kosovan ones arriving at Dover in 1997 and 2000 as a result of the overflow from the Balkans across central Europe). In August 2000, the United Nations criticized the government for its record of race relations, expressing 'deep concern' over the number of racist attacks and attitude towards asylum-seekers in Britain.

In spite of this resistance towards multicultural Britain, we are continuing to see the notion of any single version of 'Britishness' being re-examined, re-made and mythified by the non-English. The act of asserting ethnic/cultural difference over cultural Otherness manifests itself in the formation of new styles and modes of cultural production, which implicitly reject earlier assimilationist projects. These manoeuvres, or what we might call the pull between 'translation' (Bhabha, 1990; Rushdie, 1991) and 'tradition' (Robins, 1991) have signalled themselves as contradictory impulses: there are those which 're-identify' with places and 'cultures of origin'; those which produce symbolic forms of cultural identification; those which have developed 'counter-ethnicities'; those which have revived traditionalism, or cultural and religious orthodoxy, or political separatism, and so on (Hall, 1992: 308). In actuality, Britain is now incontrovertibly 'mixed-race' and 'cross-cultural', a fact accommodated for in the 2001 National Census, which for the first time, introduced a 'Mixed' category as a possible 'ethnic origin'. Whilst there are few signs of a tangible redistribution of resources, a broadening of access or a challenge to the disproportionate number of White male leadership within key institutions, we are also seeing a new type of corporatized commitment to multiculturalism, and an uncharacteristically sensitive response from some unexpected quarters in respect of this. The question of whether Black people can also be British has now been replaced with the question of how far we are permitted to be so. And, perhaps more significantly, at what points are we denied Britishness?

critical approaches to reading race on television

These major turning points and continuities in Black-British social and political history have had an important bearing on Cultural Studies, the primary discipline through which race and representation has been studied. Research can generally be split into three areas: first, as part of more general debates about identity, ethnicity, culture and representation (Gilroy, 1993a; 1993b; Mercer, 1994; much of Hall's work; hooks, 1992; Dyer, 1993; Owusu, 2000); secondly, work which focuses on representations of race in British film and cinema (Pines and Willemen, 1989; Mercer, 1988; Malik, 1996; Young, 1996; Wambu and Arnold, 1999); and thirdly, analysis of the British (Twitchin, 1988; Daniels and Gerson, 1989; Pines, 1992) or European television context (Frachon and Vargaftig, 1995). There are other studies that have looked at film and television in Britain (Givanni, 1995; Bourne, 1998), covered both Britain and America (Snead, 1994; Ross, 1996; Cottle, 2000), commented on ethnic minorities and the media in general (Ainley, 1998; Runnymede Trust, 2000; Cottle, 2000) and studies on Blacks in American cinema and/or television (Pines, 1975; Bogle, 1991; Cripps, 1993; Diawara, 1993; Gray, 1995). There have also been a number of industry-commissioned reports on the relationship between ethnic minorities and the media, which have tended to use an empirical, quantitative approach and focus on questions of policy (codes and guidelines), employment (patterns and monitoring), audience (habits, tastes and demands) and the domestic context (ownership, reception trends within a household) (Cumberbatch and Woods for the BBC and ITC, 1996; Halloran et al. for Channel 4, 1996; Sreberny and Ross for the BBC, 1996; Sreberny BSC/ITC, 1999). Within this diverse range of theoretical and methodological approaches, a number of different arguments, views and positions on Black representation have emerged, but two significant absences have prevailed. The first, relates to questions of sexuality and gender, which remain perfunctory, underdeveloped and de-emphasized (see Young, 1996). Secondly, many of these studies, while they often criticize the strategies of absence and exclusion in delineations of Black people on screen, are themselves vague in their use of the supposedly all-encompassing term 'Black', and fail to consider in any substantial way, how South Asian people have been represented. There is another problem which has arisen from the all-encompassing term 'ethnic minority media' which often fails to contextualize the distinct practices *between* different mediums, particularly television and film (Ross, 1996; Bourne, 1998). Issues which relate to television's commissioning structures, scheduling, exhibition, viewing practices, recruitment procedures and production frameworks, etc., need to be situated within the distinct institutional context of (public service) broadcasting. (Would we 'throw in' television when studying French or for that matter (non-Black) British cinema?)

representation and meaning

How we are seen determines in part how we are treated;

how we treat others is based on how we see them;

such seeing comes from representation.

(Dyer, 1993: 1)

The term 'representation' can be used in two main senses. The first relates to representing/speaking for someone/thing, thus playing a symbolic interpretative role by expressing *someone's* viewpoint from *somewhere*. Here, there is an assumption that someone else can 'fill the place of' or substitute that experience for the sole purpose of 'representing' it. This type of representation is about acting as the embodiment of someone/thing and about standing for/corresponding to that someone/thing (e.g. claiming to represent or stand for 'the Black community'). Here, someone/thing is being represented through or by someone/thing. This entails the belief that someone/thing is 'representable'. The second possible use of the term is to refer to the process by which an image/impression of something or someone is reproduced. Here, 'representing' is essentially about portrayal and description through language (oral, visual, still, moving); it is an expressive, communicative process. In both these senses of the term, signs and symbols are used to convey meaning, often to represent or stand for some aspect of an 'external' reality. For our concerns, we may agree that far from simply reflecting or presenting 'reality', the work of representation does, in fact, (at least partially) construct 'reality' and, more than that, serves an important role in how social relations develop and in how ideologies[11] are constructed. I refer to 'ideologies' here because they can be understood as 'sets of political ideas and values' that might belong to the specific interests of a particular group, hence the Marxist notion of a 'dominant ideology' which is imposed arguably through consciousness (Marx) or structures (Althusser). The term 'discourse', in relation to 'ideology', helps us to understand the textual process by which meanings are constructed. Discourse analysis considers the content and context of verbal and non-verbal codes and systems of representation. It emphasizes that there are no pre-given ideologies which are adopted and then simply represented, but that ideologies themselves are formed through discourse. Michel Foucault's work is particularly useful here for its emphasis on discourse serving not the 'will to truth', but the 'will to power' (Foucault, 1982). Foucault was less interested in 'the great model of language and signs' than in 'that of war and battle'; more concerned with the 'relations of power, not relations of meaning' (Foucault, 1980: 114–15).

The work of linguistics (the scientific study of language) and semiology (the study of signs and meaning) also plays an important part in our study of racialized representation. Just as the discursive approach emphasizes the effects and manifestations of representation (its 'politics'), the semiological approach interrogates how language produces meaning (its 'poetics') (Hall, 1997). Lacanian psychoanalytic theory can help us work through one of the ways in which television representation, a principal signifying system, works; this approach suggests that who speaks and who is spoken of are never identical. The positioning of the 'I' subject and the discourses (the mode, form or genre of language) within which they stand (the symbolic) are always therefore 'placed', and serve to structure identity. So when discourse is constructed, it always speaks from somewhere in the cultural and social field. The process of representation and 'televisualization' constructs its own relationship with the enunciator and the enunciated. It could be argued then that traditional 'unaccessed voices' (those perceived to be on the margins of a society) are commonly located as the subjects of articulation (the enunciated) with television itself as the subject in articulation (the enunciator). As such, the dialogic transaction between the enunciator and enunciated can be adjudicated by the medium. Television then, can play an important role in determining the exchange between speaker and addressee and, like other systems of representation, can guide the audience towards a particular reading which generally corresponds to the dominant social, cultural and political values of a specific time or context. Moreover, as Barry Troyna argues in relation to journalism in general, 'to a greater degree than any other profession or institution, it controls the debate about itself' (Troyna, 1981: 8). It is useful to call upon the notion of 'hegemony' here (as developed by Italian Marxist, Antonio Gramsci), which helps us to understand the struggle within popular culture to make particular ideologies synonymous with the 'common-sense' of the people (or what Albert Einstein called 'the collection of prejudices'). The constant state of cultural flux makes 'culture' not something which you do or do not have, you can or cannot get, you 'own' or are controlled by, but something, like politics, which we are all an active part of – even when we are silent or excluded. As Stuart Hall explains, cultural hegemony functions as an always shifting, never permanently set, form of cultural leadership, and is never totally conquered. This 'tug-of-war', the struggle between competing ideologies and interests, is precisely what allows popular cultures to function and makes television a critical site of this public cultural contestation, because 'it is always about shifting the balance of power in the relations of culture; it is always about changing the dispositions and the configurations of cultural power, not getting out of it' (Hall in Morley and Chen, 1996: 468).[12]

Meanings (and myths), as well as being constructed through what is being represented and by whom (the sender), are also mediated through the audience or 'reader'. As such, a third 'subject-position' is at work; that of the 'overhearing audience'. 'Significations', as Joost Van Loon puts it, 'can only become myths if they are mediated by and anchored in the historicity of this third party' (Van Loon, 1995). John Fiske explains that, 'a reader is constituted by his socio-cultural experience and thus he is the channel through which message and culture interact. That is meaning' (Fiske, 1982). Following this, we might agree then that meaning is produced both through our conceptual systems and through the things around us (people, objects, events) (Hall, 1997: 15–64). As such, no representation, in itself, is mean-ingless; all representations mean something – although never just one thing. Since meanings and ideologies are never fixed, they can also be re-worked and re-negotiated. But whilst we are all integral to how meanings and under-standings are constructed, each of us is located differently in relation to power and knowledge, and thus holds different degrees and types of power in relation to cultural production.

'Televisualization', in itself, is a process concerned with the mobiliza-tion of logos, symbols and signs (which it sometimes formulates itself) and as such, is a movement from *signification* to *representation*. The study of representations of race therefore needs to consider television as part of a 'machinery of representation' (Hall in Curran et al., 1986), which produces and circulates a number of different (and often competing) ideologies. I am concerned with those ideologies that underpin how racial identities are con-structed within television representation by arguing that aspects of process and power play an integral part in how meaning, difference, identity and subjectivity are formed to produce a 'racialized regime of representation' (Hall, 1997: 245). But, what exactly do we mean by 'representations of race?' Briggs and Cobley (1998: 281) neatly summarize the 'raw ingredients' needed to develop a discourse around 'race':

1   the person's own 'racial' identity (e.g. 'White');

2   other 'racial' identities to which that person's 'racial' identity can be opposed in a power relationship (e.g. 'Black' vs. 'White');

3   a discourse that asserts the centrality of race as a defining feature of a person's identity (e.g. racism);

4   other (non-'racial') identities to which that person's 'racial' identity can be opposed/complemented in a power relationship (e.g. 'race' may be outweighed by 'gender').

analysing race on television   There are three valuable critical approaches that I want to draw upon here. The first, is the active-audience thesis, an approach to media audience studies that emerged in the 1970s, and which shifted the emphasis from what the media 'do' with audiences, to what audiences 'do' with media images (Halloran, 1970). This was especially useful for the newly emerging theories around race, ethnicity and the media, because it identified that each reader/viewer was able to actively decode and interpret meaning in different ways, instead of being textually-constituted or 'locked' into any one ascribed meaning. In turn, some also recognized that our social relations (ethnicity, for example) help us to structure understanding (Morley and Brunsdon, 1978). The second, is Stuart Hall's model of 'encoding/decoding' (Hall, 1973) which gave this new audience studies approach a more 'workable' sociological and cultural perspective, making it possible to relate to the ways in which various media texts and readings can be actively encoded and decoded. While Hall agreed (like effects theorists) that the media do have the power to set agendas and cultural frameworks, he also stressed that viewers themselves are active, and decode messages in different ways. As such, he argued that there can be more than one reading (dominant, negotiated or oppositional) from the same message although television can promote a 'preferred reading'; this generates a dominant reading by those whose social situation or political views are most akin to the preferred reading (see also Hall in Cohen and Young, 1973). In essence, Hall stressed that there is a lack of transparency between the ways in which messages are encoded and decoded and that the media operates according to an open, not closed message system. The third useful 'tool' for our discussion, is the basic psychoanalytic framework, particularly in relation to the complicated relationship between texts and audiences and the 'politics of the look'. Psychoanalysis has traditionally revealed two limitations in relation to our focus area: the first is that its basic tenets of identification and subjectivity have been less readily applied to studies of television, which tend to be understood through more 'grounded' modes of analysis such as effects studies, social readings and textual analysis; and the second is that much psychoanalytic screen theory (such as Laura Mulvey's seminal 'Visual Pleasure and Narrative Cinema' in 1975), while it has considered issues of gender, has overlooked the question of race and failed to consider racial distinctions *between* spectators). The various works of Frantz Fanon (1952/1986), Homi Bhabha (1983), Sander L. Gilman (1985), Joel Kovel (1988) and Kobena Mercer (1994) have however been critical for using psychoanalysis to acknowledge the racial aspects of identity and looking relations.[13]

The work of three specific media research centres during the 1970s and 1980s was to prove particularly influential in studies of race and television. The first was the Centre for Contemporary Cultural Studies (CCCS) in Birmingham,[14] which developed the issue of 'agenda-setting' (of how the media establish and organize a particular set of issues) especially in relation to news and documentary reports on race. *The Empire Strikes Back* (CCCS, 1982), a study of Black-British race relations in which a certain amount of attention was paid to questions of cultural representation, was a landmark text to emerge from the centre. The second was the Leicester Centre for Mass Communications Research. Focusing specifically on the mass media and racial conflict, Hartmann and Husband found that, although direct effects on media audiences were unlikely, news reports kept within a British cultural tradition (e.g. derogatory to foreigners). They argued that these reports worked within an established cultural framework, which in terms of Black people was, 'more conducive to the development of hostility towards them than acceptance' (Hartmann and Husband, 1974: 208). The third centre was the Glasgow University Media Group with their work on news. Through content analysis, they combined elements of the manipulative theory and hegemonic theory to critique the ways in which television news is constructed (various studies were published in 1976, 1980, 1982 and 1985). Although their work focused on specific cases such as the Miners' Strike, the Falklands War and organized labour, their basic argument was that news tends to focus on effects rather than causes, is neither neutral nor natural, and actively manufactures representations, often under the guise of impartiality. This built on the important argument laid by Althusser in relation to the media in general as an ideological state apparatus which reproduces dominant ideologies.

Stereotypes became increasingly central to debates around race and representation in the 1970s and 1980s, and were criticized for being crude simplifications that select, reduce and essentialize the definition of a type of person, style, event or institution with the effect of popularizing and fixing the difference of the original 'type'. Since the 1960s, the sociological term 'stereotype' had been widely used to refer to this representational practice by which a given social experience, person, style, etc. is simplified so as to produce a reductive image/impression. Many of those who were critical of the media's representations of Black people also began to call for 'positive images' in order to balance out the 'negative images' which were often used to depict Black people and their experiences. The emphasis, therefore, was on changing the 'relations of representation' (Hall in Mercer, 1988: 27). Important as they were in identifying the media's widespread dependence on stereotypes, there was in fact, an inherent contradiction in many of these arguments: on the one hand, there was a general acknowledgement that 'representation' and 'reality' were two distinct entities; and on the other, there was a demand that representations of Black people were drawn in more 'accurate' ways. Thus, pronouncements of 'misrepresentation' were readily applied by those who also recognized that film and television do not simply reflect reality, but construct a reality of their own. Moreover, many wanted to see more 'realistic' depictions of Black people, whilst also resenting the supposition that there was any one 'real' Black experience that could be represented. There was also a general assumption that all stereotypes are negative, and thus by simply eliminating them, representations of race would become more 'balanced'. Of course, 'positive images' can also be stereotypes, and stereotypes can, in fact, be reproduced as forms of resistance (see Neale, 1979–80: 33–7, and Bhabha 1983: 18–36). Leaning too heavily on the 'stereotypes/positive and negative image' rhetoric can be limiting for three main reasons: in the first place, 'typing' has to be recognized as an inevitable and necessary system of representation; in the second, there can be no absolute agreement as to what 'positive' and 'negative' definitively constitute (can the image of a gold-medal winning Black sportsman only be considered as 'positive'?); and in the third, the validity of 'positive' and 'negative' as racial categories of representation themselves need to be questioned since they do little to displace the assumptions on which the original stereotypes are based (see Malik, 1996: 208–9).

It is nonetheless important (since stereotypes are the primary device through which representations of race circulate in media texts), to make some comment about the ways in which stereotypes function as a representational practice. Stereotypes are shorthand; they are ubiquitous because they help us to decode people (see Malik, 1998: 310–11). In fact, they rely on quite convoluted processes, enabling the reader to associate one aspect of a stereotype with many other things; creating a complex web of beliefs from, at first sight, a glib categorization. Hence, a representation of the 'unassimilable Asian immigrant', the 'Black street mugger' or the 'bogus asylum-seeker' tells us more than just that; our stream of consciousness builds on the basic information (issues of language, cultural values, social background etc. automatically follow) to create a quite detailed (though not necessarily accurate) profile of what that person constitutes. We often find it easier to blame/focus on the stereotypes than to focus on why, how, when and by whom they are produced. Stereotypes are social constructs designed *to* socially construct. They do not simply come into being from nothing and they are not 'used' in the same way by everyone. The way in which we apply stereotypes in cultural production is as revealing as which stereotypes we select to represent, so the question of *who* has the power to wield and circulate stereotypes in cultural production is an important one. For example, in his influential paper 'The Whites of their Eyes' (1981), Stuart Hall identified what he called 'television's basic grammar of race' (1981: 39) which, he argued, consisted of three types: the slave-figure, the native and the entertainer but he used the basis of this imagery to address precisely where those types had derived from, whose interest they served, when they appeared and how they manifested themselves on screen.

By the mid- to late-1980s, a series of debates began to emerge which pointed to the limitations of discussing race and representation within dualist ('right' or 'wrong, 'good' or 'bad', 'positive' or 'negative') terms, and shifted the emphasis to how a multiplicity of views, both of and from Black people, could be transmitted via the media.[15] This moved from challenging stereotypes themselves as 'wrong' or 'negative' (which presumed that there was a 'right' or 'positive' way of categorizing Blackness), to a position which questioned that there are any definite (racial) categories to represent at all. This signalled a 'cultural turn' described by Stuart Hall in his influential paper 'New Ethnicities' (delivered at the 1988 ICA conference), as representing the 'end of the innocent notion of the essential black subject' (Hall in Mercer, 1988: 28); a new liberatory position from which the Black artist could speak and a more diverse expectation of 'Black representation' to articulate difference not just across communities and individuals, but within them as well. Thus, it began to be argued that rather than Black simply being good or positive (as in the 1960s Black Power slogan 'Black is Beautiful'), 'Blackness' was in fact something which could not be defined in any simple or singular way. Of course, this also involved accepting that not all Black films are good, not all 'realistic representations' are positive, not all Black artists are non-sexist, non-racist etc., and that Black audiences/critics/ producers themselves had to move away from a black=good/white=bad orthodoxy (see Williamson in Mercer, 1988; Mercer in Rutherford, 1990: 43–71; Hall in Mercer, 1988).

What had become increasingly clear by the end of the decade was that, 'the polarisation between essentialist and anti-essentialist theories of black identity has become unhelpful' (Gilroy, 1993a: x). The concept of 'diaspora', advanced by leading Black-British theorists such as Paul Gilroy, emerged out of this need to produce a development of thought, and became a particularly useful system of representation and unit of analysis through which the plurality and diversity of Black-British communities could be understood. The central assertion here was that Black people are, in fact, part of a diverse people, a diaspora. A diasporian (for example, an African, Caribbean or Asian person in Britain) has multiple ideological (though not necessarily physical) connection-points including 'home', histories and new space, thus resulting in a 'diaspora space', inhabited not just by 'migrants', but also by the 'natives'. Many Black artists had used this space in the 1980s, to bypass the dominant regimes of representing 'race' and to form a new identity politics based around issues of migration, colonization, displacement and marginalization. It was precisely this new emphasis (on syncretism not integration, on fluidity not fixity, on the processes of differentiation as much as the differences themselves) that began to take centre stage in new expressions of cultural and political 'Blackness', not as something passed down from one generation to the next or from one Black person to another, but as an indeterminate, dynamic and contingent disposition. Importantly, this timely extension of cultural thought and expression stretched beyond local boundaries and communities to transnational networks across the US, Caribbean, Europe, Africa and Asia in the form of 'diaspora politics'. This critical turn was also differentiated by its break from Western thought (British Cultural Studies included) with its traditional, orthodox, Eurocentric and gender bias and its focus on national cultures and traditions, further emphasizing its international, global perspective and proposal to review absolutist notions such as cultural difference and nationalism through the notion of a 'Black Atlantic' (Gilroy in Grossberg et al., 1992: 188).[16] It was argued for example that when reviewing and commenting on new Black-British film practices, a new model of criticism needed to develop which moved away from the grammar of Euro-American mainstream film theory. Kobena Mercer wondered, 'whether a more adequate model of criticism might not be derived from the critical practice performed in the films themselves' (Mercer, 1994: 56) and developed a notion of 'interruption' which would entail a more direct relationship between the critic and the text (see Mercer, 1994: 53–66; Crusz, 1985: 152–6; Henriques in Mercer, 1988: 18–20; Gilroy in Grossberg et al., 1992: 187–98). The new emphasis on the hitherto under-developed fact that we are all ethnically positioned, and that we all occupy an ethnic space, also triggered a new set of discussions around 'Whiteness', an important intervention in 'defamiliarizing' and interrogating what is typically deemed 'colourless' by the group that does not want to be ethnically located. This recognized Whiteness as containing races, ethnicities and cultural identities of its own (Gaines, 1988; West, 1990; hooks, 1992; Dyer, 1997). Studies of 'Whiteness', important as they have been for their emphasis on 'race' as a social and political construct and for their concern that 'race' is not only reserved for certain categories of persons, have however, remained exceptions to the rule of 'race studies'.

Gilroy's emphasis on the 'relationship between ethnic sameness and differentiation' (1993a: xi), and on Black cultures, traditions and cultural production 'as a changing rather than an unchanging same' (1993a: 101) insisted that a break be made with both the omnipresent, polarized, totalizing and authoritative essentialism and with the anti-essentialism which absolutely overemphasizes or utterly refutes theories of tradition and cohesiveness amongst Black people. That is to say, to accept that in spite of the connections, there is no 'pure' Black cultural, political or religious form, that all identities are pluralized, and that all representations do, in fact, 'work' differently. These developments in Cultural Studies have mapped a critical lineage to the kinds of debates around race and representation that we are part of today. Gilroy has since progressed his ideas around diaspora and a Black Atlantic in *Between Camps* (Gilroy, 2000), an extension of his previous work with a renewed emphasis on moving beyond 'race thinking' in understanding our current global scenario. Others are also criticizing the over-dependence in British, and now international Cultural Studies, of the 'diaspora, ethnicity, hybridity' mantra and, impact notwithstanding, are questioning its appropriateness for an extension of debates around race and representation (Bakari in Owusu, 2000; Mercer in Gilroy et al., 2000). Mercer is concerned that this 'postcolonial vocabulary' has become sanitized, simply replacing earlier notions and debates around integration, adaptation and assimilation (Mercer in Gilroy et al., 2000: 234). In keeping with Gilroy's global style, many of his theories and indeed those of other leading Black British cultural commentators, are enjoying an extended, internationalized presence vis-à-vis the new technologies, particularly on the World Wide Web, which (despite its sometimes disturbing ungovern-ability) has become essential for the development, not just of diaspora web communities, but as an indispensable knowledge portal and area of exchange for those concerned with critical debates in the field of race and representation (between academics, critics, visual artists, writers, students and so on).

Reflecting on this introductory chapter as a whole, there are a few closing points worth making. The first, is that Black people, whether in grass-roots political struggle, intellectual discourse or on a more individual-ized, personal level have fought a very active campaign for equality and recognition in Britain, which has paved the way for our current claims to and relative ease with 'being British'. The second is that British politics and culture has been characterized by an omnipotent racialization of thought and debate, be it in relation to imperialism, immigration, nationalism, citi-zenship, community, society, inclusion, pluralism or diversity (or through the official trajectories of Black struggle, Equal Opportunity, Cultural Diversity and now Globalization). No area of British life has gone untouched by these issues, be it education, law, government, media, welfare, and so on. And the third related point is that recent struggles around difference and nationhood, like the Empire-rooted circumstances of Britain's postwar years, cast a certain doubt on whether Britain's national story has ever really been ful-filled without 'the Others'. Or to use Cornel West's point, "Whiteness" is a politically constructed category parasitic on "Blackness" (West, 1990: 29). We shall now begin to chart some of the complicated ways in which this national story has been narrated on British television.

notes

1 Commercial television's regulatory body was the Independent Broadcasting Authority until 1991, when it was replaced by the Independent Television Commission (responsible for ITV, Channel 4, Channel 5 and satellite and cable

broadcasters in Britain). The 2000 White Paper proposed a single super-regulator, Ofcom, to oversee the standards of the entire communications sector.

2   The fact that they have not been laid out in any detail in the aforementioned 2000 Communications White Paper also means that we have no formal inscription of these directives in a critical piece of long-term legislation.

3   See Raymond Williams' explanation of liberal and liberalism. Williams argues that 'liberalism' is 'a doctrine of certain necessary kinds of freedom, but also, and essentially, a doctrine of possessive individualism' (Williams, 1977: 148–50; 150).

4   All three Race Relations Acts (1965, 1968 and 1976) were initiated under Labour governments. Note the 1965 Race Relations Act established the Race Relations Board to monitor the act; the 1968 Act established the Community Relations Council to liaise with the government; and under the 1976 Race Relations Act, the RRB and CRC merged to form the CRE. The Race Relations (Amendment) Act 2000 made it unlawful for public bodies to discriminate on grounds of race or ethnicity.

5   'Official' discrimination was widespread in the form of legal quotas and laws (e.g. Edward Boyle's ruling in 1965 to restrict the proportion of 'immigrant' children in any one school, hence the implementation of school bussing procedures in heavily-represented Black and Asian areas such as Southall).

6   C.L.R. James, a Caribbean who came to England in 1932, before a 'Black Power' movement had even been conceived of in those terms, 'pioneered the idea of an autonomous black movement which would be socialist and not subject to control by the leaderships of white-majority parties and trade unions' (James, 1977: 8).

7   Singh, who founded the Indian Workers' Association in 1938, was hanged in 1940 after he shot Sir Michael O'Dwyer who had headed the 1919 Amritsar Massacre.

8   See Sivanandan's 'Race, Class and the State' (1976) for an important class-based analysis of the Black experience in Britain.

9   The SUS laws (which allowed arrest on suspicion of loitering with intent to commit an offence) had been introduced in the late-1970s, under Section 4 of the 1824 Vagrancy Act. Under SUS, research found that Black people were 14–15 times more likely to be arrested than Whites (Stevens et al., 1979). In 2000, William Hague, the Conservative Party leader, blamed the Macpherson report for introducing 'politically correct policing' and decreasing stop and search, and related this directly to the murder of a Black school child, Damilola Taylor in a run-down estate in Peckham, South London. The 2000 Home Office Report, 'Statistics on Race and the Criminal Justice System' directly contradicted this, noting that Black people are five times more likely to be stopped and searched than Whites, and four times more likely to be arrested.

10   According to the 1991 Census, 5.5 per cent of the population (just above 3 million) were from 'non-white ethnic communities', most were concentrated in five to six cities, and about half were born in Britain. Prior to the official results of the 2001 Census, the ethnic minority population was projected to be just under 4 million (around 6.7 per cent of the population, Office of National Statistics, *Annual Abstracts*, 2001).

11   See Eagleton, 1991; Strinati, 1995; Hall, 1982; and Williams, 1977.

12   See Bennett (1986) for a critique of structuralism and culturalism and the usefulness of Antonio Gramsci and his concept of 'hegemony' in studies of popular culture. Also see Hall in Morley and Chen, 1996, 411–440.

13 See Lola Young (1996) for a detailed account of different psychoanalytic approaches to the reading of race.

14 Stuart Hall joined the Centre in 1964 and became its acting director in 1968 and subsequently its director until the late-1970s when he moved to the Open University.

15 For example, at the 'Black People in British Television' event which was held at Cinema City, Norwich (13–15.5.88) and the 'Black Film British Cinema Conference' at the Institute of Contemporary Arts in February 1988. Also see Mercer, 1988; Twitchin, 1988.

16 Amos and Parmar in CCCS, 1982; Gilroy in Grossberg et al., 1992: 187–98; Gilroy, 1987: 49–57; Mercer, 1994: 20–1; Isaac Julien's critique of Alan Lovell's *Screen* article on the Black workshops, 1991: 64–8; Paul Willemen's reference to *Screen's* 'theoretical super-ego' (Willemen, 'An Avant-Garde for the 80s', *Framework*, 1982, 24).

the racialization of the black subject in television documentary

The historical development of the television documentary genre and the context within which modes of public communication were set and subsequently began to operate, are particularly useful when tracing the shifting representational strategies of 'Blackness' and 'race'. Documentary realism has been the principal mode through which Black people have been represented on British television. The identification of 'race' as an Issue worthy of documentary intervention in the interests of public communication and 'the public', and as relating exclusively to non-White people, must be seen as a powerful force in how common-sense notions around Black people in British society have developed. The focus of this chapter is the active role television played in mediating how 'race' came to be framed around a 'Blacks as social-problem' agenda, particularly in these early mainstream discourses of truth, and how challenges to these hegemonic narratives of race and nation became central to how (anti) 'Blackness' subsequently came to be articulated and 'claimed'.

the emergence of television's 'social eye'   The British cinema work of the 1930s and war years largely aspired to integrationalist ideals of mutuality and national identity; a shared sense of 'our' world. There was a clear incorporative strategy of locating the audience ('the people') *inside* the society ('the nation') that was being addressed. The radical and democratizing potential of film continued to be realized by cinema activists in the Free Cinema Movement of the 1950s (led by British New Wave directors such as Lindsay Anderson). This emerged alongside the growth of the so-called New Left in the late-1950s and represented an emerging concern with sociological notions of class, culture and community as laid out in the seminal work of, for example, (Hoggart, 1957; Williams, 1958). Many of these films displayed a deep commitment to civic education, social justice and to the notion of a Welfare State system. The *sociological* dimension of a lot of documentary of this time emerged from the documentarists' self-proclaimed, social-democratic objective to focus on social and occupational change, social problems, and the lives and circumstances of ordinary people. Another formative sense of documentary was of its instructive role in relation to 'the public', of 'informing the people' (Dziga Vertov – *Kino-Pravda/Camera-Truth*), thus being a classic form of public service with its important and sensitive positioning of 'public communication', 'public knowledge' and 'public opinion'. During television's formative years, the impact of the medium was yet to be fully realized – by politicians, the public or indeed by the BBC itself. There was a somewhat casual approach to programming, and the first time a complete programme would be seen, was when it went on air. When television was resumed after the Second World War (the service did not run between 1939 and 1946), such indifference diminished as technology and working practices became more sophisticated, internal structures were reorganized and the corporation expanded (see Swallow, 1966 and Corner, 1995).

Early television documentary continued the reformatory tradition, the process of democratization and the public service agendas that had hitherto been established by previous generations of documentary workers, but also developed in accordance to the distinct cultural agendas and technological and political determinants of the early BBC years. Reithian ideals of the BBC as a national cultural institution with a collective personality, made early BBC documentaries an important form of 'public service broadcasting', with the responsibility of informing and educating the public on certain issues. The narrative authority and exclusive position of the BBC made it Britain's official public voice, playing a critical role in uniting and elevating the nation within the broader context of loss and decline (see Chapter 1). The mythology of the camera as a tool of authority, which can effectively record an untouched and complete 'reality', secured naturalism as television's dominant language and indeed as one of the medium's classic myths (Hall, 1975; Williams, 1977). The live nature of the medium in the early years further accentuated the effect of naturalism, which was essential in establishing the truth-claims of television documentary with the audience. Despite the talk of immediacy, large production teams were still needed, filming was slow and cumbersome (reeling out of cables) and television camera equipment heavy and awkward, so that there was little chance of catching spontaneous, natural social action or 'real life'. The introduction of lightweight 16 mm television cameras in the early 1960s, added to the sophistication with which truth could be mediated, with filmmakers now able to move out of the studio with greater ease and create a closer sense of intimacy with their subject.

It was the BBC Talks Department (later to become 'Current Affairs'), which saw itself as directly addressing political affairs. Quite apart from this, a documentary tradition developed which dealt specifically with 'the social'. The social investigations worked within established, hybrid formats of interviews, observation, exposition and dramatization, and when ITV arrived in 1955, became more focused on 'fly-on-the-wall' and drama documentary. The social subject, as constructed in documentary programming of the 1950s and 1960s, was usually an oppressed, troubled one, positioned in direct relation to social crisis and problems in contemporary Britain and it was through them that inequality and the need for social change in modern Britain was explored. This overwhelmingly anthropological approach (where the documentarists would step in, gaze at, study and observe) or what was termed 'social realism', was produced in an attempt to make us, the viewer, understand the social subject better – to de-alienate them. These projects mostly fit into a humanist, roughly assimilationist paradigm, based on the assumption that the members of 'the British community' needed to co-exist in such a way as to assure the health and prosperity of 'the nation'. Hemmed in by these notions of welfarism, the 'socially-responsible' documentaries were emotive and sentimental, working within a politically vague, emotive and reformist discourse (wanting to resolve and improve the situation).

Special Enquiry (BBC1, 1952–57) was a major social problem discourse of the 1950s. Norman Swallow, the producer of the BBC monthly series, hoped for *Special Enquiry* to be a television version of *Picture Post* (Swallow, unaddressed memo, 27.2.52), the photographic journal (1938–57), described by Stuart Hall as geared towards 'the democratization of the subject' (Hall, 1972: 83). It was structured from 'our'/the audience's point of view and used mixed modes of documentation (filmed reports, reconstructions, narration, a studio-base and 'non-official' voices). *Has Britain a Colour Bar?* (BBC, Tx: 31.1.55), part of the series and the first full-length television documentary to examine the problems faced by Black immigrants, was presented by Robert Reid and narrated by René Cutforth, and focused on race relations in Birmingham, a Midlands-region of England. Asked why the colour bar issue was selected for the *Special Enquiry* series, the producer, Anthony De Lotbiniére later reflected that there was no conscious effort to cover the subject but that it was seen as both a sensitive and topical issue ('Black and White in Colour' archive interviews).[1] There had of course already been evidence of racial tension in Camden in 1954, and the recent arrival of West Indian workers to areas such as Birmingham prompted the team to trace the impact of their presence. The events of the 1950s had put the 'official goodwill' between Britain and its new Black immigrants under significant strain, but there was still a dominant sense amongst many Black people that despite – or even because of – the watershed events of 1958, the degree of 'tolerance' towards race and immigration would increase; that 'common sense' would realize that Black people were being discriminated against.

Despite its naturalistic effect, *Has Britain A Colour Bar?* was carefully staged, with effects produced, scripts co-ordinated, opinions rehearsed and reactions anticipated. As Lotbiniére noted, 'You could try to get the truth, but you could never do it without falsifying it' (see note 1). There were, for example, no vox pops in *Has Britain a Colour Bar?* so that the 'direct' testimonies about racism were in fact, previously rehearsed and the house-owners who were shown objecting to Black lodgers were acting for the cameras (thus setting up the model of a colour bar). Central to the production of the documentary then, was the role played by the White programme-makers' background *assumptions*, or what Steve Neale, in another context has called, 'cultural verisimilitude'; an aesthetic of 'truth' dictated by a dominant group of what it considers to be credible and accurate according to the common sense and mores of society (Neale, 1981). For example, rumours of Black people banging the bar when ordering a drink led to an elaborate re-enactment of this ritual in a Birmingham pub for the purpose of the documentary. Cutforth's commentary explained, 'That's the way you order a drink in Jamaica – but it puts people's backs up in Birmingham.' Although this scene was intended to exemplify the hostility which Black 'newcomers' often faced, this 'bar banging' was also used in the documentary as an example of cultural *difference*, and the general viewer was invited to read this as authentic because of the claims to realism generated from the aesthetic of naturalism through which the text worked (of course, the general audience were never told that these events had been staged). It is worth asking, using this simple example, whether by documenting this supposed ethnic custom and focusing on alleged cultural 'personal habit', the programme reflected or constructed how racial difference was perceived by the White audience to whom the programme was absolutely addressed (most of whom had very little direct experience of Black people).

Has Britain a Colour Bar? followed a distinct narrative logic which was to become the basic narrative structure of the race relations documentary – the master narrative of 'race relations' on television. Not only was it a logic which articulated around 'our' (White British people's) cultural values in opposition to 'theirs' (Black people's), but it was primarily the product of underlying assumptions about difference, always presuming that 'the norm' did not apply to the racial 'Other'. One only has to look at the BBC's Rough Outline Treatment of the programme (structured around six categories, 'Arrival', 'Employment', 'Housing', 'Crime', 'Miscegenation', and 'Overcrowding') to see the already anticipated 'racial problems' and the possibilities it created for producing a high sense of drama and conflict (BFI 'Black and White in Colour' archives). As the programme stated, 'they look *different* and they sound *different* and their tastes in matters of food are *different* . . . but let's face it, *they are* different' (my emphasis). At the heart of *Has Britain a Colour Bar?* was a liberal caution, an endeavour to explain racial difference whilst also urging official equality. Whilst this may have positioned it as a landmark programme, the documentary also presented racial difference as problematic (a position mostly expressed by a working-class person in the programme) and thus rationalized and justified the evidence of a colour bar that was found in Birmingham, whilst simultaneously disidentifying the documentary-makers from any obvious tone of racism. As the *Daily Sketch* acutely observed, 'with scrupulous fairness the BBC balanced each blow against the West Indians with a defence of them' (quoted in Corner, 1991: 47). Many White viewers disagreed, seeing the programme as a biased defence of Black people. One letter sent to the presenter after the airing of the programme said, 'You and your black friends ought to be put up against a wall and shot' (Reid, 1960: 980).

the 1960s: from social subject to social problem

During the 1960s, mainstream documentary slots such as *World in Action* (Granada TV), *This Week* (A-R/Thames TV/ITV) and *Panorama* (BBCTV) regularly represented Black people in four main areas of documentary. The first were investigative 'social' reports (of the kind we have been discussing) on housing, miscegenation, employment and 'false equality' in relation to the Black-British presence. The second were programmes on foreign affairs and the non-British Black experience, with a focus on famine, South Africa and Rhodesia in the mid-1960s, key individuals such as Martin Luther King, Mohammed Ali and US-centred movements such as the Black Panthers and Black Muslims. The third were arts and sports documentaries profiling, for example, the work of James Baldwin, Ralph Ellison and George Lamming. And finally, there were a number of historical documentaries looking at Britain's imperial past. Notable social documentaries of the late 1950s and 1960s (all screened on ITV), were *Black Marries White – The Last Barrier* (1964), *Smethwick* (1964, *World in Action*), *The Bottom of the List* (1968, *World in Action*), *Mixed Marriages* (1958, part of the indicatively named *People in Trouble* series), *Coloured Foster Children* (1966, *This Week*), *Coloured School Leavers* (1965, *This Week*), and *Coloured Voting – Hidden Issue* (1964, *This Week*). *The Colony* (BBC, 1964, Dir.: Philip Donnellan) stood out as a rare example of its time, focusing on social factors such as housing and employment, and accessing Black people directly so that their views on Britain could be expressed in a relatively unmediated way. A railway signalman from St Kitts, a bus conductor from Jamaica, a nurse from Barbados and a family of singers from Trinidad each narrated their own stories, a rare break from the omnipotent White narrator in race documentaries (the certified voice of 'the Black experience').

Some of the key incongruities in relation to television's dominant approach to race had developed in actuality programming by the mid-1960s. In the first place, Black people (both in terms of audience and within the documentary text itself) were referred to and spoken about, but rarely spoken to. This made the sociodemocratic impulse of a lot of early race-related documentary work necessarily contradictory, because in spite of the fact that much of it was arguing the case for universality and tolerance of cultural differences, the very language in which it spoke and the modes of address selected, excluded Black people from its concept of 'nationhood'. The classic liberal technique of *talking on behalf of* 'the victims' while simultaneously arguing that they are silenced, marginalized and denied access, was a key feature of this postwar humanist discourse. By working within this 'dialectic of inter-subjectivity' (based on the assumption that something cannot be questioned), these programmes presented themselves and were dominantly construed as authoritative, and left the Black-British social referent and viewer in an ambiguous position in relation to the text's spatial framework and indeed, to ideas of British society. Despite the broad Black presence, there was simply no access for an anti-authoritarian response to this, and given the scarcity of media outlets, this kind of programme functioned as a monolithic information feed. The lack of access, the technically laborious procedure and the reliance on predisposed agendas and assumptions about other ethnicities, established a set of narrative and production structures, which offered no real opportunity for alternative positions to challenge the assumptions or break with the narrative authority (best maintained through the didactic, mediatory commentary/interview-technique) of the documentarists.

Take for example, *Racial Discrimination* (1967, part of *This Week)*, which atypically included Black people in the studio discussion. Llew Gardner opened the programme with this address: 'Good evening. I'm White. Most of you watching this programme are also White, which the way things are in this country is fortunate for us.' Gardner turned to an Asian studio-guest and said, 'I would like to ask Mr Nandy what it's like to be a coloured man living in this country of ours?' Although *Racial Discrimination* showed 'ordinary' Black people speaking of discrimination, they were set up alongside a number of White 'experts' who proceeded to undermine their experiences of racism. Thus, Martin Jukes representing the Engineering Employers' Federation spoke of the 'difficulty in introducing coloured workers into factories'. Another 'specialist' argued, 'A lot is said to be prejudice that is nothing of the kind.' And the Chairman of the Race Relations Board, Henry Bonham Carter, reassured the viewers, 'Perhaps it is worth remembering that things aren't as bad in this country as they are in some other countries.' This was a common set-up; the privileged (usually middle class and male) White 'expert' positioned as the 'streamliners' and managers of race relations, with 'ordinary' (usually semi-skilled or skilled working-class) Black people situated as isolated cases, pushed to the margins of the broader debate and located outside the dominant consensus (liberal, middle-class, established values) of the programme. This is important to note, because it was an early sign of the way in which television, by and large, tends to work alongside and in partnership with other institutions and élite groups (the government, the police, the legal system, educationalists). Social Whiteness (a term I have taken from John Downing in Newcomb, 1997: 1333), a position from which these 'primary definers' were situated, was always assumed to be and constructed as the norm, and Whiteness (or – what was much the same thing – to appear to have no 'obvious' race) was treated as an unavoidable privilege compared to 'Black disadvantage'. This imaginary and binary 'ours' and 'theirs', 'us' and 'them', made the general liberal discourse around 'race', assimilation and inclusion appear both clumsy and confused. Following on from this, the second major contradiction was that, despite their obvious liberal intents, many of these programmes were already working within a framework that defined, albeit politely, ethnic minorities as an inevitable social problem. Rather than addressing the grassroots politics of (British state) racism 'head-on', they tended to construct Black people and the issues they faced as the 'social problem' or simply reduce them to 'administrative issues' (Scannell, 1979: 106), thus maintaining the image of harmonious 'race relations' (based on notions of formal equality, social opportunity and education) that saw no difference. Racism was never really discussed using the word 'racism', but in terms of 'race relations', which, in turn, worked as a kind of shorthand for Blackness and Black immigration. As such, the 'problem of race' was externalized, rather than being seen as an internal problem within the living fabric of British political life. Later on, such loopholes within this overriding liberal approach were to be manipulated in verifiably shrewd and persuasive ways by those with less reformist objectives.

The 1960s saw television social documentary take on unprecedented tones of hostility and fear in relation to the Black subject and produce a new racialized language of social control. The libertarian resolve and customarily timid suggestion of discrimination in the earlier texts now slowly began to be squeezed out, or at the very least, was certainly not pronounced in such empathetic terms. The emphasis began to shift from 'disadvantage' to the 'problem of the immigrant' *for* White people and the 'character' of English society. *The Negro Next Door* (A-RTV, 1965), part of the public affairs documentary series *This Week*, investigated how White people were reacting to 'Negroes' living near them, a bluntly opportunistic enquiry following Peter Griffiths' openly racist electoral campaign the previous year, as epitomized in his slogan, 'If you want a nigger neighbour, Vote Labour.' *The Negro Next Door* represented a critical shift from the documentary of social *description* (as in *The Colony*) and social *criticism* (as in *Has Britain A Colour Bar?*) to the documentary of social *protest* – although here it was weighted against a Black presence (these three categories of social commentary are taken from De Nitto, 1985: 330). The opening commentary, overlaid with images of Black children playing in the street without a parent in sight, set the agenda from the outset:

> In a street like Roseville Terrace Leeds … neighbours are important. You can't escape them, you're always aware of them. For fifty years the people living here have learnt to cope with the problem of proximity. The walls are thin, the lavatory is outside. In the past five years, the problem has taken on a new meaning. Now the people of Roseville Terrace have Negroes for neighbours. Today, 15 of the 53 houses in this street have coloured families in them and for the people next door, this is a new and sometimes bewildering experience. Ten years ago, there were hardly any coloured people in Leeds. Today there are 9000.

Now the bias of this opening address is very clear. First, it was assumed that living conditions would further deteriorate because of Black neighbours; now 'the problem has taken on a new meaning' with 'Negroes for neighbours' – a new crisis. Secondly, the audience was encouraged, from the outset, to read 'the problem' from a White perspective, so that the emotionality resided exclusively with the White neighbours. It was implied that the local tradition, morality and prosperity of White neighbourhoods – 'the indigenous population' – was under threat from 'the newcomers.' Thirdly, there was a focus on statistical information with the implication that the apparent acceleration in numbers (from 'hardly any' to 9000 within ten years) in itself denoted a current crisis. But *The Negro Next Door* was a classic race relations documentary for another reason; it tenaciously structured its material for dramatic effect by setting up Black and White as necessarily conflicting. It did this by loosely structuring the programme in three parts: the first addressed 'the problem' from the White neighbours' perspective; the second, although far more abbreviated, looked at it from the Black neighbours' perspective; and the third brought the two groups of neighbours together in an attempt to resolve 'the problem' – or as it turned out, to witness a conflict. Despite this seemingly instinctive reformist structure, the Black neighbours, because they were only discussed in terms of problems, were shown to be in need of rehabilitation, whereas the White neighbours were only required to 'tolerate'. Although the White women that were interviewed displayed an outpouring of racist fears (Black people were referred to as violent, dirty, unhygienic, uncivilized, unwilling/unable to communicate and 'integrate', overpopulated, unconcerned with their children's welfare and hygiene and ultimately as primitive/unable to cope in 'civilized Western' society), at no point did the narrator (Desmond Wilcox) interject or 'correct' them. The commentary simply continued, 'For those two women, still perhaps confused and uncertain, the obvious fears and myths are mixed up with their desire to be good Northern Neighbours, to be Christian.' The final scene of *The Negro Next Door* was perhaps the most revealing with respect to this preferential treatment. One of the White female interviewees turned to Wilcox and asked him 'Would you like to see your oldest daughter marry a coloured man?' The shot remained on the woman, so that the audience did not get to see Wilcox's expression. Wilcox remained silent. The woman looked at him carefully and said, 'You would not. I'm reading your face like a book. No, you would not.' A statement by Nigerian writer, Obi Egbuna, seems to exemplify the point I am trying to make here: 'When you confront him [the Englishman] personally, it is never his fault, he of course, never has racial prejudice, it is always the neighbour who is the villain. . . . This is how they have fooled the Black man in England to believe that there is little or no evidence of racialism in the Englishman' (Egbuna in Owusu, 2000: 66).

If these were the kinds of myths that surrounded African-Caribbean people in public discourse during the 1960s, then the 'culture clash' or 'between two cultures' syndrome was one commonly used to explain the Asian predicament. This projected difference and unassimilability onto the younger generation of Blacks and Asians, just as it had with their parents' generation. The 'between two cultures' logic locked the Black – often Asian – social subject at a traumatic crossroads, somewhere between their 'new' British way of life and their other 'Asian' one. As well as being predicated on the myth that there ever was a definable and homogeneous British or Asian 'way of life', this trajectory accommodated a new set of myths designed for Asians – as overly moral, oppressive (men)/oppressed (women), alien, confused and negatively bound by close-knit family structures. For example, *Asian Teenagers* (BBC, 1968) presented viewers with the image of the 'ghetto' as an essentially regressive, insular and voluntarily divisive space. Thus, the commentary began, 'Six years in Southall, Middlesex, sometimes called "little India", has taught Rajish that *they*, the English, just don't want to know about *us* the Asian teenagers.' The classic stereotypes of British-Asianness presented in the programme are too extensive to outline here, but in general there was a preoccupation with arranged marriages (described as 'repugnant to most English people. . . . Victorian is an apt description of Asian attitudes to family life and Dickens would have understood why these Muslim girls work all hours in their fathers' restaurant kitchens') and Asian culture was depicted as both sinister and exotic. Filming an Asian prayer ceremony, the commentary stated, 'For the English neighbours, it's an odd kind of happening on an Autumn Sunday morning . . . the alien forms of ritual, which could of course be mistaken for devil worship.' Although Asian teenagers were interviewed in the programme, thus allowing the programme to present itself as an 'authorized' depiction of cultural difference, the gaze was distinctly White, always judging the grounds of cultural acceptability (deeming Asian cultures and 'rituals' as odd and even audacious), and, once again, deflecting the focus from British racism. It was a case of universality (Whiteness) versus specificity (Asianness) with television (the narrator/interviewer/camera) sitting 'innocently' between a conflict situation and problem which it had in fact set up.

In displaying its democratic sensibilities, these documentaries safeguarded the 'victims' of discrimination, whilst also demonstrating the moral integrity of its expurgators (i.e. racism was disassociated from the documentarists and from television's values) even if it underpinned its own discourse. The typical 'democratic' structure of the text (of asking 'both sides') gave the illusion of balance, and the generalist titles and approaches – *Asian Teenagers*, *The Negro Next Door*, *Mixed Marriages*, *Coloured School Leavers* – implied that a typical situation existed and was simply being addressed by the programme. The aspiration towards equilibrium and the liberal attempts to 'give Blacks a fair treatment' within these social documentaries highlighted that racist opinion can, in fact, operate within the liberal consensus. Discussions were primarily set around the degree to which Black people were 'integrated', rather than what it was, on a grass-roots level, which was preventing this integrated utopia from happening. The 'social problem' was that Blacks were not fitting neatly within or simply accepting the liberal consensus ideal of an integrated society, often because they were burdened with inescapable cultural difference and its accompanying deficiencies. With everyone shown to be trying so hard to get on, these 'social problems' were never quite worked out or eliminated, leaving the Black social problem as impenetrable and insoluble.

powellism and the break with 'the tolerant centre'

In time, the gradual deconstruction of the social democratic postwar consensus which followed a number of key social changes (such as unemployment, post-imperialism and the end of the postwar boom) gave way to a range of extreme views on British race relations, with the effect of unsettling the hold of 'the tolerant Centre'. As such, the overriding social consensus of the postwar years was interrupted by political and cultural pluralization, creating a gap between television's unifying project and the social, economic and cultural interests of an increasingly differentiated British nation. As the clear demarcations of political alliances became increasingly blurred, modern forms of neo-conservative populist venting began to unfold, one of which was the anti-immigration bandwagon (see Mercer in Grossberg et al.,

1992: 424–49). During the 1960s, conservative and liberal thinkers generally agreed that immigration control was a prerequisite to 'good race relations'. This logic was summed up most memorably by the renowned Labour
politician, Roy Hattersley, who argued, 'Without integration, limitation is
inexcusable; without limitation, integration is impossible' (Hattersley in
Rose, 1969: 229). The issue of numbers and internal/external flow was high
on the political Right's agenda at the time, and whilst the liberal Left were
keen to be seen to exercise cultural and racial sensitivity, they also appeared
to be anxious to appease racist opinion in their own ranks and concerned
about being publicly perceived as a 'soft touch' (hence the 1965 White Paper
on Immigration).

The most notorious bearer of the anti-immigration movement was the
Conservative MP, Enoch Powell, a maverick voice who, during the 1960s,
influenced public awareness and approaches to 'race' in an unprecedented
manner, paving the way for the formation of a new public mood towards
race and national identity. Powell vocalized a new populist and patriotic
modality of tribal racism that did not simply present itself as a White/Black
dichotomy, but more fundamentally as a matter of national pride/identity
versus chaos, consensus versus conflict and (White) Britain versus 'the
Others'. In a 1995 BBC interview, three years before his death, he reiterated
his position when he said, 'What's wrong with racism? Racism is the basis
of national identity' Powell measured the crisis of race in his infamous so-
called 'Rivers of Blood' speech which he delivered before about a hundred
people at the Annual General Meeting of the West Midlands Conservative
Political Centre in Birmingham on 20 April 1968 (two days before the introduction of the second Race Relations Bill). He forewarned, 'In this country
in fifteen or twenty years' time the black man will have the whip hand over
the white man' (quoted in Seymour-Ure, 1974: 103). The speech was not
recorded for television, but it is estimated (according to a Gallup poll) that
within two days, 86 per cent of the British adult population had heard edited parts of the speech (Curran and Seaton, 1988).[2] This was a classic case of
the media setting the agenda, and begs the question of its role in amplifying
a crisis or 'moral panic', following Powell, over the dangers of immigration,
and of the degree to which it has, since then, insisted on infusing the public
memory with Powell's metaphors (the excreta through the old woman's
letterbox, wide-grinning picaninnies, the rivers of blood, the whip hand). For
example, the phrase 'rivers of blood' is a product of sound-bite editing, not
Powell's precise words which, drawing on Virgil, said, 'I seem to see "the
River Tiber foaming with much blood" ' (Collings, 1992). Meanwhile, the
media, which made the speech publicly known by simultaneously celebrating, replaying and condemning its content, overlooked the impact that this
kind of debating (usually based around the aphoristic questions, 'Is he/isn't
he racist?', 'Is his proposition right or wrong?') was having on Black Britons

(programmes were always set up according to what Powell thought of Black people, never around what Black people thought of him).[3]

A new tone of fear about the Black presence and a growing emphasis on 'numbers' began to occupy many of the documentary programmes in the late 1960s and early 1970s. Pre-Powell, the usual approach was what Stuart Hall has called 'inferential racism' (Hall, 1981: 37): always starting from the premise of White superiority and tolerance and the assumption that Blacks were 'the problem'. The BBC's 'Great Debate', *The Question of Immigration,* hosted by Robin Day, also constructed the debate in terms of numbers, while foregrounding Enoch Powell's scare-mongering forecast of trouble. As Hall says about 'the problem of immigration' as laid out in this programme: 'The *logic* of the argument is "immigrants=blacks=too many of them=send them home". That is a racist logic' (Hall, 1981: 46). Throughout this period, Enoch Powell courted the media, and Powellite rhetoric and language – no matter how cryptic and politically complicated it could be – began to have an important bearing both on societal attitudes towards race and on the public vernacular of British racism itself. Powell's blend of highbrow, populist and inflammatory language seductively touched on, released and intensified social fears and uncertainties related to 'race', change and 'otherness'. The legitimacy and cachet of Powell's parliamentary position at the time separated him from earlier, more marginal, anti-immigration 'extremists' such as Colin Jordan and Oswald Mosley. The media presented itself as straddling the middle ground by merely relaying the views of a generally respected and intellectual Conservative politician to the public (for example, on *The Great Debate – Enoch Powell and Trevor Huddleston* (LWT/ITV, 1969)).

The blanket coverage of Powell across different media forms, especially following the now legendary 'Rivers of Blood' speech, pointed to a clear divide between those calling for Powell's dismissal from the shadow cabinet (Edward Heath sacked him from the cabinet following the April speech) and those proclaiming 'we back Powell', but television also needs to be recognized as itself soliciting such 'pro' or 'anti' positions. On a state level, many politicians saw Powell's views as a green light, and now felt able to register *their* fears about Black immigration, which had been festering since well before the 1948 Nationality Act. Many White Britons (who were being told by Powell that they were a silenced majority), now also felt quite justified and determined to express their hostility towards a Black presence. To be 'with Enoch' simply became a matter of choice and Powell's divisive views on race continued to be sought by the British media. Despite a range of critical or hostile press responses to Powell, television (in keeping with its ethos of neutrality) tended to take on a largely non-evaluative position, never leading the debate, or noting the positive effects of immigration or highlighting non-Black immigration (particularly Southern Irish, Italian, other

European). By implicitly allowing Powell to set the agenda, television never doubted that immigration was innately problematic and needed to be strictly controlled. Interestingly, Powell located the media itself ('a tiny minority, with almost a monopoly hold on the channels of communication, who . . . will resort to any device or extremity to blind both themselves and others [to the effects of immigration]') as one of the 'enemies within' (Powell, 1969: 300). Most of all, he condemned the media's apparent location at 'the centre' of a liberal consensus, a criticism which was also beginning to emerge, for quite different reasons, from some minority groups who felt sidelined by a supposedly impartial mainstream media.

the rise of access and anti-racist interventions in the 1970s and 1980s   By the 1970s, television itself was being intensifyingly located at the centre of debates around race, and the impact, uses and powers of the medium were increasingly being noted (not just by Powell, but in, for example, the UNESCO reports, 1974, 1977, 1986). During the 1970s, a number of 'alternative' (although they shared some characteristics with the earlier set of social discourses) race-related documentaries began to materialize. Some had an overseas or historical emphasis, but others such as *Asians on the Shop Floor* (*Man at Work*, BBC, 1972), *See For Yourself* (ITV, 1972), *Black to Front* (ITV, 1978) and *Singh* (*Worktalk*, BBC, 1976) were focused on Britain, often on the timely issue of unions and workers' (cultural) rights, or on the rise of right-wing, fascist militancy (*World in Action*, 1971). For the first time, Black people were now becoming involved in the production team and, occasionally, a Black-directed or produced production would emerge (for example, *Breaking Point*, ATV/ITV, 1978, Dir. Menelik Shabazz; *Struggles for a Black Community*, Channel 4, 1982, Dir. Colin Prescod; Newsreel Collective's *Divide and Rule – Never*, 1978). Alan Horrox, who worked on a four-part series on race, *Our People* (Thames TV/ITV, 1979), suggested that some social documentaries were working against 'a growing conservatism at every level of programming in television' (Horrox, 1979: 83). *Our People* for example, combined statistics, historical information and factual source information to examine the institutional racism of immigrant laws; racial discrimination in housing, employment and education; the history of imperialism and the call for immigrant labour. It also looked at the recent increase in racist attacks and the response of anti-racist organizations. *Our People* was targeted at a 'swayable' audience, 'the great number of people in the "middle ground", for whom racism is part of everyday culture, and who are open to accepting racist arguments and explanations if no better alternative seems available' (ibid.). But this was also a mass majority audience, whose 'middle ground' race politics had been reinforced precisely by the ever-converging BBC and ITV positions on 'race relations'.[4]

As a result of various internal and external critiques of television bias, the medium began to open out to audiences, new producers and unexplored modes of production. The word 'access' became central in considerations of the medium's effects, as did what television as a (multi-ethnic) 'public sphere' really meant. The first set of television access slots, mostly political and campaigning in approach, had their roots in BBC Local Radio of the mid-1970s, and were influenced by the rise of access work in Canada and the USA. The BBC's Community Programmes Unit was established in 1972, and headed in the 1970s by Mike Fentiman who later explained the department's mission to 'give airtime to the unheard, the rarely heard, the socially inarticulate and so on' (quoted in Dowmunt, 1993: 164). The first programme to come out of the Unit was *Open Door* (subsequently *Open Space*), which was broadcast on BBCTV from spring 1973. Specific slots such as *Black Londoners* were open to the public to make programmes from a 'community' viewpoint. This moment marked a shift not only in the politics of representation, but also in terms of the politics of production, with Black people now becoming more actively involved.

In the name of access, 'neutrality' and 'democracy', these spaces were now also being extended to those who had previously been thought too contentious or provocative to be (explicitly) granted airtime on British television, such as extreme racist organizations. An edition of *Open Door* entitled *British Campaign to Stop Immigration* (1976), was a racist, anti Black-immigration project which critiqued, amongst other things, equality legislation. Thus, we saw one man explain how 'his area' had been taken over by immigrants. Mid-polemic, the words 'Censored – By Race Relations Act' were sprawled across the screen, implying that the effects of a liberal consensus were indeed a conspiracy of silence (which Powell had long ago identified in the media). Another edition of the *Open Door* slot, *It Ain't Half Racist, Mum* (1979), the first (mediated) television access slot to address the question of Black representation, was 'a programme *about* the media and racism, *on* the media, *against* the media' (Hall, 1981: 47) made by the Campaign Against Racism in the Media (CARM). By showing examples from mainstream television programmings' depictions of race, Stuart Hall (who co-presented the programme with Maggie Stead) explained CARM's aim 'to make the media, for once, "speak" against the media's dominant practice, and thus reveal something about how they normally function' (ibid.). Many of those involved in making the programme were aware that the BBC was uneasy about the programme because they felt it, 'undermined their professional credentials by suggesting that they had been partisan where they were supposed to be balanced and impartial. It was an affront to the liberal consensus and self-image which prevails within broadcasting' (Hall, 1981: 37). The issue of access also laid open broader questions about the paternalism of that which is supposed to be a public service institution and 'owned' by the nation: 'Access', as Carl Gardner argued, 'is something that the BBC *gives* to other people, despite being itself a public service paid for by *our* money' (Gardner, 1979: 19). Other *Open Door* programmes such as *Black Teachers* continued to effectively criticize institutional (in this case, educational) racism. The Southall Defence Committee used the slot to 'pad out' information and re-educate people about the politics of the 1979 Southall disturbances (see p. 17). *Southall On Trial* (1979) used direct testimonies, maps, photographic evidence and commentary to retell the story of exactly why so many had protested and of how the peaceful protest had ended in violence and death. The programme-makers offered an alternative viewpoint to the 'official' news coverage of the incident, by emphasizing the use of provocation, police brutality and unfair legal procedures, thus pointing to the racism that exists within institutions such as the law, the police and the media, rather than depicting 'race' or 'Blackness' as the source of 'the problem'. The 'subjective' stance that access programming was required to declare and the fact that it was explicitly authored, meant that these programmes were likely to be read in a different way to the mainstream current of master race relations documentaries.

There was certain resistance to the emergence of these 'alternative' voices, particularly when they didn't operate within undisguised access slots. So for example, Black filmmaker Henry Martin's film *Grove Music* (1981), although it had an obvious focus on music and the emerging sound of Black-British reggae bands, also warned of racial unrest. Although bought by Channel 4, once the riots did in fact start in 1981, Martin had to fight against the decision to ban the film. When it was eventually screened (it stayed on a shelf for three years), it was aired late at night with no mention in the television listings or to Martin himself until 7 p.m. that evening (Martin, interview with author, 16.5.96). Similar struggles were experienced by the Black independent film workshop, Ceddo, with their film *The People's Account* (Dir. Milton Bryan, 1986). The film, which was in fact banned by Channel 4, focused on the uprisings of 1985 and particularly on the views of many in the Broadwater Farm Community. When *Death of a Hells Angel* (LWT/ITV, 1985, part of *The London Programme*), a unique investigation into the death of John Mikkleson, a young Black man in police custody was made, the police involved in the case put out a high-court injunction which was upheld by the Court of Appeal, thus banning the programme from television, until a further settlement which allowed it to be screened.

Institutional evasion tactics were more explicitly played out with David Koff's film *Blacks Britannica* (US, 1978). Although the independent production was made for the US (WGBH-Boston), it was based on Britain's colonial heritage and on the Black-British experience from a Black-British perspective. As part of an American series which aimed to access new viewpoints, *Blacks Britannica* was editorially controlled by a group of mainly Black radicals, and by resting between Latin American and European traditions of political filmmaking, it also opened up new ways of approaching the documentary form. Despite such advances, WGBH was pressurized to put out a re-edited version of the film because of concerns that it presented a damaging critique of Britain's race relations record (the BBC and CRE were involved in the dispute). A court battle ensued in the States with Koff and colleagues contesting directors' copyright since they were dissatisfied with the altered version of the film. The planned airing on PBS was cancelled and, for the next four years, was under federal court injunction not to be seen by more than 19 people at any one time. As Black-British cultural practitioner, Colin Prescod, who was involved in the production recounts, 'The whole thing was about denying what the film was saying, which was that things are very bad; the measure of how bad they are is their youth and the measure of how bad it is for the youth is that they are about to explode. . . . In 1982 Channel 4 purchased a copy but it has never been shown' (Prescod, interview with author, 19.11.96). When the riots did happen in 1981, WGBH withdrew their case and said they would destroy their version of the film. The impact of the original version of the documentary was telling (it played to packed houses in venues such as The Other Cinema in London and various community centres). What became apparent in these encounters between a number of overlapping constituencies of tastes, interests and politics, was that the media space which Black people could potentially occupy, although highly regulated, had to be regarded as a significant site of struggle. 'Race facts' had rarely been challenged in this way; the 'race relations' case was assumed to have been proven. It also illustrated that critical opposition to liberal and conservative attitudes on race, racism and immigration (the defining positions and themes of Black representation) had themselves only been allowed to work within a narrow and regulated range of opinion and thus had only been willingly accessed when they were considered as legitimate forms of opposition. Television audiences had grown accustomed to the medium's preponderant attitudes on matters of race: a position which was not only promoted as and widely assumed to be independent, liberal and centrist, but which also framed Black people as socially moot and as essentially marginal from British society. Such is the power and effect of the dominant consensus constructed by popular representations of race, that even those programmes designed to dismantle 'untruths', are often subsequently perceived as untruthful themselves because they are seen to work against the grain and outside the inter-textual framework of mainstream common sense. In this sense, meanings of cultural Blackness, even when they emanate from alternative spaces, are inevitably mediated by their relation-ship with other signs of Blackness, and this, in turn, impacts on the way they are read.

breaks and continuities in the 1990s

We will return some of these issues around access, 'alternative representations' and Black-produced documentary in more detail within the context of multicultural programming (Chapter 3), but I want to make some comment on the key shifts within documentary, and indeed on the entire tone of television, during the 1980s and 1990s and also point to some of its stubborn, racialized con-tinuities. The two main shifts for our concerns, were: first, that as a result of developments in ethnic minority cultural politics (Chapter 1), the overall look of television had become increasingly pluralistic and multiculturalized; and second, that as a result of the governing regulatory and economic forces, there was a general move from the political, public and campaigning empha-sis of the earlier set of documentaries, to ones based more on personal iden-tity, talk, consumerism, lifestyle and characters. Leisure documentaries, or ones with a more human angle, were occasionally fronted by new Black-British 'crossover' personalities (e.g. ragga star Apache Indian (*Apache Goes Indian*, Channel 4, Tx: 19.8.95), Jazzie B (*Frontline*, Channel 4, Tx: 29.6.94), Madhur Jaffrey (*Madhur Jaffrey's Flavours of India*, BBC2, 1995), Ainsley Harriott (*Ainsley's Barbecue Bible*, BBC2, 1997), and Chrystal Rose (*The Chrystal Rose Show*, Anglia/ITV, 1993–96). Many of these pro-grammes were part of a broader shift towards hybrid 'lifestyle' formats (travel shows cum documentaries cum cookery programmes), which offered a more socially inclusive look, audience user-friendliness, and marked a more extensive break with long-running landmark documentary strands, particularly on ITV (such as *World in Action*, *First Tuesday*, *Weekend World*, *This Week*, which all ended in the 1990s) to short series and one-off documentaries (see Anderson, *Broadcast*, 20.3.98, and Campaign for Quality Television, *Serious Documentaries on ITV*, January 1998). Previously marginalized voices were now emerging as a subaltern part of 'non-specialist' programming. Traditional notions of authored access were reinterpreted in the updated form of 'docu-soaps' and 'video diaries', and a glut of 'accessed' narratives – from popular light entertainment such as *Beadle's About* (ITV), to documentary series such as *Modern Times* (BBC2) to viewer-narrated, 'human-document' slots such as *Video Diaries* (BBC2) and *Video Nation* (BBC2), were now aided by the sophistication of camcorder technology. During the 1990s, it was clear that the character of access had changed – it was no longer about a political struggle over the 'ideological state apparatus', but about making programmes and covering issues with a mainstream tabloid agenda (crime, money, social issues, health, celebrities, the Royal family) and in ways that were more audience-accessible; this updated version of access was now more implicitly incorporated and being popularized to occupy the ever-expanding mainstream. It was part of the commercial drift, underpinned by the basic fear that by making things too difficult, too challenging and 'inaccessible', viewers would switch over to one of the many other channel options now on offer (John Humphreys, *Guardian*, 30.8.99).

In the face of such changes, the BBC Community Programmes Unit and BBC Education continued to produce some exceptional analyses of Black-related issues. The BBC TV Continuing Education and Training Initiative's five-year Mosaic project was launched in 1989 to bring together educationalists, BBC Education and other specialists from ethnic communities to work on a range of anti-racist training programmes and education initiatives such as the *Black and White Media Shows* (I and II, 1984/5), *Living Islam* and *Racism and Comedy*. BBC Education's *Black and White in Colour* season (Tx: 27.6.92–3.7.92), which featured the two-part documentary, *Black and White in Colour* (Dir. Isaac Julien, Tx: 27.6.92, 30.6.92), traced the history of Black representation on British television from the 1930s to the 1990s through archival footage (see Malik in Newcomb, 1997: 184). The season broadcast a number of British programmes featuring Black people, as well as exploring the American experience of Black programming. One particularly interesting production to emerge from the Mosaic initiative was *Birthrights* (BBC2, 1991–93), part of the BBC Education Department's effort to invest in Black independent film production (see Chapters 3 and 9) (an arrangement followed by the channel's Black history series, *Hidden Empire* in 1996) and to explore 'questions of culture and identity and from a black perspective' (*Birthrights*, BBC memorandum) by focusing on Black culture, history and identity. Many of these documentaries – *Who Stole The Soul?* (1991, Dir. Ngozi Onwurah) on the resonance of music of Black origin; Gurinder Chadha's moving film on elderly Asians in Southall (1992, *Acting Our Age*, Umbi Films); and *Crossing The Tracks* (1993, Reel Life), a homage to the ways in which youth culture is 'changing Britishness' in its cross-fertilization of ethnic styles, music and language, presented by dub poet, Benjamin Zephaniah – exemplified a critical break from the framework of the Black problematic.

Despite such developments, the master-codes of the 'official' race relations rhetorical documentary style (liberal, polite, social problem discourses) were still much in evidence through the 1990s and arguably, because of the new ratings-focus, being narrativized and dramatized in unprecedented ways. This growing commercialization also coincided with the rise of Black media professionals in mainstream broadcasting spaces, particularly within investigative journalism, especially when it involved 'race', 'community' or

Black stories which Black researchers and producers were more likely to be assigned to. Accordingly, we began to see more Black people involved in the making of these mainstream Blacks-as-social-problem narratives (*The Peacemaker* (*Witness*; Channel 4, 1998), *Forbidden Love* (*Inside Story*; BBC, 1998), *Victims of Fear* (*This Week*; ITV, 1990)). Let us take the example of a critically-acclaimed and largely Black-produced edition of *Panorama* entitled *Underclass in Purdah* (BBC1, 1993). Its press release claimed the programme would break the stereotype of a successful Asian community and examine how Pakistanis and Bangladeshis were part of an emerging underclass because of crime, drug abuse and family breakdown (*Panorama* News Release, 28.3.93). The double marginalization of the Asian community under investigation here – their vulnerable class status and their 'specific' ethnicity and religion (Islam) – was reinforced by the textual approaches used to 'explain' them. *Social* problems were collapsed into *cultural* and *religious* ones (thus 'Underclass' – a specific term used for a sub or low class socio-economic group, was understood through 'Purdah' – which is a veil or curtain secluding and screening Muslim or Hindu women). The primary definers of the text were characteristically the 'official' spokespeople and the documentation functioned metonymically in-so-far as the illicit images (drugs, prostitution, family violence, battered women) filmed in parts of the Manningham (Bradford) area were presumed to be representative of the entire British Muslim community. Thus the commentary stated, 'Those not looking for girls in Manningham are usually looking for drugs' and 'Most Muslim-Asian families prefer to leave the British way of life outside the front door', and a pimp explained, 'Most of the girls are run by Asians you know – they're all Asians – all the Asians are mixed up in drugs and you know gambling and all sorts of things really'. The 'expert' advice of White policemen, the secret filming of young schoolgirls, an interview with a professional (non-British) cricketer who was expected to speak as a professional Pakistani (Imran Khan), and an interview with Tariq Modood, a British-Pakistani academic from the Policy Studies Institute who concluded that, 'the main reason for the difference between Muslims and the rest of the Asian community is not racial discrimination' all produced mixed messages, a lack of grass-roots analysis, and an emphasis on supposed 'self-inflicted' community problems. A battered woman recounted, 'He was more backwards, you know . . . 'cos he's not brought up in this country. He's from Pakistan, which meant we wouldn't get on anyway. He was completely different to me. I was more westernized than him.' The documentary concluded, 'In many ways, Pakistanis and Bangladeshis find themselves in a worse position today than when they first arrived in Britain 30 years ago. . . . Muslim Asians are now asking themselves how they got into this position when other ethnic groups are doing so much better.' *Underclass in Purdah* was indicative of a more general shift from focusing on 'society' to 'self-help solutions', breaking with what Werbner has described as 'the one-way deterministic approach which defines immigrants as victims' (Werbner in Werbner and Anwar, 1991: 141), to a focus on points of anxiety which Black people are experiencing, and often depicted as responsible for creating.

A key image of British-Asians in the 1990s focused on the threat and manifestations of what was depicted as religious fundamentalism, particularly in relation to British Muslims (via notions of Islam) who became *the* ethnic Folk Devils during the 1990s. The public discourses around 'the Salman Rushdie affair', and particularly the 'book-burning' of *The Satanic Verses* by a group of British-Muslims in 1989, indicated a shift from crude racist biological essentialism towards supposedly more rational (cultural, religious) explanations of difference, which accommodated distinct forms of Islamaphobia. The typical media response to this 'religious fundamentalism' was a more widespread 'liberal fundamentalism'; defining how we were to arrive at our judgement of *all* Muslims – except of course, Salman Rushdie (and other media élites such as Tariq Ali and Farrukh Dhondy), who was now in the safe hands of Western liberalism and fair-mindedness (see Parekh and Bhabha, 1989). The boundaries between religion, culture, politics and history, and 'Muslim Pride' and 'fanaticism' were collapsed into one. Television news provided very little thoughtful analysis, and made a series of generalized assumptions that *all* British-Muslims supported Ayatollah Khomeini's fatwa. Such discrimination had very real, local effects on the everyday lives of many British-Muslims who had to deal with this new burden of purportedly unassimilable difference. Other events – the resignation of White headmaster, Ray Honeyford, following his comments on multicultural education and Muslims (1983); the debates around religiously independent schools; the Gulf War (1991); Jemima Goldsmith's marriage to Imran Khan (1996); and the outrage over the prospective 'beheading' of two British nurses in Saudi Arabia (1997) – have also triggered anti-Islamic discourses. When the two British nurses (Deborah Parry and Lucille McLauchlan) were charged with murder and threatened with the death sentence in Saudi Arabia in September 1997, the studio-discussion programme *Thursday Night Live* (Carlton/ITV, 25.9.97) whipped up general condemnations of both Islamic criminal codes and Islamic culture, and confused Islamic law with Pakistani law (the programme opened with an image of the Koran, the 'build-up' to a beheading and photos of Muslims branding swords). A *Panorama Special* (BBC1, 21.5.98) aired on the nurses' release, depicted the Saudis according to the nurses' anecdotal 'evidence' and claims of sexual harassment. At around the same time, we were witness to another form of patriotic media favouritism with the frenzy over the Louise Woodward US murder-trial in 1997–98, and exhaustive reports on her supporters' 'yellow ribbon' campaign. The media's partisan approach on these occasions is even more unmistakable when we juxtapose it with the comparative apathy to non-White British criminal cases, such as that of Krishna Maharaj, a British-Asian, who has had a death sentence pending over him for over a decade in the USA. We are not talking here about guilt or innocence, but about obvious inequities in the mainstream media agenda regarding what is in 'the national interest' (it is left up to the minority press or random one-off, usually regionally-aired documentaries to fight the marginalized corner, for example, *The London Programme* special on Maharaj's case, *Dead Man Talking*, Carlton, 1997). I want to return to some of these issues in the next chapter where I will outline, in more detail, the institutional responses to redressing the obvious inequities (in terms of access, modes of address and subject-matter) that we have so far been discussing.

notes

1   The 'Black and White in Colour' archive interviews are unedited versions of the interviews conducted as part of the BFI's Black and White in Colour project.

2   Note *Panorama: A Profile of Enoch Powell* (BBC, 1968). Following his death on 8 February 1998 and to mark the thirtieth anniversary of the 'Rivers of Blood' speech, Channel 4 screened a mock trial entitled *The Trial of Enoch Powell* (LWT for C4, Tx: 20.4.98) based around these core themes of Powellism.

3   One important exception here was an edition of the BBC social documentary series *One Pair of Eyes* (1968) entitled *One Black Englishman* in which author and poet Dom Moraes spoke of the effect which Powell's 1968 speech had on him. A later edition in the series entitled *Return as a Stranger* (1970, produced by Anthony De Lotbiniére) saw Moraes return to India.

4   The 1986 Peacock Report was later to make a criticism of the BBC's and ITV's overly 'comfortable duopoly'.

the institutionalization of the black voice on television: questions of access, multicultural programming and cultural diversity

The 1980s saw important breakthroughs in terms of accessing the Black voice, particularly through the provisions of the Multicultural Departments, which explicitly positioned Black representation on the agendas of British broadcasting institutions. The inclusion of Black faces and characters, the exploration of 'Black Issues', the training and recruitment of Black programme-makers, and the designation of these Black 'specialist units' stemmed, to a large degree, from the debates around access and public service broadcasting during the 1970s and 1980s. I want to look back at some of those developments here, particularly in relation to non-fiction multicultural programmes. But I also want to bring the story up-to-date to consider why terrestrial broadcasters today are having to find new ways of addressing and attracting Black audiences in a pluralist Europe, devolved Britain and in a (media) society that is fast outgrowing the simple notion of 'multiculturalism'.

Apart from *Asian Club* (BBCTV, 1953–61), a live studio discussion programme for people of the Commonwealth, set up to commemorate 21 years of the BBC's General Overseas Service on which the radio version of *Asian Club* had been broadcast for ten years, British television had no targeted multicultural programmes until the 1960s. In 1965, the newly formed Campaign Against Racial Discrimination demanded that the BBC provide programmes which made Britain's Black communities feel a more integral part of British society, and Asians in particular argued the case for a separate programme. Many Asians, having come from traditions of pluralism in terms of language, countries (Bangladesh, India, Pakistan) and religion (mainly Muslims, Sikhs, Hindus and Christians) thought it only natural that they were catered for in the name of diversity. Two programmes followed: *Apna Hi Ghar Samajhiye* (*Make Yourself at Home*), which began in October 1965, and was broadcast early on Sunday mornings both on BBC1 and on the BBC Radio Home Service, and *Nai Zindagi Naya Jeevan* (*New Life*) (BBC1, 1968–1982). Both programmes were mainly presented in Hindustani (a hybrid of Urdu and Hindi) and produced by the Immigrants'

Unit, the first BBC bi-media department, set up by Hugh Carleton-Greene (who became Director General in 1960). These were classic 'public service broadcasts'; integration services for 'immigrants' designed to 'help integrate newly arrived Asian immigrants into their new environment through practical advice, and act as a link with the Indian sub-continent through performances and interviews with items on abroad' (BBC Multicultural Programmes Department, BBC Pebble Mill Pamphlet, 1995). In 1966, the BBC launched the English-speaking strand, *Look, Listen and Speak*, and in 1977, it broadcast *Parosi* (BBC, 1977–78), a drama series intercut with discussions in Hindi and English, centring on the lives of two Asian families in Britain.[1] Those seen to be most in need of tips for 'integration' (more so than African-Caribbeans whose language, dress and religions were often similar to the English), were Asians, so it was for them that this narrowcasting was devised. Somewhat confusingly, the BBC was not at ease with admitting this assimilationist agenda; on the launch of the new service, BBC producer, David Gretton stated, 'this service will make no attempt to "integrate" its audience; though, to the extent that they are willing to assimilate, we shall be on their side' (*Radio Times*, 7.10.65). In 1977, the BBC introduced *Gharbar* (*Household*) (1977–87), a programme for Asian women screened on Wednesday afternoons which was primarily concerned with 'women's issues' such as health, hygiene, marriage, housekeeping and career advice. Meanwhile, *Nai Zindagi* became *Asian Magazine* (1982–87), a weekly half-hour Sunday-morning magazine programme. The homogenizing impetus behind many of these 'social service' programmes represented a liberal position which favoured cultural co-existence and the inevitability of a racially-integrated system and thus posed a striking contrast to the hovering proposition of voluntary repatriation which was making itself publicly known in many of the mainstream documentaries of the 1960s. At a time when many Asians inevitably felt alienated from the primary sources of information and entertainment in Britain, these programmes indicated that efforts were being made to address non-English viewers. At the same time, they were also based on an explicitly integrationalist project – a dominant assumption that any problems which Asian people faced in Britain could be eradicated by the assimilation of 'Asianness' into 'Englishness' – which was predicated on the *difference* of the Asian immigrant.

diversifying the public service ideal: multicultural programmes – 'what say you'?
We have already mentioned how during the 1970s, many of those involved in media research, such as the Centre for Contemporary Cultural Studies (CCCS), the Commission for Racial Equality (CRE),[2] the Glasgow Media Group and the Campaign

Against Racism in the Media (CARM), began to debate the issue of 'agenda setting', particularly in the context of news and current affairs reports on race (Chapter 1). In the last chapter we began to see how some of the more direct anti-racist interventions in television documentary (*It 'Aint Half Racist Mum, Black Teachers, Southall on Trial*) first emerged out of the television access slots of the 1970s which acknowledged criticisms that (despite the existence of a dominant public service ethos) television was tightly controlled and actively manipulated. Various committed individuals such as Darcus Howe, Gus John, John La Rose, Stuart Hall, Cecil Gutzmore and Ambalavaner Sivanandan were also pushing the question of institutional discrimination onto the agenda of various media organizations. The newly-formed CRE responded to the 1978 Government's White Paper on Broadcasting by arguing that, 'good race relations and equality of opportunity in Britain' needed fair media reporting and access (CRE, 1979). Despite Britain's unique philosophy of public service broadcasting, and the fact that television remained the most popular medium amongst Black audiences (Anwar and Shang, 1982), it was trailing behind many other countries in its ethnic minority programme output (Anwar, 1978) and was not matching the ethnic programmes and specialist formats of other media (mainly the press and radio).[3] By the late 1970s, the limitations of television approaching 'public service' as a social democratic paradigm of universal citizenship gradually began to give way to a more pluralist conception of 'the British public'; a shift from an undifferentiated mass to a number of distinct identifiable groups making up a whole nation. This positioned television as a central player in the shifting political discourses and ideas around race and nation.

Non-BBC targeted programmes first emerged at a regional level, with the pending (1980) reallocation of ITV franchises which made regional companies keen to be seen to address the different needs of their local audiences. (Of course, varied Black markets – in terms of taste and quantity – exist in different regions across the country, but those with low ethnic minority populations tended to have a patchy response to minority communities.[4]) ITV companies with comparatively large numbers of Black potential viewers such as the capital's London Weekend Television (LWT), began to experiment with schedules by using low-risk, off-peak slots to respond to calls for locally relevant minority programmes. These included: *Here Today, Here Tomorrow* (ATV/ITV, 1978–79), three films on British Asians presented by Pakistani actor, Zia Mohyeddin; *Here and Now* (Central TV/ITV), a weekly multicultural programme; and *Babylon* (LWT/ITV, 1979), a six-part series presented by Lincoln Browne targeted specifically at young Black Londoners under the initiative of John Birt (then head of Factual Programmes at London Weekend Television and later to become BBC Director General). Birt set up the London Minorities Unit (LMU) to acknowledge the capital's diverse minority audiences, and to target series for gay, Black and elderly (i.e. minority) audiences. At the time, Birt insisted that, 'the London Minority Unit's programmes are neither exclusively by or for their particular communities (although they are in part both these things) but they are emphatically *about* these communities' (Birt, 1980: 6). This commitment to 'crossover' audiences was to be a feature of the first set of Black actuality programmes during the 1980s, but was also to develop as a source of tension in terms of address, content and reception.

The LMU went on to produce *Skin* (LWT, 1980), a 30-minute documentary series broadcast on Sunday lunchtimes aimed at Asian and African-Caribbean communities, but also, as the executive producer, Jane Hewland stated, meant to appeal to the interests and concerns of White audiences. Despite its ambitious forecast, *Skin* was widely criticized for assuming that the British Asians and African-Caribbeans constituted a politically monolithic Black audience and for following in the tradition of mainstream documentaries by *explaining* the Black minority to the White majority, thus being yet another programme *about*, but not *for*, Black communities. *Skin* also tended to be very problem-oriented; essentially structured around the points of difference between the 'visible ethnicities' (a range of Black and Asian communities who, it was hoped, would all identify with the programme) and the 'invisible ethnicities' (White majority), with 'Blackness' generally discussed in relation to racism and White society. As Trevor Phillips,[5] who worked as a researcher on the series in his first television job, recalls, this bias weighed the series down:

> we were always going on about discrimination, always talking about racism. There's nothing wrong with doing those things as such, but . . . the experience of being black or Asian in a capital city is a bit more than waking up every morning and thinking 'Who's going to discriminate against me today? What job am I not going to get?' – because life isn't like that for people. (Phillips in Pines, 1992: 147–8)

The *Skin* initiative was however, an important early sign that the multicultural consensus had begun to establish itself, and that statements of good intent and equal opportunities procedures were now being applied in aspects of television policy. In 1980, the Black Media Workers' Association (BMWA) formed as a pressure group, bringing together Black and Asian mainstream and independent media practitioners. It began on a small informal basis with Mike Phillips, Julian Henriques, Diane Abbott, Parminder Vir and Belkis Belgani and was officially launched in February 1981 focusing on what Gary Morris categorized as two key aspects: one, 'concerns of the profession' which included monitoring press depictions of race, improving the independent Black media and liaising with media unions on these matters; the other was 'concerns of the black community', which included the establishment of a video group, attracting grants and accessing Black groups to the mainstream. In their first research report, the BMWA argued that racist practices in the media could only be tackled if more Black people were 'actually involved in reporting and editing, programme-making and developing images of black people for public consumption' (Brown, 1983: 52). The BMWA folded after five years, partly because the key players in it moved on to develop their own specific careers (spanning from politics to journalism to filmmaking), but also because the ideals of the group itself gradually began to fragment as it drew in different types of Black media workers who wanted a number of apparently incongruous things (Ainley, 1998). Black activist effort during this period was considerable, but the reasons for its demise said something significant about why so few Black institutional frameworks have fully established or sustained themselves over long periods as part of a broader anti-racist movement (for example, CARM and CARD also closed). As Imruh Bakari, a Black British filmmaker, argues: 'Where is the agenda of the Black Media Workers Association today? That should have existed until now. It should have been an institution' (Bakari, interview with author, 10.12.96).

In response to the growing debates about the influence, content and power of television, the BBC had set up the Independent Programmes Complaints Commission in October 1977, to consider viewers' complaints about particular radio and television broadcasts. In the same year, the Annan Committee which had been commissioned to research what form a new fourth channel might take, emphasized the importance of a liberal pluralistic model of broadcasting. This it saw as a free marketplace in which balance could be achieved through 'the competing demands of a society which was increasingly multi-racial and pluralist' (Annan, 1977). The new Channel emerged under the control of the Independent Broadcasting Authority (IBA), and was to commission programmes both from existing ITV companies and from independent practitioners (as a means to encourage diversity), and proposed to appeal to 'tastes and interests not generally catered for by ITV' and 'to encourage innovation and experiment in the form and content of programmes' (Blanchard, 1982). 'Minority groups' who had been campaigning for diversity generally welcomed this initiative, and detailed discussions for the internal structure and programme content of the fourth channel subsequently began.

Channel 4 began transmission in November 1982. Black programming was built into the structure of the Channel and, as such, it was the first time ever that someone had been specifically appointed to commission programmes for a non-White British audience. The first Commissioning Editor for Multicultural Programming was Sue Woodford who was to be succeeded in 1984 by Farrukh Dhondy who maintained the position until 1997 when it was taken over by Yasmin Anwar. Channel 4 also signified a new pattern of organized production by breaking with the prevailing in-house model within broadcasting and operating as a 'publishing house', commissioning work from different production units. There was of course a certain irony in Channel 4, with its commitment to a diverse conception of the national audience and societal vision, emerging in the teeth of a recession and against the methodologically individualistic governing forces of a Thatcherite government (Margaret Thatcher famously declared that there is 'no such thing as society . . . it's our duty to look after ourselves and then to look after our neighbour', *Woman's Own*, 31.10.87). But this was a channel that had been vociferously fought for by those who realized the importance of an alternative third space to the BBC and ITV duopoly. In time, the channel was also to have varying degrees of impact on the look, feel and approach of the other channels, particularly on BBC2, the other 'alternative' channel on which the BBC's multicultural programmes have traditionally been screened. Britain began, in a clearer sense, to operate a symbiotic model of broadcasting which accommodated public and private in a way that pertained to the interests of 'the general public'.

In general, early Channel 4 Black programmes were actuality-based. This was largely a matter of economics, given the considerable expense involved in drama production compared with magazine and documentary programmes. By the mid-1980s, Channel 4 had built up a large number of 'Black programmes', including *Black on Black* (1982–85) (produced by Trevor Phillips) and *Eastern Eye* (1982–85), live studio audience Black magazine programmes targeted towards African-Caribbeans and Asians respectively. The programmes began on controversial ground, since many had hoped that Sue Woodford (given Channel 4's proposed commitment to Black minorities and its commissioning, not producing role) would have turned to an emerging Black independent company, rather than the well-established London Weekend Television, to produce the channel's flagship Black programmes; posing as an early sign of the potential loopholes within diversity mandates. *Black on Black* and *Eastern Eye* focused on news, current affairs, cultural events and opinion, both nationally and internationally (a 'familiar mix of people and politics, culture and comedy, music and mayhem', Phillips, LWT Memorandum, 8.1.85). The regularity with which the programmes were broadcast (26 one-hour slots per year for each programme) was unique, because for the first time there was a permanent weekly presence of Black people on screen, a record that has since gone unmatched. *Eastern Eye* also covered a range of light and serious issues both home and abroad, and was produced by Samir Shah (who, like Phillips had been a researcher on LWT's *Skin*) and executively produced, together with *Black on Black*, by Jane Hewland (see Figure 2).

Figure 2

Eastern Eye, London Weekend Television for

Channel 4, Presenters Aziz Kurta and Shyama Perera

Courtesy of Channel 4 Picture Publicity

While Channel 4 was proactively addressing Black-British audiences, the BBC – with no Black programmes to speak of (apart from its traditional formats which emphasized links with 'home') – inevitably felt considerable pressure to do the same. In the early 1980s, the BBC attempted to match these two programmes with it's own versions – *Ebony* (BBC2, 1982-89) (the *Ebony* production unit was set up in 1982 for African-Caribbean programmes), and the aforementioned *Asian Magazine*, which was subsequently converted into the English-spoken, forty-minute Saturday morning magazine programme, *Network East*, in 1987. *Ebony*, like *Black on Black* was a studio-based magazine programme scheduled in a relatively peak-time slot (compared to *Black on Black* and *Eastern Eye* at 10.50 p.m.). Again the awkwardness over how to speak accountably *from*, *about* and *to* Black communities was a problem. Some argued that these early Black programmes should have done for Black audiences what other programmes were failing to do: use the space to redress the overall media racial imbalance. Sivanandan argued, 'what *we* want on *Black on Black* and *Eastern Eye* is an unbalanced view. We don't want a balanced view. The whole of society is unbalanced against us, and we take a programme and balance it again?'

(Sivanandan, 1983: 7). This was just one of the pressures that many early Black programme-makers had to face; that their 'marginal' space needed to be significantly different to mainstream programmes whilst not alienating a mainstream audience. Trevor Phillips later admitted that whilst *Black on Black* was for a Black family audience, he wanted to show how Blacks 'could behave like everybody else' (Phillips in Pines, 1992: 150). The BBC's and Channel 4's varied approaches to the Black-British diaspora and the anxiety over terminology in their definition of 'Blackness' (the BBC's decision to lump together both Asians and African-Caribbeans in a non-White category in *Skin* and Channel 4's decision to set the two apart in *Eastern Eye/Black on Black)* were bound to draw criticism. Where the former was seen to deny important cultural differences, the latter was criticized for overlooking the complexities of recent developments in racial politics in Britain, which had brought many from the Asian, African and Caribbean diaspora together under the unifying category 'Black' (see Gilroy, 1983: 131). Since 'the Black community' did not live as a homogeneous entity, television – along with other forms of media and arts (music, literature, radio, the press) – became a central medium in producing and disseminating the various meanings and ideologies that came to be associated with 'Blackness'.

In 1985, one of Farrukh Dhondy's first controversial decisions as the new Channel 4 Commissioner for Multicultural Programmes was to axe *Black on Black* and *Eastern Eye*. At the time, he urged the need for the Multicultural Department to commission a Black company with the task of developing current affairs output. *The Bandung File* (1985–89), produced by Dhondy himself together with two of his political co-workers, Tariq Ali[6] and Darcus Howe,[7] subsequently replaced the two programmes, operating under the newly formed, Black-led, independent company Bandung Productions, which Dhondy insisted could 'tell a story that no other British television company can tell' (Dhondy in Robinson, 1985–86: 17). Reporting from a uniquely 'Southern' outlook, *Bandung File* spanned a range of subjects from international affairs (*President Nyerere in conversation with Darcus Howe and Tariq Ali*, 1985), to the arts (*Profile of Vikram Seth*, 1986; *Linton Kwesi Johnson In Concert*, 1985), to home affairs affecting Black Britons (*Till Death Us Do Part – Labour and the Black Vote*, 1985). Indeed, *Bandung File* and *Black Bag* (which replaced it in 1991), can be considered amongst Channel 4's more successfully analytical and insightful Black programmes, with Dhondy's privileging of, at times, hard investigative journalism over what he defined as 'grievance programming' (a preoccupation with the manifestations of racism). *Black Bag* for example, examined the relationship between Asian newsagents and newsprint wholesalers, the intricacies of the Asylum Bill, and politics in the Punjab. The subsequent demise of such investigative journalism series by the early 1990s was to leave the responsibility for the coverage of key Black political issues to those few remaining generalist documentary slots such as Channel 4's *Dispatches* and the BBC's *Panorama*.

For some, Farrukh Dhondy's relative autocracy as the longest-running commissioning editor in the history of Black broadcasting (1984–97) was shrewdly misdirected. Like his predecessor (Woodford), Dhondy's recruitment practices were heavily criticized for side-stepping both existing and new Black talent. In addition, he made a number of controversial comments that appeared to work against the interests of the Black communities he was employed to make programmes for (see Dhondy, 'Black is a Point of View' *Broadcast*, 10.8.84: 20). When I spoke to Dhondy, a short while before he relinquished his post to Yasmin Anwar, he described how he saw his position and defined what he took 'multiculturalism' and 'public service broadcasting' to mean:

> What makes multiculture is colonialism and the transfer of populations. When they lived where they were, they were quite happy, there was no multiculturalism, there was unique culture in separate parts. Multiculture is when you import lots of Muslims here. . . . I feel that television ought to be editorially-led, ought not to be done by committee, ought not to have pretence at democratic opinion forming and giving people whatever they like. It ought to have a head sitting in charge of it saying 'I think this is what the public want to have'. Between that and Channel 4, that's what I think; between that and what I do for Channel 4 there is the commercial reality. I know there are certain things I ought to do, even if I do not like them. I ought to run Hindi film seasons. (Dhondy, interview with author, 1.9.96)

Given Dhondy's background and interests (he was part of the *Race Today* collective, a playwright, journalist and active member of the Black Theatre Co-operative), it had been hoped that he would be able to liaise favourably with Black artists and communities. However, his rather dictatorial style and the manner in which he exercised his commissioning role gradually drew criticism, as did his curious disengagement from aspects of the multicultural reality 'his' audiences lived on a daily basis. This autocracy was of course also accommodated by Channel 4's commissioning structure, which is fundamentally subject to individual commissioner's tastes, a thorny arrangement when it comes to satisfying the varied tastes of a poorly represented group and avoiding being cornered into the 'burden of representation' (Mercer, 1994: 81). In 1992, Alan Fountain (then Channel 4's Senior Commissioning Editor for Independent Film and Video) argued that, 'Channel 4 is an institution which has no policies, the policies are in a sense the tastes of the commissioning editors' (quoted in Givanni, 1995: 43).

One of the few series to foreground Black opinion in the 1990s was *Devil's Advocate* (Channel 4/LWT, 1992–96), a set of studio debates, very much in the sensationalist, personality-led and infotainment style of emerging factual programmes. Although the series quite obviously courted publicity by juxtaposing differing opinion on a 'Black subject' and through the confrontational tactics of its frontman, Darcus Howe, the best of the series managed to critically and engagingly profile Black figures such as Bernie Grant, Nigel Benn and Imran Khan and discuss issues ranging from the changing face of the Notting Hill Carnival, to the rise of new Black literature and the role of teenage magazines. In one memorable edition, which questioned the right-wing columnist Paul Johnson about his views on repatriation, Johnson, quite obviously feeling harassed by a vocal, multicultural studio audience, turned on presenter Darcus Howe, fists waving, declaring:

> This programme is extremely dangerous and destructive. The net effect of this programme is to set one race against another. You are indeed the Devil's advocate. You are doing the work of the Devil. . . . We should try and keep the tone of the discussion with which we treat these [race] problems as low-key as we can. . . . What I fear is that programmes like this don't help. (Paul Johnson on *Devil's Advocate*, 1996)

Johnson's outburst highlighted the pervasive 'fear' that 'outspoken' Black programmes, rather than being part of a liberal (well-mannered, polite, repressed) broadcasting rationale, were divisive and in opposition to it, and pushed the limits of acceptability and 'public service' too far (see Howe in the *New Statesman*, 15.11.99).

In any case, the very presence of specialist units and racially-targeted programmes has elicited disparate opinion about whether/how they can provide for Black audience needs and whether or not they encourage the 'ghettoization' of Black programmes, experiences and programme-makers by containing them at the margins, thus always ensuring they remain peripheral to mainstream production and representation. Part of the problem of course, is ingrained in the very fact that multicultural programmes consolidate Black audiences and programmes within particular slots. The fact that we still have *Black Christmas* (1995), *Indian Summer* (1997) and *Caribbean Summer* (2000) seasons are indicative of how poorly integrated Black programmes are in the mainstream schedules across the television year, an add-on mentality which best reflects itself in the appalling scheduling of Black programmes in 'graveyard slots', or against other prime-time audience pullers. On a commissioning level, there is a general fear (although it has been systematically denied by those who head the Multicultural

Departments) that the actuality of minority units allows other commission-ers/departments 'off the hook', since they rely on the specialist units and/or channels to cover 'race-related' topics and to have a conscience about Black audiences' needs (ITV, which is exempt from these kinds of social responsi-bility guidelines, has a depressingly poor track record in terms of an ongoing, network Black screen presence). In the early 1990s, journalist Alkarim Jivani, claimed that in a 1990 PACT meeting (the Producers' Alliance for Cinema and Television), 'at least one commissioning editor admitted that if there wasn't a multicultural unit, he would look harder at proposals from black programme-makers' (Jivani, 'Multiculture Clash', *Impact*, 1992: 27). There is little doubt that the Multicultural Departments have provided real opportunities for a number of Black producers and accessed new voices, but the individual tastes, policies and attitudes of commissioning editors, the concentration of production companies commissioned by them, and the types of narratives and formats broadcast, have often differed from the ideal of expanded diversity. Perhaps an even bigger problem, is the ingrained pre-sumption that the multicultural units *do* meet the Black public's needs.

The BBC's Multicultural Departments for example, particularly since the 1990s as part of a broader emphasis on unchallenging ratings-pullers, have demonstrated an overriding interest in emotive issues such as sex, crime, violence and abuse. Take for example, *All Black* (BBC2, 1993) and *East* (BBC2, 1990–), Black current affairs series commissioned under Narendhra Morar and defended by him on the grounds that, 'If a series is current affairs, then I'm not surprised it's going to be hard-hitting', and that his department refused to 'shy away from controversial issues' (Morar, inter-view with author, 17.7.95). But the sensationalist choice of topic (rent boys, prostitution, pornography, polygamy, abortion of female foetuses/suicide rates, self-mutilation), the hypothesis journalism (presenting recent findings in a report, then setting out to prove them), and the voyeuristic way in which the analysis was often conducted in these series (awkward dramatic recon-structions, darkened rooms, anonymous case studies) routinely veered towards a sordid picture of Black-British life. The myth of a static, political-ly naïve, Asian community, particularly in relation to the traditional icono-graphy of the passive female condition in Asian cultures, was also a common subject, feeding into racialized fears and stereotypes of cultural difference. Of course, to defend the importance of the issue is quite different from defending the way in which it is examined. These documentaries were also broadcast at around the same time as Channel 4's *Doing It With You . . . Is Taboo* (October 1993), a three-part series looking at inter-racial relation-ships from the perspectives of Black women and men, which constantly veered towards voyeurism and reiterations of mythologies around Black sexuality – of Black men and women as better lovers, of 'jungle sex', of exotica (Ross, 1996: 136).

Highly-regarded journalists such as Fergal Keane ('Who Really Killed Aung San?', 1997) and Mark Tully ('Last Among Equals', 1996; 'Tiger Trap', 1998) have been involved in notable editions of *East*. There is little doubt that the kinds of issues covered in these 'minority' programmes would be overlooked elsewhere on British terrestrial television. I am not arguing here that documentaries should only show us the 'good side' of our lives and our communities or be too scared to provoke or even disturb, but coming from the Multicultural Departments themselves, there are inevitably expectations that while such issues might get covered, the terms of the debate might start elsewhere and that they might break with the traditional race documentary approach of always locating 'the Black experience' in relation to the problematic and usually in relation to the same types of 'racial problems' and stereotypes. This is a tricky issue – how to present investigative journalism about and addressed to Black audiences, without alienating a mainstream audience, which does not intensify raced stereotypes or offend its target audience, and which has the BBC bosses coming back for more. The balancing act involved in holding onto cultural aims while competing equally in the mainstream marketplace inevitably puts further pressures on minority perceived programme-makers. A more practical issue emerges when we consider that a series such as *East*, the BBC's flagship current affairs series, because it is only screened for a few months a year and in predetermined slots, it does not pick up on events as they unfold, leaving the coverage of big community issues such as the troubles in Kashmir, the 1995 Bradford riots, and the 2001 Indian earthquake in the hands of mainstream news and the occasional documentary. There have of course been important exceptions to emerge from the BBC2 Multicultural Departments such as *Will to Win* (BBC2, 1993) on the history and ethos of Black people in sport, and *Sikhs* (BBC2, 1997), which traced the history and ethos of Sikhism. *East* has often touched on some very hard investigative lines and offered some interesting editions (a focus on political parties' relationship to British Asians, 1995; cricket and national identity, 1999; institutional racism in the prison system, 2000 and the clashes between the police, Pakistani and English youth in the Oldham area in 2001).[8]

The structural inconsistencies, and I am talking specifically about the BBC here, have prevented its Multicultural Departments over the years from having any clear sense of programme identity, any considered direction or any consistency in terms of on-screen output. This is a significant loss for the BBC and for its Black licence-fee holders, many of whom still feel failed by the Corporation and its claim to 'ethnic minority provisions' (Sreberny-Mohammadi and Ross, 1996). The politics around the department are complicated, but to briefly summarize: it was not until 1989, when the *Ebony* production team (part of the BBC General Programmes Unit since 1985) became the African-Caribbean Programmes Unit, that the BBC appointed its first Black editors to develop targeted multicultural programmes. Vastiana Belfon only lasted about a year as Editor of African-Caribbean Programming, and after about 18 months of low morale, internal strife and makeshift operations, Colin Prescod took over from Belfon, and Narendhra Morar oversaw Asian Programmes. The main productions (all documentary or magazines) were *Network East, On The Road, Black on Europe, Ebony People, Hear Say, All Black, East* and *Out of Darkness*. The hasty disbandment and then remodelling of the two departments as one umbrella Multicultural Programmes Department in 1992 under Morar's much-criticized management (largely because of his shoddy approach to African-Caribbean programming) did little to boost morale or faith in the future of the department. A repeated attempt to divide the single unit back into two (in late 1995), reallocate resources, and further disperse the African-Caribbean Department (now based at BBC Manchester under Dele Oniya) into news, drama and entertainment output, inevitably continued to put the personnel and output under considerable strain. Confusion over the department(s)' name ('Ebony Unit', 'Multicultural Programmes Unit', then 'African Caribbean Unit' and 'Asian Programmes'), its Editors (Belfon, Morar, Prescod, Dele Oniya and Paresh Solanki), and its geographical location, has exposed a piecemeal, ambivalent response by the BBC towards its licence-fee-paying Black audiences (Malik, 1995: 13–14). Black talent within the departments has unsurprisingly moved on (Oniya for example, has since moved to ITV's Carlton Television) reflecting a broader problem for the BBC in holding on to key Black personnel. Greg Dyke, appointed as the new BBC Director General in January 2000, made an early decision to close down BBC Pebble Mill (where Asian Programmes is based) and relocate its departments, hinting at an unpredictable future for Asian Programmes. Although these are essentially just 'packaging' problems, combined with the commercial drift that all broadcasters are part of and the complex unfolding of ethnic minority cultural politics over the past two decades, this muddled legacy has prevented the creation of a solid base from which to address the various representational needs of Britain's Black and Asian communities (Cottle, 2000). Unfortunately, it is the programmes and the audience-share, rather than the structural framework, which are the major determinants in how these 'minority' production units will maintain themselves as sustainable entities in the future. Many of the programmes are prime examples of the types of 'products' least likely to sustain themselves in our so-called 'third broadcasting revolution', which also happens to be increasingly bent towards a 'commercially-sensible', mainstream tabloid agenda that tends to ignore minority-perceived issues. Later BBC Asian programmes such as the imported Pakistani drama series, *Manjdhar* (1999) and *Paranda* (2000), the Asian video show, *Surfin' @s.i.a* (2000), and the multicultural youth discussion show, *Café 21* (1997– 1999) have looked dated and have no doubt been hampered by poor scheduling and low-budget demands. Meanwhile, a number of landmark Black programmes have emerged from other BBC departments such as News/Current Affairs (e.g. *Black Britain*, a Black-oriented news programme), BBC Education and the BBC Community Programmes Unit which spearheaded the *BBC Windrush Season* (BBC2, 1998).[9]

When I worked for BBC Asian Programmes, I got some independent insight into the internal production structures. I felt that there was deep-seated inferential racism within the corporation, a lack of considered critical reflection about programme aims and strategies, internal bidding for commissions and funds which called for a market mindset that seemed antithetical to the worthy issues we found ourselves covering, a general fear of challenging the governing forces of scheduling, budgets, programme-direction and management, an overwhelming culture of silence, defensiveness, careerism and acquiescence, and a hierarchical departmental structure which did not encourage too many ideas and opinions below producer level.[10] Although there are no official figures, there are undoubtedly many people who do watch and enjoy the BBC's targeted output, and the reasons why others are offended by particular Black series and programmes are complex: some Black viewers are certainly relatively conservative and/or prejudiced about particular 'taboo' subjects (such as abortion, pornography, homosexuality); and others may feel such enquiries are an indictment and intrusion on their communities. But we cannot disassociate the reasons for offence from other signs and meaning of Blackness in the public sphere: some Black viewers are inevitably conscious of what generalized or racist impressions other people (particularly a White, mainstream audience who might not 'know better') might form of them – a double rejection of the passive audience-thesis because it is not just about Black viewers actively making meanings of the text here, but also about how those meanings are, in turn, partially dependent on critically assessing 'what other people might think' (see pp. 99–100 on 'ethnic sitcoms'). There are others who are critical of the authorship of these programmes. A certain Muslim constituency would frequently lobby outside the BBC Asian Programmes' Pebble Mill offices protesting over what they identified as an anti-Muslim bias emanating from the department. Internal, unofficial attempts were often made to 'balance out' the Pakistani Muslim input and output by, for example, placing Muslim researchers and presenters on 'Muslim stories', and vigilantly paying as much attention to Eid as to Diwali and Vaisakhi. These dynamics raise a whole other set of concerns about religious (over)sensitivity, authorship, essentialism and internal production structures, not to mention the very valid claims of neglect by other ethnic groups who are generally overlooked by the Multicultural Departments at large.

targeted multicultural programmes – the last phase?   There were signs by the early to mid-1990s that there was a decline in commitment to on-screen innovation and diversity. The drift towards a culture of commercialism, triggered by increased competition, lighter touch regulation and technological developments, had begun to side-line limited meaningful access for alternative voices and position these 'worthy' areas as necessarily antithetical and surplus to future requirements and the language and logic of the marketplace. The 1990 Broadcasting Act required Channel 4 to raise its own revenue from advertising (previously the responsibility of ITV which partially funded Channel 4), and the Channel's subsequent quest to boost revenue (thus attracting the largest audiences possible) appears to have directly contradicted many of its 'socially-geared' policies. In 1992, ten years on from the launch of Channel 4, Andrea Wonfor, then Channel 4 Controller of Arts and Entertainment, discussed her idea of what 'progression' constitutes: 'There's a limit to how many pro-grammes people can take on the Third World, environment or racial issues. . . . They're all extremely important parts of the mix, but the Channel is beginning to have a broader brief, which is healthy' (Wonfor, *Guardian* 2.11.92). What this 'broader brief' in fact meant, was an increasing depend-ence on US imports (*Frasier, Friends, Ally McBeal, Sex and the City* were all expensive buys for Channel 4) and home-grown 'safe options' for peak-time programming on the two alternative, higher cultural profile channels (BBC2 and Channel 4), thus further squeezing out any obvious signs of Black programmes in prime slots. The emphasis was now on bankable stars, high-profile personalities and on accessible, unchallenging and risk-free program-ming which would guarantee larger audiences.

The 1990 Broadcasting Act had obliged all terrestrial broadcasters to commission at least 25 per cent of their original productions from outside sources/independent producers, usually on a single-project basis. The Act offloaded some of the public service burden from commercial organizations, and triggered a shift towards lighter touch regulation (see p. 7–11). In time, we began to see a demise in institutional commitment and the beginning of a single project-led commissioning structure,[11] which was essentially a strategic necessity in order to cut staffing and operating costs: it involved a move towards short-term contracts, multi-tasking, freelance and part-time workers (see Sparks in Hood, 1994). The squeezing of production fees, the intensified competition for commissions, and the project-by-project con-tracts had a broader impact on the independent sector, both in relation to film and television commissions (see Chapter 9). In the main, Channel 4, forced to snap into the reality of the free market, gradually stopped dealing with smaller (Black) independent companies in favour of those (usually White-led ones) with a large capital-base, high-profile and formidable repu-tation, and thus began to narrow down its independents to a core set of 'preferred suppliers'. These companies were often run by established media personnel who, at the appropriate moment, had chosen to 'go independent', and between them dominated the independent sector, and were also the ones to produce so-called 'Black programmes' (Humphrey Barclay Productions, Barraclough Carey Productions for example). Even those who headed the Multicultural Departments were unable to commit themselves to commissioning smaller, lower-profile companies over those high-profile (mostly White-led) ones, which tend to have a larger capital-base and are quick to 'deliver the goods'.

In any case, the fact that the average Black current affairs programme (the Multicultural Departments' core output) usually brings in less than a million viewers – when 9–10 million is considered 'mainstream' – had inexorably left it commercially undesirable in an increasingly competitive marketplace with its new emphasis on secondary markets and 'value pricing'. By the mid-1990s, the amount of targeted Black programming had gradually begun to decrease. In 1997, the European Media Forum ascertained that between 1988 and 1995, Channels 4's 'ethnic minority' programming was down from 163 to 64 hours of programming per year (a drop of 61 per cent) and that multicultural output had dropped from three to one per cent of the channel's total output (see Phillips, *Guardian*, 13.10.97: 6–7). Since 1999, Channel 4 has been obliged (following ITC recommendations) to deliver at least three hours of multicultural programmes per week (these do not necessarily have to come out of the Multicultural Programmes' Department but at least one hour has to be screened in peak-time), and everyone who pitches an idea to any Channel 4 department now has to explain how it relates to multiculturalism, thus marking an attempt to make its multicultural remit more resonant across the channel. Subsequent Channel 4 programmes such as *Electric Avenue* (1999), looking at a range of people living in Brixton; *Love in Leeds* (1999), based on a group of multi-racial women looking for love; *New Model Army* (2000), a detailed insight into young Black people's experiences of being in the British army; and *Position Impossible* (2001), a populist documentary about the *Kama Sutra* presented by British-Asian comedian Sanjeev Bhaskar, have indeed embraced Yasmin Anwar's conception of a 'new multiculturalism' based on broad-based, socially inclusive, 'cross-cultural' appeal (see Malik, 1997: 5–7). Mark Daniels' challenging *Classified X*, David Okuefuna's outstanding *Hitler's Forgotten Victims* (both part of *The Ba Ba Zee* (1997) late-night documentary strand), *England, My England* (1999) and *White Tribe* (2000) (both written and presented by Darcus Howe), and Trevor Phillips' *Untold: Britain's Slave Trade* (1999) have seen significant efforts by Channel 4 to address the issue of race, ethnicity and identity as a universal issue. Other Channel 4 programmes (such as the share-tips afternoon programme, *Show Me The Money* (2000) and business-ideas show, *The Real Deal Show* (2000)) have offered a more integrated, effortless multicultural approach. These are all convincing reasons for the continuation of the department.

The bigger question remains, however, of whether the increasingly complex and changing realities of the Black-British diaspora have outgrown the premise of Black programming? The answer surely has to be that when Black audiences and media-workers feel as though they are being adequately served and accessed by mainstream British television, then that is the time when the Multicultural Departments have served their purpose (to diversify, innovate and ensure that other routes and points of access open up). But until this has been demonstrated conclusively – and we are not yet there – a need remains for a regulatory structure which demands an area of dedicated 'diversity-conscious' programming alongside the mainstream, although as we know this does not correspondingly mean that all Black viewers' needs will adequately be met. This is not about there being no 'Black programmes' on British television, because unlike the USA, we have no solid evidence in Britain that 'White' programmes, or programmes that do not feature Black people are not watched by Black people or that there is any obvious racialization structuring audience preferences of terrestrial channels.[12] Outside the multicultural units, there is the bigger question of why (and despite the emergence of Black programmes and specialist, trainee and other targeted schemes) on a personnel level, British television companies remain remarkably White.[13] In 1985, The Erlich report, the first BBC monitoring exercise to assess Black employment within the Corporation, revealed a huge under-representation of Black workers, apart from as 'caterers or cleaners' (Erlich, BBC, 1986: 3). The industry's self-awarded brownie points for commissioning research which adopts the 'counting ethnic-heads' method, also raises the decisive question of what exactly we expect that percentage of ethnic minority representations and/or media employees to be representative of?[14] It bears repetition that the *cultural* value of ethnically diverse representations is as – if not more – important as its *numerical* standing, and the cultural significance of Black representations are not exclusive to Black audiences. Moreover, the value of these interventions needs to be carefully assessed: how are the trained-up members of the schemes valued within broadcasting institutions? What are the realistic opportunities that they can aim for after the scheme is completed? Are these schemes effectively implemented or simply brandished about, by those who employ them, like trophies of progression and liberalism? For example, the BBC's short-contract culture (sometimes as little as three or six months), coupled with its seasonal multicultural programming and slow-paced promotion, means an erratic employment pattern and low morale for many of its employees.

But outside the multicultural Departments, television is still 'hideously White'; a phrase used by Greg Dyke early on in his BBC Director-Generalship in an interview with Scottish-Asian journalist, Anver Khan

(*In the Mix*, BBC Radio Scotland, 7.1.01). Dyke was alarmed by the lack of ethnic minority personnel as he walked around BBC departments and at only spotting one senior Black person out of 80 Whites at a BBC managers' lunch (note also Dyke's speech at the CRE Race in the Media Awards, April 2000 and Dyke, *Breakfast with Frost*, 4.2.01). The efficacy of Dyke's 'Diversity Tsars' (Linda Mitchell as Head of Diversity since March 2000, and Peter Salmon (following Tony Hall) as 'Diversity Champion' from January 2001) is called into question by Dyke's own criticism of the prolongation of the Corporation's Whiteness. Dyke's assertion, although more or less stating the obvious, must have come as a bit of a shock to Black people working within the BBC, many of whom have felt and known this coded culture of Whiteness, but are also well-acquainted with not hearing it openly affirmed, particularly by senior management. In terms of personnel, one of the principal problems is the persistent under-employment of Black people at senior producer, senior director and executive levels. Some of the most senior Black figures in British broadcasting (Waheed Alli, Ben Robinson, Samir Shah, Narinder Minhas) have moved to the independent sector, signalling a decrease since the late 1980s in the number of Black executives working directly for the five channels. Apart from Andi Peters (former BBC *Blue Peter* presenter who went on to become Commissioning Editor for Channel 4 youth programmes), Yasmin Anwar (ex-BBC), Patrick Younge (who left the BBC in February 1999 to join Yasmin Anwar at Channel 4) and Paresh Solanki, there are still too few Black people with the power to editorialize or who are actually reaching the industry's boardrooms. Rare exceptions here are the former deputy chairman of the CRE, Ranjit Sondhi, who has been a BBC governor since August 1998, and Waheed Alli, who was a board director of Carlton Communications until November 2000.

In conclusion, the type of liberal freedom sought today is not essentially about ensuring access to resources or 'multiculturalism', but about 'market liberalism'; the *economic* freedom to do as well as one can, leaving the broader contextual questions to market forces – addressed only if they meet the needs of a profitable cultural marketplace. But these new modes of populism are inclined to exclude the 'minority' cultural needs, sensibilities and heritages of distinct ethnic groups. Ironically, cable and satellite, without claims of 'responsibility', 'quality', 'intervention' and 'public service', are now providing many Black-Britons with programmes that they want to watch and are willing to pay for (Asians and African Caribbeans have an estimated purchasing power of around £7 billion and £5 billion respectively). Black-British viewers were amongst the first sub-demographic group to turn to pay-TV models and have, since the early 1990s, increasingly moved away from free-to-air programming. Colin Stanbridge (Managing Director of Carlton Broadcast) had forewarned that, 'In the not too distant future it is projected that 25 per cent of the Carlton region will be from ethnic minorities. We literally cannot afford for them not to be watching our pro-grammes' (Stanbridge in Smith, 1996: 32). Trevor Phillips advised, 'this is not a problem for the blacks. It's a problem for our industry' (Phillips in Smith, 1996: 31). By the mid-1990s, a significant 73 per cent of Asians who received cable or satellite tuned into the Asian channel, Zee TV,[15] and over a half of ethnic minority communities said they were willing to pay for target-ed channels (Smith, 1996). Numbers have been rising ever since, and it would appear that new avenues are being forged through which each person can be granted their 'cultural rights' in more specific and varied ways. Given this option to customize viewing preferences and easy access to a whole range of dedicated channels and programmes (from Pakistani to Turkish to African-American ones), why should those who can afford these alternative delivery systems bother to tune in to terrestrial multicultural programmes, many of which are screened at awkward times, appear tokenistic, outdated or misdirected in their address?

The remarkable twist, of course, is that terrestrial broadcasters, dic-tated by economic issues such as the licence-fee (that is, the need for the BBC to maintain significant audience-share to continue to justify it), demo-graphics and advertising, are now being forced to draw in Black viewers. In the face of competition, many franchised regions are currently being faced with the alarming reality that ethnic minorities are watching over 20 per cent less of their channels (namely LWT, Carlton and Central who between them cater for 70 per cent of the total ethnic minority audience in the UK).[16] The business model of broadcasting institutions (commercial or public) is such that they are dependent on viewing figures; there is little economic sense in any business manager turning a blind-eye to a large proportion of its cus-tomers. As marketing becomes more sophisticated, global and lifestyle-based, and new media forms (particularly the Internet and digital channels) are basing themselves on the nirvana of one-to-one relations with their users, so British terrestrial channels begin to look increasingly insular and isolated to British and international onlookers. What these late acknowledgements of migrating audiences also reveal is that British broadcasting can no longer sustain itself, on a local or global basis, if it continues to model itself on a simple homogenized nation-state paradigm. The increasing number of 'mixed race' and hyphenated identities mean that audiences are becoming more and more ethnically and culturally diverse, placing new pressures on the medium (including Black programmes) to move away from its prevailing White versus not White binary logic.

Terrestrial broadcasters are now paving the way for a targeted-channel future. In 2001, the BBC began to remodel itself as a 'digital terrestrial mul-tiplex'; seven digital services across five channels with new channels BBC3 and BBC4 (youth entertainment and arts-based accordingly) added to the existing digital channel, News 24, and the terrestrial BBC1 and BBC2 (which will continue as the mainstays of the BBC until analogue transmission is switched off at the end of the decade) (Dyke, MacTaggart Lecture, Edinburgh Television Festival, 25.8.00). Channel 4, still a state-owned broadcaster, with its new digital entertainment channel E4 launched in January 2001 and its division to accommodate a commercial (mainly digital) arm, 4 Ventures Ltd, seems to echo ex-Chief Executive Michael Jackson's earlier declaration that, 'we don't want to define ourselves as a minority broadcaster' (Jackson, *Variety*, 8.2.99). In the light of these changes, we need to consider: (1) the possibility that what we *think* Black audiences want to watch and what they actually choose to tune in to, might be two very different things; (2) the strong evidence that the open market, as has been proved by various cable and satellite channels, often means identical products, poor quality and an investment in cloned genres, formats and personalities; and (3) that representations of nuanced, local and indigenous differences might be overtaken by universalized and homogenized global ones (what kind of preferred national image will British broadcasters want to project?). Diversity of brands does not guarantee diversity of product and as with all cultural change, these new shifts in the marketplace are full of pros and cons. Besides, the issues we have been discussing – regulation, ghettoization, delivering diversity on-screen and ethnic minority provisions – may become even more pressing in the sprawling new media world.[17]

notes

1 *Parosi* was written by Dilip Hiro and Naseem Khan and starred Roshan Seth, Zohra Segal and Cleo Sylvestre.
2 The CRE is a non-political, law-enforcing body that offers free legal aid, investigates allegations of discriminatory practice and implements and monitors equal opportunity programmes. Since 1992, it has held the annual Race in the Media Awards (RIMA).
3 Examples include *Geet Mala* (BRMB), *Jhankar* (Beacon), *Meeting Place* (Pennine) targeted at Asian radio listeners and *Rice & Peas* (LBC) aimed at African-Caribbeans.
4 ITV has 15 regional broadcasters. At the 1996 CRE 'Channels of Diversity' conference, many regional companies (HTV and BBC Scotland) admitted that they had not adequately addressed issues around ethnic minority employment and programming.
5 Trevor Phillips was Head of Current Affairs at LWT until 1994, and then LWT Executive Producer/Factual Programmes. He now oversees the independent company, Pepper Productions, was a candidate for London Mayor, and has been Chair of the Greater London Assembly since 2000.
6 Ali was an active anti-capitalist campaigner in the late-1960s and famously spoke in the anti-Vietnam war demonstration in Berlin in 1968. In 1997, he became one of the presenters on BBC2's late-night political discussion programme, *The Midnight Hour* (which Trevor Phillips also used to present).

7 Howe, one of the most 'outspoken' presenters on British television, was former editor of *Race Today*. He organized the New Cross March in 1981, and was involved in the Mangrove Nine trials in the late-1960s following police raids at the Notting Hill Mangrove Restaurant. He was co-founder of the IRR with Sivanandan.

8 Aside from its documentary strand, since 1994 the BBC Asian Programmes Unit established the 'Asia 2' strand which featured light entertainment series such as *Bollywood or Bust!* and *Q Asia*.

9 The BBC2 season included the four-part documentary *Windrush*, produced and directed by David Upshal with Trevor Phillips as series producer. The Windrush effect could be seen across the UK, with 'Windrush Days' organized by councils and the BBC basing its African-Caribbean On-Line portal around the series.

10 I worked in the department between June and December 1999.

11 Note Channel 4's *TV With A Difference* (1989) and *Workshops in the Nineties* (Alan Fountain).

12 Although the USA and UK television contexts are quite different, it is useful to note that recent viewing trends have seen Black and White US audiences over the age of 21 becoming increasingly polarized in their viewing tastes, whilst young White Americans are increasingly crossing over to watch all-Black shows (see Gray in Cottle, 2000: 118–29).

13 Such training schemes reached their heyday under Birt's Generalship – the BBC Television Training Trust (est. 1990), Television Production Trainee Scheme, the RJT as the radio equivalent, and Black Screen (launched by the BBC in 1993; see Frances-Anne Solomon interview, *Black Film Bulletin*, Summer 1994: 14–15).

14 The BBC set themselves a target of an 8 per cent ethnic minority workforce by the year 2000 which it reached (but there is no departmental/job profile break-down available on this) (see Cottle, 2000: 100–17). In 2001, Greg Dyke set a new target of an 8–10 per cent ethnic minority workforce by 2003.

15 Zee TV was previously known as TV Asia. Other Asian-targeted channels include Sony Entertainment Television, Ice-TV, Namaste, B4U, Channel East and Asianet.

16 Although the two companies serving the London region (Carlton and LWT) have 5.5 per cent and 6 per cent respectively of workers coming from ethnic minorities, the overall ethnic minority percentage in London will reach 30 per cent in 2001 and 12 per cent of the Midlands (www.cre.gov.uk).

17 The Runnymede Trust Report recommends that 'the regulatory framework for digital TV include, at least in the short term, protection for programme suppliers which offer channels targeted at particular cultural interests' and 'that the implications and workings of the new digital universe be closely monitored' (Runnymede Trust, 2000: 172).

the packaging of black identities in television news narratives

As with documentary, the discursive organization and production of television news is central in how the moral judgement and consensus about community, citizenship and social inclusion is constructed. Gramsci's notion of hegemony is particularly valuable in understanding news frameworks as a central knowledge system through which this (national) common sense about in-group cohesion and out-group difference, is established, disseminated and authorized. The domestic rituals involved in watching news, and the fact that it is engaged with as a matter of course, makes the 'truth' of the news text and those who tell it (the news-makers or the enunciators) appear both natural and legitimate. News, as an everyday routine structure, meta-discourse and archetypal 'classic realist text', can therefore be considered as a critical site in how the imagined community and geographies of 'nation' are framed, and in how the nation narrates itself to itself. Unlike other aspects of the news media such as the press, television hides the actuality of editorial control and claims to operate within the narcissistic framework of impartiality (that it is a fair, balanced and complete recording of reality), as established in the early years of television, and more specifically as the offspring of notions of 'public service' (see Chapter 2). But like documentary, news presents reality mimetically; it might 'reflect reality' but it does not represent reality itself.

racially-coded news bias   Its truth-claims set news up as a primary site for early criticism based around the genre's agenda-setting, its recurrent exclusion of minority viewpoints and perspectives, and in how 'objectivity' is manipulated, albeit inadvertently, to reflect racist ideologies and fears (Hall et al., 1978; Hartmann and Husband, 1974; Troyna, 1981). As Denis MacShane, former president of the NUJ pointed out in the late 1970s, there is a difference between 'talking simply of "raising professional standards" and admitting openly that the intervention is political and inviting journalists to consider the political role they play in reporting racist issues' (MacShane, 1979: 91). This is not to suggest that everyday 'negative'

Black news images are the product of collusion or of a general racist conspiracy, but that they do, in part, result from the non-interventionist political culture, common-sensical racial ideas, deluded ideals of objectivity, and mechanically shared (rather than critically negotiated or questioned) news values that dictate news production processes. I want to argue that news, on the whole, is a negative genre, so, whilst this 'reporting of the negative' is not exclusive to Black people, when Black images do come to the fore, reports often touch on recurring aspects of racial and cultural difference as if this were the source of the problem rather than situating this 'information' within a considered context. Context is important here for two key reasons: first, because in terms of race and racism it has all too often been denied; and secondly, because there is an abundance of *mis*information about 'race'. Lack of context is a growing problem, as British television news bulletins get shorter, more sound-bite based and work largely to evade the contextualization and complexities of such issues, and as hard documentaries which may have once provided more detail, are on the decline (Barnett et al., 2000). In our current condition of expansion, we are seeing the rise of 'alternative' national and international news services and sources on the internet (www.africana.com, www.blackbritain.co.uk), but television news still dominates our public knowledge and has regulatory responsibilities and expectations that it will hold certain guidelines about coverage in place.

The common assumptions that if the news camera shows us something then it must be true, and that bad news is 'real', touch at the heart of the problem of race reporting and of television as a whole; the medium is capable of producing very powerful images without always placing them in a discerning context. Such images can be wholly arbitrary to the full context of the situation, but are signposted as *the* representative moment. Such shortcomings can add to a tacit and trusting acceptance of racist thought. Take for example Paul Condon's statements about the preponderance of Black muggers which triggered an intensive 'Black mugger' crackdown operation, months before the 1995 Brixton riots occurred. Over consecutive days, Condon appeared on virtually every channel's news bulletins to state that, 'many of the perpetrators are very young Black people' (*Black Britain*, BBC2, Tx: 30.7.96) and, 'At the end of the day, we've got to react to the facts' (*London Tonight*, Carlton/ITV, Tx: 2.8.96). The natural conclusion for many viewers may have been, 'the majority of young Black men are criminals', a reductionist simplification which may have been further confirmed by the subsequent riots (which we shall go on to discuss). Like Condon, the overwhelming majority of the news reports substantiated and relied upon the common-sensical link between Black youth, crime and statistics, as if this were the fundamental starting-point of the debate (thus, the 'increase in crime means ...', 'latest crime figures suggest ...'). As such, they discursively reproduced racist ideologies about 'racial crime' through the supposedly neutral discourse of news, instead of, as an example, juxtaposing this with the racial profile of other crimes. Reports were always constructed in terms of authority (the ubiquitous Paul Condon as official spokesman of the Metropolitan Police and 'primary definer' of the subject) versus anonymity (any Black youth), and fact (racially-coded statistics) versus sentiment ('Black community' angry about being called muggers). We can relate this unfolding of 'news truth' to any number of perceived 'race issues' such as immigration, asylum-seekers, police/community relations, and inner-city regeneration, which although they are not 'negative issues' in themselves, are overwhelmingly reported in terms of the negative, problematic and 'our generosity'. Coverage of the urban riot, the Black crime or international aid also carries this national self-image of tolerability, patience and benevolence. We are less often made aware of what the Others put up with in terms of hostile policing, everyday racist social practice, institutional discrimination, ill-funded services, or even what they might add in a positive sense. Because Black people are rarely seen in non-race related news stories, this bias offers a particularly problem-oriented and negative overall sense of Blackness.

Since the first news broadcast (*BBC Television News*) in 1954 (soon to be followed by the *Independent Television News* in 1955), the majority of news coverage involving Black people has operated under the 'race relations/racial tensions/community relations' paradigm (Hartmann and Husband, 1974; Troyna, 1981). This has facilitated a broader preconceived reasoning that 'race' is a highly controversial subject and only needs to become an issue when Black people are involved. As with broadcasting overall, where Black people continue to be under-represented in news is at a strategic level (making coverage decisions, integrated in general 'non race-related' news output and accessed to renegotiate and provide contexts), which is arguably where it counts the most in terms of shaping the agenda of 'truth'. This is where it becomes particularly important when, how and where Black people are and are not seen and empowered. The question of policy is particularly relevant in the context of news and current affairs, because it is here, more than anywhere else, that notions of professionalism and balance are consolidated in television. In 1996, the BBC under John Birt announced that it was to exercise monitoring to ensure 'fair representation' in news and current affairs output. It also introduced *Black Britain* (BBC2, 1996–), an 'alternative' news series offering a more integrated form of Black news production that was designed to broaden existing terrestrial news provisions for Black audiences. In 1999, Tony Hall, then BBC News Chief Executive, urged BBC editors to readdress this issue in specific relation to indifferent Black news-viewers. He wrote: 'The BBC receives more than £200 million in licence fee from people from ethnic minority groups but we know from our research that this important audience is not tuning in to our output and that they don't feel that the BBC connects with their lives' (BBC internal letter, 'Portrayal in BBC News', 1999). Migrating Black news audiences are all the more meaningful because on a personnel level, the genre has been held up as a success for Black representation, because many of the reporters, newscasters and journalists who work in network and regional television news are Black. Black news presenters such as Wesley Kerr, George Alagiah, Zeinab Badawi, Shahnaz Pakravan, Moira Stewart, Anya Sitaram, Krishnan Guru-Murthy, Daljit Dhaliwal and Phil Gale have boosted the overall presence of Black people on British television. In addition, some of the most high-ranking Black executives and personalities in British broadcasting (Trevor Phillips, Trevor McDonald, Samir Shah) have been involved in News and Current Affairs. Sir Trevor McDonald, tagged the 'nation's favourite' newsreader, became Britain's first Black reporter when he moved to ITN from the BBC World Service in 1973, and stands today as one of the most prestigious and regularly seen Black people on British television. But this veneer of equity and dispersed editorialship hides a deeper imbalance in terms of news knowledge, news agendas and news bias, particularly when it touches on racial lines. As George Alagiah puts it, whilst recent years have seen various attempts by the leading broadcasters to make news reports look more diverse, by interviewing more Black people and sourcing out Black experts, 'the BBC has been dominated by a white male culture. It has a certain way of working and networking' (Alagiah, *Connections*, CRE magazine, Winter 2000–1: 6–7). In response to an industry-commissioned report (Cumberbatch and Woods, 1996) which deduced that Trevor McDonald made up 3 per cent of the total number of representations of ethnic minorities on British television, the then Chairman of the CRE, Herman Ouseley responded:

> Trevor McDonald appearing several times over is counted as 'ethnic minority representation', and that is seen as a symbol of ethnic minority success. That is how it's often evaluated, and thrown back at ethnic minorities who are campaigning for equality and justice. So we are given the erstwhile chairman of the 'Better English' campaign [Trevor McDonald] as our sole role model. (Ouseley in CRE, 1996: 30)

Black newscasters, however welcome, also represent 'exceptional talent' compared with the more general view of Black people contained within the news stories they deliver. The overriding 'Englishness' of the news discourse, in its language, style and mode of address, inevitably plays an important part in the boundaries of acceptable difference. Channel 4 newscaster, Zeinab Badawi, has argued that, 'As far as working in television goes, I am treated as an insider – foreign, but so Anglicised that I could be regarded as British' (Badawi in Twitchin, 1988: 133). Since the 1960s, the BBC and its commercial rivals have battled to see who can provide the most comprehensive, robust and insightful news programming. The contemporary news style is, in crude terms, divided between BBC1's and ITV's briefer image-led bulletins and BBC2 (*Newsnight*) and Channel 4's (*Channel 4 News*) more analytical and dialogue-led approach. Channel 5, meanwhile, has taken deliberate steps to develop alternative news formats and agendas to create a more accessible and 'modern mainstream' news approach. Broadly speaking, it is only *Newsnight* and *Channel 4 News* (broadcast on the 'alternative channels' to what is perceived as the mainstream consensus), which actively determine to cut across the predisposed agendas, public images and political language that dominate news information in Britain, and only multicultural or Black-based factual programmes (*Black Britain*, *Eastern Eye*, *Black on Black*, *Bandung File* for example) which have attempted to explore Black-related news stories from a more critical standpoint.

subjective notions of 'balance'   The classic bystander logic of television emanates from the liberal tenets of freedom of speech, democracy and mediated tolerance, but such notions of 'good news journalism', and 'non-interference' by the state, with TV simply acting as a communicator of different viewpoints, are, as I have been arguing, themselves highly subjective. Take for example, coverage of the extreme Right (see Troyna, 1981). In the run-up to the 1974 General Election, John Tyndall, the Chairman of Britain's then leading racist party, the National Front (NF), insisted that, 'every opportunity to cultivate the mass media, and particularly the press should be exploited' (Tyndall, *Spearhead*, 1974: 76). Putting all their resources into an electoral effort, the NF were granted a Party Political Broadcast on television, and the National Activities Organizer of the NF, Martin Webster, boasted, 'We are laughing all the way to the bank. Where else can you get simultaneous five minute broadcasts on the BBC and the ITV for thirteen and a half grand?' (Webster, *Guardian*, 12.10.74). Whilst such broadcasts were not directly part of a news bulletin, they were customarily broadcast at either side of the evening news and were set up as 'official' information feeds designed to brief the electorate about different political manifestos. The accepted practice of press partiality at least warranted open critiques of the NF (e.g. 'The "Menace" of the Front', *Daily Mirror*, 4.11.77) (although the press also generally operates within a narrow repertoire of positions on 'race') compared with television's strained attempts to remain aggressively neutral (see Hall on *Nationwide's* coverage of the Anti-Nazi League and National Front, 1981: 45).[1]

Lamentably, these 'professional' ideologies of Open Airtime do not belong to a bygone era; extreme Right groups who can afford it are still legitimized by television in this way. In the run-up to the 1997 General Election (the European Commission's European Year Against Racism), the British National Party (BNP) were granted uncritical access to several minutes of peak-time viewing in a pre-Election broadcast (Tx: 25.4.97). It needs no further argument that the thrust of the broadcast fed (without breaching the programme code, www.itc.org.uk) into certain popular racist fears around immigration, and of Britain under threat from a foreign invasion. There had been mild protests prior to the screening by some BECTU (Broadcasting Entertainment Cinematograph and Theatre Union) members outside the BBC, by Anti-Nazi League campaigners outside the Channel 4 building and a further 'Pull the Plugs on the BNP' protest, but there was no mention of this opposition on terrestrial news channels. Channel 4 eventually decided not to screen it, but only because it was untransmittable under ITC guidelines relating to a specific legal issue around participators' consent, not because of any moral or ethical position. Channel 4 even requested an edited version to dodge the guideline, but the BNP failed to deliver in time for the scheduled screening. Meanwhile, the other channels each put out different versions of it (the BBC screened the original BNP broadcast, the ITV regions made some alterations 'for legal reasons' and Channel 5 made necessary changes *on behalf of* the BNP). The BBC defended its decision by maintaining that essentially, 'the BBC is publisher' and that the broadcast did not 'impinge the law or the channel's guidelines' (*Right To Reply*, Channel 4, Tx: 3.5.97). Interestingly, the previous day's Prolife Alliance broadcast had been banned by the BBC on the grounds of it being against 'taste and decency'. As broadcaster Mark Lawson commented, 'It seems a confused culture in which a campaign broadcast is not allowed to show what does happen to foetuses but a man is permitted to say what he would like to happen to non-White people' (Lawson, *Guardian*, 16.4.97: 5). What the airing of the broadcast made clear, was that despite certain regulatory policies that command degrees of objectivity and cultural sensitivity in television news and current affairs, these do not necessarily eliminate racist material, and broadcasting channels do have a considerable degree of autonomy and can exercise their editorial control *when they see fit*. Few would disagree with the impeccable liberal credentials of the 'freedom of speech' hypothesis, but it is also the responsibility of broadcasters to ask with what exceptions, and to what degree this logic should be applied, and to question whether classic liberal non-interventionism should always override all other factors. Surely there is a contradiction between the fact that if you field enough candidates and can afford the £15,000 deposit, you can get a five minute television broadcast whatever you plan to say, and British broadcasting guidelines on taste and decency which insist (at least on paper) that material cannot be aired if it is offensive to public feeling or incites crime/disorder. News programming, especially when governed by the special conditions of electoral broadcasting, has not yet adequately resolved this contradiction.

news and racialized crisis   If blatant anti-Black sentiment can work within the ethical codes of British broadcasting, then what can we determine about how Black people have been situated in relation to news' moral centre? We know from their recurrent appearances in certain types of news stories since the late 1960s (immigration, 'race rows', and most of all crime, law and order), that they have typically been positioned in relation to crisis (the motor of news narratives). The codes of these racialized geographies 'create a kind of network, a *topos* [location] through which the entire text passes (or rather, in passing, becomes text)' (Barthes, 1990). Stuart Hall explains:

Blacks become the bearers, the signifiers, of the crisis of British society in the 70s: racism is its 'final solution'.. . . This is not a crisis *of* race. But race punctuates and periodizes the crisis. Race is the lens through which people come to perceive that a crisis is developing. It is the framework through which the crisis is experienced. It is the means by which the crisis is to be resolved – 'send it away'. (Hall, 1978: 31–2)

So we can recall that certain moments – the mid-1950s, the late 1960s, the early to mid-1980s, the late 1990s – are now popularly remembered as moments of 'race troubles', when there was 'a breakdown in race relations'. The predominant early newsreel footage was of Black Commonwealth citizens coming to Britain in the postwar years – Lord Kitchener (Aldwyn Roberts) singing 'London is the Place for me' as he stepped off the *Empire Windrush*, various 'waves' of immigration from the Commonwealth, images of 'the newcomers'. Later in the 1950s, when there were clear signs of racial tension in Nottingham and Notting Hill, the panic-inducing news coverage largely focused on the problem of 'mob violence', 'riot terror' and rogue Teddy Boys. This was not specifically related to British racism or police ineptness, but to the presence of a 'colour problem' in particular geographical areas and housing estates. Thus, following the 'Shameful Episode in Notting Hill' (British Pathé, 1958), a BBC news bulletin warned, 'Something new and ugly raises its head in Britain – racial violence . . . the injured victim, a Jamaican, is taken to safety.' However excited the tone, there was still a certain politeness ingrained in these bulletins. Later reports – Kelso Cochrane's funeral in 1959 (attended by over 1000 people who walked silently in procession across the 'troubled zone' of North Kensington); waves of immigration following the bulk expulsions from Kenya (1968), Uganda (1972) and Malawi (1970s); stories about illegal immigrants and Heathrow detentions; the 1980s riots; the unfolding of the Stephen Lawrence case in the late 1990s; the murder of the 10-year-old Nigerian schoolboy, Damilola Taylor in 2000; the 2001 Oldham riots – all located Black people as an integral component in social adversity and deeply associated with trouble and/or bound by victimhood. It bears repetition that television news dictates when these issues become significant: 'ethnic minority areas' (Brixton, Southall) only come under public scrutiny during a riot; Stephen Lawrence's murder only entered the public conscience when his parents and lawyers pushed it onto the 'official' agenda and towards a public enquiry; anti-racist/fascist campaigns are only followed when in direct conflict with the NF or BNP; the famine is only considered a crisis when millions have died of starvation, and so on. Equally, news decides when something is not newsworthy: for example, when 13 Black teenagers died in the New Cross fire in 1981, the news media treated the case with overwhelming silence; the spate of Black deaths in custody and everyday racist crime are rarely reported (www.guardian.co.uk/racism); domestic affairs are overwhelmingly prioritized over foreign ones. We are not encouraged to invest in the unfolding of events over long periods of time or in the political nuances or consequences of a situation, particularly when the issues are complex and cannot easily be choreographed in a tightly-timed news package. In turn, crisis and conflict become the *leitmotifs*, which attach themselves to Black subjects in wider contexts, genres and debates (see pp. 149–51 on crime series). The effects of agenda-setting are considerable, not just because it allows news to set the grounds for discussion, but also because it defines when it is time for narrative closure or exposure.

Bearing some of these patterns of race reporting in mind, I want to focus on one of the leading images of Blackness in news – the inner city riot. Like the global image of starving, helpless Black sufferers dependent on the West to break out of a cycle of crisis, the pathologies around urban – read Black – youth are connected to issues of poverty, youth and to the familiar binary oppositions between normality and deviance, civilization and barbarity, civil disorder and cultural etiquette. Just as the plight of Sudan, Ethiopia and Rwanda have come to define 'the Black condition' in a foreign context, so civil unrest in 'troubled zones' such as Notting Hill, Southall, Brixton, St Paul's/Bristol, Handsworth and Bradford have clarified the domestic one. The familiarity of these parables and the representational language through which they are mimetically told, has helped to cement them as fact, and they have, in turn, become prototypes of Blackness; self-evident and intrinsic, and uncritically referred to in broader contexts. The media's preoccupation with 'youth as trouble' was, of course, nothing new, although in the 1970s it took on a specific 'racial' angle with the image of the street criminal, the mugger and the inner-city rioter (see Hall et al., 1978).

Howard Tumber has researched extensively on the 1981 inner-city riots; the first major television riots captured in routinely extended news editions.[2] Lord Scarman, who was asked by the Home Secretary to report on the April 1981 disturbances in Brixton, pointed out how the civil unrest had been 'captured' on television:

> The British people watched with horror and incredulity an instant audio-visual presentation on their television sets of scenes of violence and disorder in the 'capital city' the like of which has not previously been seen in this century of Britain. These young people brought about a temporary collapse of law and order in the centre of an inner suburb of London. (Scarman, 1981: 1).

Dominant news narratives struggled to make sense of Blackness *through* the riots and comprehend the riots through Blackness. Because many of 'these young people' were Black, and because the 'inner suburb' of Brixton was highly Black-populated, the racialization of the inner-city space (the common playground for street racism and reaction) was a basic representational code in the riots coverage. Such distinctions between urban and rural Englands, left the inner city as reminiscent of a colonial space, both characteristic of and inhabited by the wild, untamed and in-need-of-civilization (with authentic Britishness found in the quite different England of the leafy suburbs or countryside). 'Civilization' here was culturally aligned with 'social order' – and it was to this that Black people, through 'official public discourses' such as news, were presented as a threat; and in that sense constituted a 'menace to society'. When identifying the causes for 'Black criminality', public discourses, although they often appear to be 'liberal' and intrinsically humanitarian in their emphasis on a 'cycle of deprivation' thesis based around social conditions, economic insecurity and 'enforced idleness because of unemployment' (Scarman, 1981: 14), in fact, redirect the root of the problem back *within* Black communities, *within* their locality, lifestyle, family set-up or neighbourhood, and *within* the ideologically-charged category 'Black working class youth'. The common emphasis on inter-generational conflict, gangs, and 'street culture', further collapses 'race' into 'culture', and 'racism' into 'disadvantage'. As Fisher and Joshua note, it is these areas of focus related to the reproduction of culture (such as language, family, cultural values etc.) that are the prime 'targets for racist state intervention' (Lawrence in Sivanandan, 1983: 98), particularly when we are dealing with people in a 'lower' class bracket which broadens the scope for disciplinary action. Again, this emphasis takes us back to one of the fundamental strains within the liberal political framework (which public service discourses such as news work through); despite its ideals of individualism and formal equality, liberalism can be profoundly assimilationist and authoritarian when it positions itself as the adjudicator of the boundaries of 'problematic citizenship'. Thus, when the Metropolitan Police Commissioner, Sir David McNee, told anti-Nazi protesters (many of whom were of course White) following the 1979 Southall riot and Blair Peach's death, 'If you keep off the streets in London and behave yourselves, you won't have the SPG [Special Patrol Group] to worry about', he was saying something more general about the way in which British 'social order' operates in relation to the Black presence. This adjudication of the boundaries of 'problematic citizenship' and 'law and order', was, of course, to become a powerful governing ideology of Thatcher's Britain.

News journalists were of course under certain pressures to provide 'a good story' that was headline-worthy, but news editors were also under huge obligation to 'ensure balance and coverage of disorder' (Scarman, 1981: 111). This was particularly difficult because journalists inevitably faced the problem of getting access to information from both the police (who were cautious about how their public image would stand) and the Black people who had rioted (who were generally concerned about how the information would be used and that the media would, in any case, juggle around the facts to tell the same story). We know of course that news is a hurried, frantic, conveyor-belt type operation which is usually negative, dramatic and tragic, and depends on the knowledge and participants that are accessible. Because of the live, amorphous nature of the 1981 riots, there was also pressure on news journalists to actively 'hunt out' trouble and linger in those areas where they forecast outbreaks of disorder. Another news convention that was regularly used was the 'live from the scene' report (usually with no live action to be captured), offering a sense of urgency and 'visual evidence' of the 'aftermath' of the riots. Once the immediate 'drama' of the first riots had happened, journalists depended more on anticipating trouble and 'news interest', than on the events themselves in order to sustain the story. As one senior editor explained, 'It's the company that has had the better riot that wins because they have had visually more dramatic pictures' (quoted in Tumber, 1982: 27). Tumber's report identified deliberate set-ups to ensure a good story – paying Black people to put a camera in their homes, asking them to throw petrol bombs for the camera, and so on (see Tumber, 1982: 11–14). When the day's events had not provided sufficient levels of 'quality' footage, a provocative line of enquiry was also often adopted. An edition of ITN's *News at Ten* in the midst of the summer riot, carried the headline, 'Was Someone Directing the Riots?' (ITV, Tx: 7.7.81). The report briefly identified someone they claimed *might* have engineered the Toxteth riots. Not only was this leading news story based on unsubstantiated evidence (blurring the line between fact and opinion), but it also represented a blatant attempt to find a quick-fix answer to a complex situation, and to simplify the complex causes of 'social violence' by locating one root cause (McNay, *Television*, Sept/Oct, 1981:15). Black youths were shown to react against the state through violent means, but there was no analysis about police harassment (the use of CS gas, discriminatory urban policing methods and racist stop and search methods) that was applied both before and during the riots. Besides, the pseudo-scientific conjecture about why the riots had happened was only developed by some and only in hindsight – after the event – when the inner city became defiled and, as such, was rendered interesting.

These representational strategies were echoed many years later in the 1995 Brixton riots. Like 1981, 1995 had been a watershed year with respect to matters of 'race' and crime. In May, Wayne Douglas, a Black man, died in police custody; in June, a local street football match in Manningham, Bradford, turned into several nights of civil disorder involving local British-Asians; in the same month, three police officers who had gagged and restrained a Black woman, Joy Gardner, on an immigration raid, were acquitted after having been charged with manslaughter; and July saw Paul Condon's aforementioned comments on Black muggers. The year ended with riots in Brixton on 14 December. Out of the four channels, only BBC2's *Newsnight* and *Channel 4 News* went some way to entering the discussion from a probing and critical standpoint. Both the BBC and ITN (for ITV) (Tx: 15.12.95) organized their reports around a formulaic structure: firstly, images of the riots ('gangs of predominantly Black youths took to the streets', ITN); second, police efforts to manage the chaos; third, an emotive case study of an injured policeman and the (White) man who had rescued him; fourth, the Home Secretary's (Michael Howard) visit to Brixton the next day; fifth, the views of Sir Paul Condon; and finally, Brixton's 'troubled past' and regeneration programmes for the area. We get an even clearer sense of the structure when we look at London's specially-extended news programme, *London Tonight* (Tx: 15.12.95), which labelled its five consecutive reports as follows:

1   '*The Battleground*': 'Clearly someone from somewhere was planning more than a peaceful vigil . . . the first signs of marchers turning into a mob . . . the first stones and bottles were thrown at the police . . . for him and his colleagues there was a chant of "Murderers" ' and 'The police weren't the only targets; the media were next on the hit-list. *London Tonight*'s cameraman was assaulted at knife-point, our engineer sustained rib injuries, the Outside Broadcast van put out of operation.'

2   '*The Aftermath*': 'Once again Brixton has been stained by the hand of violence'.

3   *'The Heroes of the Brixton Riot'*: This focused on only one person, PC Tisshaw (the injured policeman), who was filmed in his hospital-bed.

4   *'The Trigger'*: This focused on (a) Wayne Douglas' violent criminal past (rather than on his unexplained death in police custody); (b) British Black newspaper, *The Voice*'s recent front page story questioning the official verdict on Douglas's death; and (c) the 'inflammatory' rhetoric of civil rights activists who had spoken at the protest march.

5   *Condon's View*: 'In the past, the threat has been – unless you let crime flourish, we will riot. Well no civilized society can tolerate that. There always has to be a balance.'

In their quest to describe a sequence of events, these news reports worked through particular formulaic patterns (beginning, ending, cause and effect, purpose, meaning) and, as such, ordered the events within a controlled, and emotive framework. The obvious point we can note, is the lack of variation in the way the story is carried and the similarity in the ordering and presentation of the 'event', even across the two different channels. This is a common scenario: news, in general, tends to select the same stock of stories from a vast number of possibilities. *The 'herd-like' impulse* (i.e. the tendency for different news channels to carry the same story, and in similar ways) serves to suggest that there is a universal consensus about *what* news is and *how* it should be presented (mode of address, information supplied and withheld, angles provided, opinions given, etc.). These reports also established a theory by shaping supporting and selective material around it, and were thus classic forms of 'thesis journalism'. *London Tonight* (the local news programme which airs to London, the multicultural heart of Britain, and where the 'riot' took place) implicitly depicted White people as both the victims and the heroes of the riot. Brixton was shown as an innately troubled zone despite government spending programmes (i.e. 'beyond hope'); and the report supposed that 'the Black community' (be it *The Voice* or Wayne Douglas or civil rights speakers) were to blame and held an established aggregate view. Furthermore, using distinct categories and terms that disunited Whites and Blacks, civilians, 'rebels' and 'the establishment' ('The trigger' = Blacks, The Heroes/Victims = the news production team and White police) was both divisive and conflict-led. No attempt was made to humanize Douglas by interviewing his family for example, or to supply a context to his death in custody that had previously gone unreported on network television news. These selected moments reflected broader patterns of silence, marking an omission that characterizes racialized representations: there was no real explanation of how a peaceful protest suddenly turned into a riot; very little attention was paid to the original reason for the protest (Douglas' death as one in a series of Black deaths in police custody); and a hierarchical criteria shaping who was individualized and accessed to speak, and from what position (Condon, PC Tisshaw and Howard all as the official voices of authority) was set up. I am arguing that such approaches lead to a predisposed and persuasive assessment of the total context of a situation that is, in fact, utterly equivocal. Television's 'bystander' approach, which comes to the fore in 'truth' discourses such as news, means that it rarely leads the debate or disagrees too strongly with the 'official' agencies' (the police, the immigration services, the law). The total effect is a prevailing sense of cooperation, consensus and agreement between television and other institutions. These mutually cooperative structures make crime news an important player in clarifying society's moral framework and in determining what is (un)acceptable for the 'moral majority' and in the 'interests of the public'.

Since news is so much better at telling us *what* than *why*, and typically negates matters of context, the role of 'public images' (Hall et al., 1978) becomes central in building uncomplicated topographies around racial difference. Notions of the underclass, the inner city or the ghetto provide such a direct mapping, making 'race issues' and more specifically, a Black presence, all the easier to locate in one 'troubled' area and within specific 'communities'. The circulation of power and meaning is dependent on both those who are excluded from and active in the production of these images. So, whilst the producers of news programmes might *select truths*, *set agendas* and *reduce* experiences (thus producing stereotypes and public images), they often base their work on empirical truths that they choose to – or think they should – foreground. So, for example, the image of the Black male criminal is not necessarily fictitious or imaginary, and is obviously sometimes based on a certain truth. Mercer and Julien refer to this as the 'cycle between reality and representation [which] makes the ideological fictions of racism empirically "true" – or rather, there is struggle over the definition, understanding and construction of meanings around black masculinity within the dominant regime of truth' (Mercer and Julien in Mercer, 1994: 137–8). Whilst news reports might operate within this 'dominant regime of truth', and whilst some Black men may have adopted violence, often in response to feelings of powerlessness or aggressive policing, the news discourse, as an 'official' source of public information, is important for the *way* in which it invites us to understand a particular image or story in relation to 'truth' and context, and for the ways it chooses to either strengthen or weaken the links in the chain of associations around Blackness.

notes

1   This style of presentation was also apparent in the coverage of the National Front's public opposition campaigns against Czech asylum-seekers in Britain in 1997 and 1998.

2   A number of documentaries that dealt with the events: *TV Eye: 'Race Riots: The Lessons of St Pauls'* (ITV, 1980), *Panorama: The Lessons of Brixton* (BBC1, 1981), *Skin: Southall Riots* (ITV, 1981). Between 4 July and 16 July 1981, the BBC and ITN covered the Toxteth, Brixton and Southall riots for all 13 days, totalling 26 reports, sometimes up to 35 minutes long (see Tumber, 1982).

'is it 'cos i is black?': the black situation in television comedy

So far we have been looking at how images of Blackness in the 'truth' genres work through representational codes of verisimilitude, realism and impartiality in order to represent 'society'. By contrast, with light entertainment, the distinction is often made between 'television' and 'society', where the invitation to find pleasure is sold on the grounds that it acts as the direct antithesis of the routine displeasure to be found in everyday (home and work) life. Despite this, the axis of a large proportion of British humour has rested on notions of racial difference, depending on it for its narrative and temporal setting on the proverbial grounds of 'laughter as the best medicine'. But how do these comedies function in terms of 'social order', and what in these instances is being requested of the viewer: *who* is being laughed at and *why*? In particular, satire (the principal use of wit in British television comedy since the early 1960s), with its heavy social emphasis and designated political targets, is presumed to be central to the workings of a healthy democracy – a kind of relief mechanism that diffuses social tension and functions as harmless catharsis. Since comedy tends to home in on current preoccupations and particularities in present climates, it relies heavily on 'the situation' and on the effects of repetition and familiarity, making the history of 'race sitcoms' and Black comedy a useful barometer of popular opinion on race at specific moments and over time. And because it works through essentialist types, it is arguably one of the principal areas in which reductive ethnic simplifications are maintained, intensified and endorsed. It is often argued that comedy needs to offend in order to be funny, but is it really the case that if we jettison offence, we will jettison the joke, and if so are we to see this as the taunt of the bully or the fact of comedy? The innermost workings of the comedy text when it touches on aspects of racial difference, is dependent precisely on this cultural politics of representation centred on ambivalence.

The focal point of ambivalence is the Black television entertainer which we can trace back to 1936 when Buck and Bubbles made their appearance on the opening day of the BBC television service at Alexandra Palace (BBCTV, Tx: 2.11.36). Their act was a continuum of the 'Blacks as entertainers' tradition established during the Elizabethan era, and they were described in the *Radio Times* as, 'a coloured pair who are versatile comedians, who dance, play the piano, sing and cross-chat'. Many other variety acts occupied this ambiguous form of showmanship, displaying genuine talent (usually musical) on the one hand, while being cartoonish objects of fun on the other. Caricatures of Blacks as the butt of the joke continued into the 1950s (not without criticism), with the popular US television show *Amos 'n' Andy* (CBS, 1951–53) in which Andy Brown and Amos Jones (Spencer Williams and Alvin Childress) played two idle and clumsy Black fools.[1] The central question has always been one of whether images of Blackness in television comedy 'play on' or 'play off' the long-established Black clown stereotype, and whether we are being invited to laugh *with* or *at* the Black comic entertainer. The comedy figure, according to Hall, captures the 'innate humour, as well as the physical grace of the licensed entertainer – putting on a show for The Others. It is never quite clear whether we are laughing with or at this figure: admiring the physical and rhythmic grace, the open expressivity and emotionality of the 'entertainer', or put off by the 'clown's stupidity' (Hall, 1981: 40). These questions around performance and the body (to be expanded on in the next two chapters) are elemental when we consider the focalization of Blacks as entertainers (clowns, jesters, singers and dancers) throughout Western cultural history. As Jan Nederveen Pieterse observes, 'the first role blacks were permitted to perform in white society, after that of slave or servant, was that of entertainer' (Pieterse, 1992: 136). This early image of the musical comedy 'raced' clown was indeed deeply ambivalent. As Carlin explains, there is, 'the Irish clown, who is always drunk; there is the Asian clown, the Babu; there is the Negro clown – we know him well. . . . All racial clowns are sooner or later celebrated on the musical comedy stage' (Carlin, 'Clowns for all Races', *New Society*, 9.1.75).

till death us do part – (anti) racist?

The 1960s/1970s sitcom *Till Death Us Do Part* (BBC1, 1966–68, 1972, 1974–75) has been held up as the classic model which points to the knotty issues around racism, comic intention, impact, authorship and context. *Till Death*, with its direct reference to racial difference and more particularly to Black people, signalled a drastic break from television's habitually 'polite' and awkward response towards racial themes thus far.[2] Whilst Enoch Powell was having a major impact on opening up the public debate about 'race' and immigration in the political and legislative arena at precisely this time (see pp. 44–7), Alf Garnett, a die-hard believer in 'the Establishment', was stirring it up in people's living rooms, speaking the unspeakable ('coons', 'kikes' and 'wogs') and thus working against the grain of expected liberal (television) caution. The Alf creation was of a flawed, bigoted and reactionary character who lived in an East End house with his wife Elsie (Dandy Nicholls), daughter Rita (Una Stubbs) and her partner Mike (Anthony Booth). Rita represented the voice of reason, and Mike was the symbol of liberal youth designed to provoke Alf (Warren Mitchell). Writer, Johnny Speight, had designed to ridicule, through Alf, the kinds of attitudes which underpinned the British popular psyche, and later explained how, 'I wanted to create this character that was pig-ignorant and of course the nation fell in love with him' (*The Life & Times of Alf Garnett*, BBC2, 1997). Following a successful pilot, the early series of *Till Death* (fittingly broadcast alongside the celebrated 1966 World Cup tournament which England won on home soil) was soon at the top of the ratings, sometimes drawing in 18 million viewers (about half the homes in Britain) (Shulman, *London Evening Standard*, 21.2.68). Alf went on to supersede fictional status and became a cultural phenomenon, attracting seismic media coverage, largely because of the series' controversial and open focus on race, sex, religion and politics. Warren Mitchell, with no holds barred, delivered Alf's racist (and homophobic and sexist) views with force and passion, inexorably overshadowing the programme's other characters.

Within the context of news and documentary images of the Black problematic at this time, Alf's views, for many, inevitably appeared logical (if extreme) attitudes towards race, and validated their racist opinions. Alf emulated some of Powell's 'real-life' panic and, in this sense, effectively added to a newly emerging wave of popular opinion on race and immigration. Many, who took Alf's diatribes at face-value, adopted this dominant reading of the text, although this was not the preferred reading intended by Speight. Members of the public frequently told Warren Mitchell that they loved it when he 'had a go at the coons'. Speight received congratulations *and* criticism for his treatment of Black people, by both Black and White viewers. Of course, part of the problem was that Alf was a peculiarly sympathetic character (arguably because he was too stupid to keep his racist views quiet), thus winning audience identification, even for those who were open to a negotiated reading of the programme. It was this point of identification that clinched support for Alf; nothing else in the text could destroy the pro-Alf affinity. If you identify with a character on aesthetic or dramatic grounds, then a part of you, whether you like it or not, will probably identify with what they stand for, despite your own reservations. This was the real source of Alf's and indeed the programme's ambivalence. The point here is not so much whether *Till Death* can be determined as a racist text or not, because to that there is no clear-cut answer, but that it was precisely Alf's bigotry which Speight claimed he was working against. Speight later suggested, 'I never created Alf Garnett, society created him. He's a lout; a loutish, ignorant, raucous pea-brain. . . . I don't think politically correct people can see the joke' (Speight, cited from *Without Walls*, Channel 4, Tx: 25.10.94).

Speight might have been right in his analysis of how humour can function as a reactionary process, but if we are to assume that 'politically correct people' didn't get that the joke was on Alf, then we also have to say that a lot of 'politically incorrect' people didn't understand the workings of satire.

What *Till Death* demonstrated, was that a single text – and we can relate this to any media text – can produce and circulate contradictory and competing meanings and readings and can, as such, say more than one thing. Meaning is not simply enclosed within the text itself, but is actively produced outside it, in the way an audience reads it and within the context of reception and transmission. Ambiguity is further contained within us, as individual readers, so that programmes can appeal to mixed sensibilities and contradictory subjectivities at the same time (we could therefore see the programme as racist, anti-racist and/or something confusedly in-between). In fact, Speight's liberal intentions were not really the defining factor, since audiences – as well as being hugely unpredictable – are not driven by the will of good intentions or preferred meanings alone, and Speight neither controlled audience identifications completely (to make Alf a victim or hero of the comedy), nor had any hold on continuing forms of racism through which many interpreted the programme. In essence, *Till Death* was not *just* Speight's text. The ambiguity of *Till Death* proved to be workable on many levels and on two sides – both within the text and in terms of the readings it produced. As the political climate and notions of acceptability changed, there was certain pressure on the BBC, and Johnny Speight declared, 'I would write another series for the BBC but only if this censorship was stopped' (Speight, *London Evening Standard*, 21.2.68). Speight went on to pen a *Till Death* movie (1968) and further series (BBC, 1972) which often attracted an outstanding 24 million viewers, and a later version, *In Sickness and in Health* (1985–87).[3] This phenomenal success and divided impact, was later echoed in the US with its version of *Till Death*, developed by Norman Lear and packaged as *All in the Family* (CBS, 1971–83). Featuring Archie Bunker as a racist bigot who lapsed easily into racist name-calling such as 'jigaboo' and 'jungle bunny' to refer to African-Americans, the responses to Archie (like Alf) were varied (see Gunzerath, 'All in the Family', in Newcomb, 1997).

In fact, the absence of any regular Black character in *Till Death* was arguably more solid grounds for criticism, because Alf was referring to Black people in a derogatory way when they had no significant right of reply in the programme or on British television at large. At the time, because of television's overriding social Whiteness, even in Black-related discourses, this did not seem particularly extraordinary. Guyanese actor, Thomas Baptiste, made an appearance in the second episode of the first series, but even at that early stage in the programme's run, felt uncomfortable about how Alf's racism might be interpreted by the viewing public. He expressed his concern to producer, Dennis Main Wilson, and recounts, 'although I thought the script was very funny, I felt people were going to be laughing with this bigoted man, instead of at him … those jobs always represented a dichotomy for one as a professional actor – either one did them, or one refused, in which case somebody else would have done them' (quoted in Pines, 1992: 67). There had, to date, only been a few Black actors in such prominent roles. For example, British-born Black singer, actor and comedian Kenny Lynch, made a number of television appearances during the 1950s and 1960s, and an appearance in *Till Death* in 1967. He played a bigger role in Johnny Speight's next venture, the contentious *Curry and Chips* (LWT, 1969), which Speight was inspired to write after the fever-pitch response to Powell's 1968 'Rivers of Blood' speech.

Curry and Chips was illustrative of the standard tone of racial humour that was beginning to emerge at this time; it set up a multicultural scenario as the basis for racial tension. The common structure in these comedies featured a racist proponent who was blatantly narrow-minded, but delivered the racism almost affectionately (of the Jimmy Tarbuck, Benny Hill, Cannon and Ball kind). This would usually be counterpoised by a Black character who would underscore the former's racist attitudes and 'put them right', or alternatively by a White liberal voice who would urge a more empathetic approach towards Black people. Even this quarrel between racist and anti-racist claims would work through a predictable, repressed language ('they're all the same' versus 'they're not that bad'); but Blackness was always located as a source of ambivalence, discussion and Otherness. Accordingly, *Curry and Chips* set up these stock character-types: an overt racist (Norman, played by Norman Rossington), a Black worker, (Kenny, played by Kenny Lynch), a liberal factory foreman (Arthur, played by Eric Sykes), and, inexplicably, a blacked-up Irish Pakistani (Kevin O'Grady or 'Paki Paddy', played by Spike Milligan). O'Grady, complete with nodding head and mock pidgin accent (meant to denote an Irish-Asian), represented the kind of bumbling foreigner stereotype that was to be recycled again and again in other popular television comedies such as *It Ain't Half Hot, Mum* (BBC, 1974–81). Kenny, the comedy's only 'real' Black character (i.e. not 'blacked-up' like O'Grady), was as vehement as the comedy's other racist characters in his anti-'wog' stance. The relative 'acceptability' of the British-born Kenny, as well as enacting a 'divide and rule' logic between those 'Made in Britain' and 'real foreigners', exploited the differences between Asians and African-Caribbeans, and set up Kenny as a Black 'ally' to effectively enable audiences to disclaim their own identification with the racist overtones that ran through the text. There was something quite surreal, not to mention insulting, about seeing a White comedian blacked-up as a Pakistani (Milligan), who was, in turn, being mocked for his foreignness by a genuinely Black actor (Lynch).

the comedies 'about race' and ethnic sitcoms　At a time when very little was happening for them in theatre or television drama (see Chapter 8), some Black actors were being snapped up for popular comedy parts during the 1970s. *The Fosters* (ITV, 1976–77), Britain's first Black family sitcom, based on the popular US comedy *Good Times*, marked an important, early attempt to feature Black people in a family, domestic setting. Set in their tower-block home in South London, it featured early performances from Lenny Henry (Sonny Foster), Isabelle Lucas (his mother, Pearl), Norman Beaton (his father, Samuel) and Carmen Munroe (Vilma), all of whom became leading Black television performers. The hugely popular *Rising Damp* (Yorkshire TV/ITV, 1974–78) also marked a certain advance. The series was based on Eric Chappell's 1973 play *The Banana Box*, but Racist Rooksby was slightly 'watered down' into the rather pitiful Rupert Rigsby (played by Leonard Rossiter), and 'Blackness' was not *the* defining element in the comedy. Philip Smith (Don Warrington), was the intelligent, well-educated, if smug, son of an African tribal chief who always got the upper-hand over Rigsby, his irrepressible, snooping landlord. Soon after, came *Mixed Blessings* (LWT/ITV, 1978–80), a comedy based around the problems posed by a mixed marriage. Munroe played Matilda Lambert, the mother of Susan (played by Muriel Odunton), a social worker married to Thomas, a White man (see Pines, 1992: 63).

These comedies were clearly products of their time, both acknowledging the multi-racial diversity of Britain, but also written by White writers. Because Blacks, Asians or 'race' were usually the butt of the joke, these comedies tended to hit a racist note, but always in a well-meaning, benevolent tone. Take the example of *Mind Your Language* (LWT/ITV, 1977–79); never before had so many diverse races (Indian, Pakistani, Chinese, Turks, Greeks, Japanese, etc.) been seen in the same television frame, but they had also never clung so tightly to their popular crude national stereotypes (see Figure 3). Conveniently set in an English-language teaching centre, *Mind Your Language* (which starred amongst others Jamila Massey, Albert Moses, Dino Shafeek, Pik-Sen Lim and Robert Lee) set up the perfect opportunity to show the differences between various 'foreigners'. The source of humour was not just racial difference, but more specifically non-Englishness (denoted in their accents, customs, clothes and the situations they would find themselves in). The only racially 'neutral' character (that is, with no 'obvious' racial characteristics) was the English teacher, Jeremy Brown (played by Barry Evans). At the time, Humphrey Barclay (then Head of Comedy at London Weekend Television, which produced the majority of these comedies about race) defended the programme on the grounds that seeing different races on-screen would familiarize and naturalize them to a White majority viewing public. This standard defence based on an unpersuasive multicultural philosophy, supposed that some representation was better than

Figure 3

Mind Your Language (LWT), a picture of the cast

Courtesy of London Weekend Television

none, and that putting something on screen would necessarily 'unshackle' it. In fact, it is quite possible to flaunt a multi-racial society without displaying any multicultural sensibility or awareness, and laughter does not necessarily mean that we have 'overcome' racism, but that we can, in fact, be in the midst of reproducing racist ideologies. In 1985, Michael Grade (then at LWT), on being questioned by Linda Agran at the Edinburgh Television Festival, agreed that *Mind Your Language* was racist and said, 'It was really irresponsible of us to put it out.' Unfortunately, all did not share Grade's penitence, and a new series of *Mind Your Language* (using most of the original cast) was aired to 'selected' ITV regions in 1986.[4]

In keeping with television's implicit social Whiteness and broader debates about assimilation in the 1970s, many of the comedies 'about race', were actually comedies about Blacks signifying *trouble*; *trouble* with the neighbours, *trouble* with language, *trouble* with 'fitting in', so that if the White characters did display prejudice, this was deemed funny or understandable given the 'difficulty of the situation'. One such example was *Love Thy Neighbour* (Thames TV/ITV, 1972–76) starring Rudolph Walker, Nina Baden-Semper, Kate Williams and Jack Smethurst, which attempted to balance out racist attitudes by showing 'mutual racism' as a natural response to coping with cultural difference. The comedy constantly signposted the Reynolds' 'Blackness', or more accurately, television's interpretation of Blackness (limbo-dancing, voodoo/Black magic), and racism, intead of being challenged, was shown as a reciprocal, inevitable and petty process (hence the neighbours' respective use of 'nigger' and 'honky'). Again, a Thames Television spokesman suggested that such humour would, 'take the heat out of the colour question' (quoted in Twitchin, 1988: 124). This classic defence was widely used to disavow the general discourse of racist humour both in television comedy and stand-up routines. Although the stand-up circuit, and specific talent shows such as *New Faces* (ATV/ITV, 1973–78), were an important entry-point for up and coming Black British comedians such as Lenny Henry, Gary Wilmot and Charlie Williams, it also tended to work within a specific tradition that was male, working class, sexist and racist (epitomized by comedians such as Bernard Manning, Jim Bowen and Duggie Brown) and which derived from the working-men's club circuit (for example, *The Comedians* (Granada TV/ITV, 1971–85). Since 'colour' was considered as the defining feature of Black people, it was never really an option for a Black comedian to make no mention of this, although as Lenny Henry explains, this was not necessarily a submissive practice, 'because they [the Black comedians] wanted the audience to know that they knew' (Henry in Phillips and Phillips, 1998: 314). To 'know' and reiterate that Blackness was a popular source of humour was also a way of getting one foot in the door. For example, popular Black comedian Charlie Williams would joke in his thick Yorkshire accent, 'Watch out, or I'll come and live next door to you', so that the comedy often depended not simply on self-deprecation, but also apparently on a certain self-knowledge.[5] Of course, this also made many Black viewers feel utterly uncomfortable, although such humour was generally accepted as 'just good fun', and because the Black comedian would actively collude with this racist humour, it would avoid criticisms of racism.

We have already signposted that during the early 1980s, as part of shifts in ethnic-minority cultural politics, there was a new climate of cultural sensitivity towards 'minority' communities. The establishment of the Comedy Store in London in 1979 was an important sign of the times, symbolizing the demise of the old-school humour which had once formed the backbone of British comedy (racist, sexist, homophobic). 'Alternative comedy' as it became known, was widely perceived as 'left wing', 'anti-establishment' and 'politically correct'; outrageous in its directness, but selective in its new satirical targets. The non-sexist, non-racist premise of the jokes meant that Blacks, Jews and women (particularly mothers-in-law) were no longer the prime targets of the comedy. Starting as a fringe activity, alternative cabaret began to occupy the mainstream comic agenda and, along with emerging notions of youth style (see Chapter 6), influence television's approach to British comedy. What the alternative comedians collectively signalled was that comedy does need targets, but that these were not fixed in stone and desperately needed updating. Older comedians such as Jim Davidson and Bernard Manning, who relied heavily on racist rhetoric in their acts, were now increasingly seen as traditional, out-dated and conservative alongside their new leftist colleagues. Whilst television was critical in registering, packaging and circulating this change in comic mood, there were ironically, very few Black comedians in the 'alternative comedy' set.

Against this background and with the support of the newly emerging minority-sensitive targeted channel programmes, the mid-1980s introduced *No Problem!* (1983–85) and *Tandoori Nights* (1985–87), 'ethnic sitcoms' with an African-Caribbean and Asian focus respectively. These comedies represented a more integrated mode of Black production, so that Black artists were now actively involved as writers, actors and producers. *No Problem!* was the first all-Black situated comedy to come out of Channel 4 and its Multicultural Programming Department (part of the London Weekend Commission under Sue Woodford (see Pines, 1992: 14–15)) and developed out of Humphrey Barclay's interest in the Black Theatre Cooperative and the writing and performing talent it had spawned (Farrukh Dhondy, Victor Romero Evans, Trevor Laird, Mustafa Matura). Although it marked a milestone in access and production terms ('Black' patois and dialect, roots in Black Theatre and a unique sense of 'Black-Britishness'), like most comedy it was dependent on stereotypes (stand-in mothers, tough Black women, predatory Black females, macho clowns and wayward criminals) which drew intense criticism for being racialized stereotypes. For example, the fact that *No Problem!* was based around the Powell siblings whose parents had returned to Jamaica after selling their family business, was criticized for positioning 'voluntary repatriation at the heart of the situation' (see Gilroy, 1983). The ambivalent racial undertones of the text were reiterated in cheap gags about Asians ('Abdul the camel driver' and 'illegal immigrants from Finchley'), comments alarmingly reminiscent of Kenny Lynch's character in *Curry and Chips*. Similarly, *Tandoori Nights* presented a number of familiar Asian stereotypes: the Indian restaurant setting, Saeed Jaffrey as the unctuous, conniving businessman (Jimmy Sharma), revelling in what he perceived as the 'social climb' in dating White women; the rebellious Asian daughter played by Rita Wolf; and the subservient, bumbling, servile, servant-fool in Alaudin (Tariq Yunus) (see Daniels and Gerson, 1989: 50–4 for a range of reviews).

These comedies and the reactions they triggered, marked a pivotal moment in terms of Black media criticism: for the first time in television history, these were programmes that really were 'ours' to criticize, and furthermore, they had emphatically produced disparate readings and opinion. As with Channel 4's actuality equivalents, *Black on Black* and *Eastern Eye*, the varied responses demonstrated that there is no monolithic reaction to Black programmes by Black audiences, and that comedy is a particularly tricky area, 'a double-edged game, in which it is impossible to ensure that the audience is laughing with, not at, the stereotype' (Hall in Givanni, 1995: 21). *No Problem!* and *Tandoori Nights* required a lot more 'work' for Black viewers who now found themselves being cornered into negotiating a reading, not just of the programmes' laughableness, but also of the source of the humour and the effects it might produce *on other* (White) viewers. Whilst these series may have indicated a shift in terms of audience address (i.e. they were largely geared towards Black viewers), the presence and power of White viewers who were making their own readings of the comedies, was also essential to the show's representations and the reactions to it. The fact of these differently racially organized subject positions inevitably had a bearing on the overall meanings derived from the text. These first 'ethnic sitcoms' were also bound to attract disparate reading positions, since Black viewers, in the main, had not yet cultivated a tolerance of Black comedians laughing at themselves on the very public site of television. There was inevitably some disappointment that this much struggled for space on a long-awaited channel was flirting too breezily with well-rehearsed stereotypes of 'Blackness' and, moreover, located Black and Asian culture as self-conscious, comical and exotic. Many of the criticisms revealed a quite impossible burden of expectation of the series (demands for 'realistic' and 'accurate' characterizations, for Black people not to be laughed at in a comedy show, and for the series to wipe out the whole history of 'misrepresentations' of Black women in the media – see Brixton Black Women's Group on *No Problem!* in *City Limits*, No.126, 2–8.3.84)). Nevertheless, after years of lobbying and campaigning for alternative spaces and representational approaches, the roots and context of this discontent amongst many Black viewers also needed to be registered.

Interestingly, it was the comedies that set themselves up as 'ethnic sitcoms' which attracted this kind of criticism. Other sitcoms which featured Black people usually managed to avoid the critical spotlight, such as the likeable *Red Dwarf* (BBC2, 1988–96), a science-fiction comedy featuring Craig Charles (as David Lister) and Danny John-Jules (as Cat). One can only assume that its supernatural setting made it far removed from the positive/negative, realistic/misrepresentative debates that had so far characterized the debates around Black comedies. During the 1980s, *The Cosby Show* (NBC/Channel 4, 1984–92), the US-produced Black family sitcom proved to be hugely successful in Britain, arguably because it was funnier than *No Problem!* and *Tandoori Nights*, but also because it moved away from the conflict-based White bigotry/tolerance versus Black bigotry/ignorance/passivity paradigm of so many earlier comedies about race (see Gray, 1995 and Jhally and Lewis, 1992 for a range of views). *Desmond's* (Channel 4,

1989–94) is the closest Britain has come to emulating the Cosby model, although its setting, style and humour were quite different. Like *The Cosby Show*, it was an explicitly 'corrective' text; designed to work against the types of 'negative' images of comedic Blackness which had hitherto been seen on television. Black scriptwriter Trix Worrell and Humphrey Barclay were keen, 'to say something positive about black families and, more importantly, about migrant families within this country and what it is to be Black in England' (Worrell, quoted in Pines, 1992: 184). Opinions were characteristically divided about *Desmond's*, but it was one of the few Black shows to successfully reach a mainstream audience in Britain and also proved popular in the Caribbean and America where it was broadcast on Black Entertainment Television (BET). The long-running programme built its characters around different (regionally, politically and generationally) types of Black characters who congregated in 'Desmond's', a barber-shop in Peckham (South London). The series was unique as a Black comedy which was set in the workplace, and as one in which Blackness was mediated through a relatively stable and unified home family life (Malik, in Newcomb, 1997). In terms of its production, *Desmond's* also had its own distinct method of team writing, which became a training-ground for many new writers. *Desmond's* only ended when the series' lead actor, Norman Beaton, died in December 1994, and Channel 4 went on to screen two brief 'Black comedies': *Porkpie* (Channel 4, 1995–96), a *Desmond's* spin-off, starring Ram John Holder as an elderly, solitary lollipop man turned £10 million lottery winner; and *In Exile* (Channel 4, 1998), a bizarre comedy based on a deposed military dictator of the African Republic of Kumeria (played by Patrice Naiambana), in exile in Britain.

comedy milestones   Despite the general 'liberalization' of British comedy, the post-Alternative era has remained remarkably White-dominated. As Cook notes, 'it is ironic that the movement which spawned this egalitarian sea-change has remained almost as white as the working men's club circuit that it set out to counteract' (Cook, *Guardian*, 8.12.93: 4). Lenny Henry stands out as one of Britain's few Black 'household names' who reached success in comedy and made his name on British television. Having spent much of his early career working within a context of racist humour (touring with *The Black and White Minstrels* and *Cannon And Ball*), and facing others' expectations of him to be another Charlie Williams (see Henry in Pines, 1992: 213–14), his gift for creating comic characters and witty vignettes of West Indian life in Britain began to manifest itself more clearly, and he was given his own show, *The Lenny Henry Show* (BBC1, 1984–85, 1987–88), featuring caricatures such as PC Ganga, Deakus, Theophilus P.

Wildebeeste and Delbert Wilkins (Malik in Newcomb, 1997: 755–6). Henry's subsequent move into film and television drama; the establishment of his own production company, Crucial Films, in 1992; his Golden Rose award at the 2001 Montreux TV Festival for *Lenny Henry in Pieces*, and his involvement in the Step Forward comedy-writing workshops in conjunction with the BBC, have all demonstrated the consistency of Henry's success, from teen hopeful to middle age. Unlike many Black performers, he has through his work, been allowed to 'grow up', something reflected in his later drama roles as head-chef, Gareth Blackstone, in *Chef!* (BBC1, 1993–96), a series characterized by respectable production values, tight seriocomic scripts and sharp lead performances, and then as a headteacher in the prime-time drama series, *Hope and Glory* (BBC1, 1998–). These are unparalleled successes for a Black Briton on British television.

In general, the 1990s presence in the genre was dominated by the all-Black sketch show, inaugurated by *The Real McCoy* (BBC2, 1991–96) (see Gupta, *Guardian*, 20.2.99), and followed by a spate of late night, sketch-based shows such as LWT's *291 Club* (1991), Channel 4's *Armed & Dangerous* (1994), *Get Up, Stand Up* (1996), and BBC2's *Blouse and Skirt* (1996–2000). Richard Blackwood stands out here, having been given his own show, *Club Class* (1997) on Channel 5 and then *The Richard Blackwood Show* on Channel 4 (1999–), thus being one of the few Black Britons, other than Lenny Henry and footballer, Ian Wright, to have his own entertainment show.[6] In general, British television comedy remains dominated by the cult of the alternative White comedian (Caroline Aherne (Mrs Merton), Steve Coogan (Alan Partridge), Reeves & Mortimer, Jack Dee, Lily Savage), and the Black and Asian comedy circuits in Britain remain localized, experimental and small-scale. Television access for and expectations of Black comedians remain severely limited and are typically pushed to the corners of the schedule (an exception here is Mina Anwar and Rudoph Walker in *The Thin Blue Line*, BBC1, 1995–96).

It is hoped that *Goodness Gracious Me* (BBC2, 1998–2001), a rare British-Asian intervention in the genre [featuring Meera Syal, Sanjeev Bhaskar, Nina Wadia and Kulvinder Ghir] will, with its vast national and international success, have an enabling long-term effect on the Black and Asian presence in the genre. The series was the first Asian sketch show on British television. In particular, *Goodness Gracious Me* has proved that 'minority-based' comedy can be universally popular despite its use of dialogue and 'in' jokes that only a minority audience are likely to fully understand. This solicitation of extra-diegetic knowledge through bilingualism and Asian cultural references, offers the British-Asian viewer a sense of inclusiveness, as though the comedy has been tailor-made for an otherwise neglected sector of the viewing audience. In fact, Asians and Middle Englanders tuned into the programme from the start and it was estimated that the first series drew in an 85 per cent White majority audience, part of a broader 'Asian renaissance' at the time with an interest in Asian fashion, home-furnishings and culture. *The Times* attributed the show's success to Britain's comfortable race relations: 'Old Britain and its more recent immigrants are lucky. When both laugh at each other, both like each other better for doing so' (*The Times*, 7.01.98). The reasons for *Goodness Gracious Me*'s vast success are arguably a little more complicated, not least because the comedy frequently laughs at 'Old Britain', in a style that could only have materialized from this distinctly hybrid British-Asian comic register. The politically astute and omniscient cultural politics of *Goodness Gracious Me* is centred on an implicit self-awareness of popular perceptions of British-Asians and an acknowledgement that British racism and, for that matter, liberal political correctness, exists (satirical sketches on the 'institutional Whiteness' of broadcasting boardrooms, on 'Going for an English' meal in a restaurant, and on anthropological travelogues of 'exotic India' for example). Interestingly, the series is also based on traditional and updated stereotypes of British-Asians (the spiritual guru who exploits mysticism-loving Westerners, the Bollywood macho man, the restrictive parents, the Indian 'wide-boy', the inexhaustible bhangra dancer, the more-English-than-the English Asian social climbers, and so on), although it draws on a range of influences, from Jewish-American humour to Bollywood films to British television and cinema. Part of the trick of the series is the way the comedy team 'go inside the stereotype', often reverting to it, thus inadvertently raising the question, 'When is a stereotype not a stereotype?' Because these stereotypes are negotiated by Asians and deliberately subverted through visual puns, spectacle and parody, can we safely say that racist readings are not gleaned from the text? There are complex issues involved here, not least regarding the broad range of responses to the series within the South Asian diaspora itself, which touch on questions of generation (the various readings the comedy appears to have generated amongst first and second-generation Asians), geography (the comedy faced resistance from viewing authorities in India, but sold to Sweden) and morality (the complaints upheld by the Broadcasting Standards Council in June 1998 regarding a scene which some found offensive to Hinduism).

One of the most contentious and popular comedic icons of Blackness, although he is not Black, is Sacha Baron-Cohen's character Ali G; a White (Jewish) comedian acting out the style of a Black-British rap-inspired youth with the catchphrase, 'Is it 'cos I is Black?' (see Figure 4). Following his appearances on Channel 4's late-night satirical comedy programme, *The 11 O'Clock Show* in 1999, Baron-Cohen was given his own series, *Da Ali G Show* (Channel 4) in 2000. The ambiguity at the heart of this cultural phenomenon, divided opinion as to whether he is: (1) a White character blacked-up to mock a Black person (albeit deliberately clumsily and

Figure 4

Sacha Baron-Cohen posing as Ali G for Channel 4's
The 11 O'Clock Show

Courtesy of Channel 4 Picture Publicity

'inauthentically' acted out by Baron-Cohen); (2) an impersonation of a White kid who thinks he is Black (a 'Wigger'); or (3) a White comedian mocking an Asian kid who thinks he is Black. The uncertainty over the source of humour, although arguably eclipsed by the way in which Baron-Cohen skilfully selects and manipulates his satirical targets, whilst synchronously parodying 'yoof TV' and the climate of obsession which has surrounded Black youth culture since the 1990s, raised criticism from many Black comedians. Felix Dexter and Gina Yashere were critical of the media frenzy over 'Ali G', compared to its marginalization of and lethargy towards 'genuinely' Black comedians, and comedian Curtis Walker compared Ali G to Al Jolson, feeling uncomfortable about the popularity of a 'Blacked up' performer in contemporary Britain. Richard Blackwood, himself a rising star at the time of Ali G's phenomenal success, said, 'When I watch the show and listen to where the laughter comes, I think the joke is on the black man, and that is a stereotype we are fighting every day' (Blackwood, *Daily Telegraph*, 1.6.00).

These criticisms touch on broader issues around how Black comedians still feel their performance repertoires and points of access are restricted. Because of the tie-in between comedy programmes and other forms of popular culture – quiz shows, chat shows, and adverts – the overriding absence of Black comedians outside of ghettoized slots, has a broader impact on where Black light entertainers (such as Felix Dexter, Chris Tummings, Malcolm Frederick, Curtis Walker, Angie La Mar) are and are not seen. And so it takes a separately organized event (such as Britain's first 'Black International Comedy Awards' in April 2000), or 'corrective' initiatives such as Carlton Television's series *Single Voices* (2000), a set of four beautifully-acted, half-hour, peak-time monologues produced by Parminder Vir, and written and performed by Black and Asian talent (including Felix Dexter, Sanjeev Kohli and Nina Wadia), to foreground this talent. Furthermore, it is still quite common to see a group of White executives developing and directing a Black comedy show (see Charlie Hanson in Pines, 1992:192). As Black comedian, Felix Dexter says,

> TV traditions tend to be conservative, and the TV establishment is resistant to black artistes in general. When they think of a black comedian, they always think of Lenny Henry. . . .There's a self-conscious, privileged elite who have a fascination with black culture – but only because it has a quaint novelty-value. (Dexter, *Guardian*, 8.12.93: 4)

This 'novelty-value' is not just contained in the sketch-show or sit-com, but is also communicated by those leading Black personalities, who are not comedians by trade, but whose 'excessive' mannerisms position them as modern racial clowns. I am thinking here of the popular chef and presenter, Ainsley Harriott, who is often referred to as 'madcap', 'effervescent' and 'irrepressible', and is more publicly known for his endless hugging, singing, dancing and eyeballing than for his culinary skills.[7] Then there is Rustie Lee with her hearty belly laugh; and sportsman-turned-presenter, Kris Akabusi, with his affected trademark chuckle; and, of course, Frank Bruno whose pantomimic mannerisms and sporting background position him as national-hero-cum-buffoon (see pp. 132–3). One senses that these figures are popular because of, rather than despite, their folly, and that they are comical because of their rather un-English shows of emotion and self-mocking. We also see this 'novelty-value' in game shows (most obviously in the traditional TV popular hits *Family Fortunes*, *Barrymore*, *Play Your Cards Right*), where Black and Asian contestants are regularly marvelled at, joked and teased about their accents or other cultural features. This cultural practice of suffering Black fools gladly, was also to be found in Britain's popular youth show, *TFI Friday* (Channel 4, 1996–2000), which in its heyday, regularly featured an elderly West Indian café-owner, Cedric, a rare television appearance for that older generation of

Black Britons. Cedric however, was a figure of ridicule, delivering poorly-rehearsed lines, making weak social commentary, and appearing faithfully dependent on the call of his 'master' – in this case, the media mogul presenter, Chris Evans. Unlike their antecedents, there is no direct acknowledgement in these images that the starting place for the humour is 'Blackness', but there is an unsettling and deep-seated sense that this is the case; a fact of ambivalence inextricably associated with formative notions of raced clowns.

Kobena Mercer has, in another context, considered the wider manifestations of 'ambivalence'; that it functions 'as a complex "structure of feeling" experienced across the relations between authors, texts and readers – in relations that are always contingent, context-bound, and historically specific' (Mercer, 1994: 174). Mercer shifts from considering the ambivalence, as he puts it, 'inside the text' to that which functions outside it. For some, those precise comedic expressions that are seen to deconstruct and challenge Black stereotypes by working through them (*No Problem!*, *Goodness Gracious Me*, Ali G) are seen by others as signs that we are now playing the essentialist game in order to get popular and mainstream profiles. The uncertainty is such that the 'right targets' of comedy shift over time, are deemed (in)appropriate in different historical moments and are inescapably dependent on who delivers the joke, how the comedy is enunciated and the context within which it is read. Thus, when *Till Death* was broadcast again on the BBC in the 1990s, it had its more caustic moments edited out for contemporary audiences, and when Bernard Manning (once a kingpin of television light entertainment) appeared on *The Mrs Merton Show* (BBC1) in 1998, the duty logbook recorded approximately 600 complaints about his appearance and use of the word 'Paki' (the BBC put out a virtually unchanged scheduled repeat showing a few days later). A point that might help to break through the ambivalence is to consider that not all racisms work in the same way. Alf Garnett's is different from Bill Reynold's, Bernard Manning's different from Kenny Lynch's. Whilst there is clearly a new climate of racial sensitivity, we also need to consider how Black and White audiences have themselves changed and ask what it says about the traditions of British television that a central tenet of its comedy programming has been so obsessed with, and dependent on, racist humour. Comedy writers frequently pledge their commitment to irony or elevated liberal ideals to shield themselves and their comic creations from accusations of being anti-Black. This is a very British form of defence. Much of the British comedy tradition needs to be recognized as working within this culture of racism, while using the alibi of comedy to give the illusion of being outside it.

notes

1 In 1953, the National Association for the Advancement of Coloured People (NAACP) successfully campaigned to take the show (the first to feature a Black cast in primetime) off the air.

2 Two episodes which foregrounded the issue of 'race' and which can be found in the archives, are *Intolerance* (Tx: 27.6.66) and *The Blood Donor* (Tx: 12.1.68).

3 This cast a gay Black character, Winston (Eamonn Walker) (nick-named Marigold by Alf) as Alf's home-help, thus setting up an opportunity for Alf to abuse not only his racial but sexual other. Walker went on to play quite different roles as an undercover drug-officer in Lynda La Plante's *Supply and Demand* (Yorkshire TV/ITV, 1998) and in America's HBO series, *Oz* (Channel 4).

4 The US cloned *Mind Your Language* into *What A Country!* in what represented the first sale made directly to US syndication. Twenty years after it was first made, *Mind Your Language* was screened in India where it was hugely popular.

5 Charlie Williams was also the host of the popular game show *The Golden Shot* (ATV, 1967–75).

6 Although there have been a few Black women to have daytime chat-shows such as Chrystal Rose (*The Chrystal Rose Show*, ITV, 1993–96), Josie D'Arby (*Josie*, Channel 5, 1999) and Trisha Goddard (*Trisha*, ITV, 1998–).

7 Harriott struck a deal with America's NBC network in 1999 to host the *Ainsley Harriott Show* (cookery and chat) which was swiftly axed, and Harriott subsequently returned to the UK to host *Ready Steady Cook* on BBC2 from 2000.

light entertainment on television – and the black-british cultures it is missing

Part of the 'utopianism' of pleasure-related texts is that they involve an escape (on an audience, textual and performance level) from class and cultural distinctions. Popular culture implies cohesion. This makes approaches to reading race (within a supposedly 'non-racial' field) complicated; as though we are attempting to extract something 'heavy' from something supposedly 'light' and scrutinize with rigour cultural representations which are probably instinctive and based on the form of 'innocent' meritocracy known as 'talent'.[1] We can hardly ignore though, the fact of a major Black presence in the music and light entertainment field, compared with the story of absence, social Whiteness and marginalization that has so far imbued this discussion. But if this retrospective takes a significant turn here, then does popular culture in the television world also represent a shift away from the spectacle of Black Britishness *and* its discontents that we have hitherto been witness to? The primary concern of this chapter is youth, music and television and its relationship with the new Black-British ethnicities (see Hall in Mercer, 1988: 27–31; Gilroy, 1987, 1993a, 1993b). Here, we are essentially talking about the contemporary and mostly about African-Caribbeans, although youth culture does not exclusively pertain to the modern or to 'Blackness'.

Popular entertainment is one of the rare instances where we really can say that, for better or worse, Black forms of expression have shaped *lived* (i.e. not always those seen on television) cultural activity. For our concerns, the importance of mapping these 'lived cultures' (Bennett, 1986) or what Angela McRobbie has called the 'social practices of performance, production and participation' (McRobbie in Chambers and Curti, 1996: 34) is twofold: firstly, these aspects of Black cultural life have gone far in influencing versions of Black-Britishness which have, in turn, altered the shape of British (popular) culture; and second, many of these public moves and styles have helped to influence delineations of Black people in the representational site of television. But the duality of the process goes further: these routes towards individual and collective identity formation coincide with, support and shape mass consumer culture; they are both cultural practice and cultural commodity and therefore sanction Blackness as spectacle. As a key area for change and exchange, Black popular culture has become increasingly medi-agenic within the context of wider shifts towards cultural populism, mass consumerism, and diversity. It provides the commercially fruitful edge of dif-ference, whilst also fulfilling the needs of corporate diversity. One only has to look at the impact of popular versions of Blackness, such as rap, hip-hop, Ali G, or the neologism of the Budweiser advertisement 'Whassup' phrase to see its influences being played out.[2] If we take a moment to think about the examples I have just mentioned, then we can see the kinds of culturally-loaded and socially contradictory issues at stake here: these images are all, in a sense, mutated versions or the flip-side of the very kinds of 'street, amoral, reckless, uncivilized' images of young Black men, which have been projected and located at the heart of race crisis in Britain, as defined in the television news discourse for example. Different inflexions of this spectacle of Black masculinity – of the Black delinquent on the front page of a news-paper and the Black style-icon on the front covers of glossy style magazines – hang together, sit side by side and are never incompatible with 'the facts'. If Black popular culture carries this dual image of vice and aspiration, it also has to distribute these associations within a television culture that is enmeshed with common sense racialized discourses (news, documentary). That is, it has to shed positive light onto an otherwise denigrated trope of Blackness, to enunciate the 'positive' as well as the 'negative'. We are not simply talking about one-way, frivolous appropriation here, because televi-sion and lived Black youth cultures each have a greater, more complex and symbiotic role to play in the production, circulation and consensus around the expression of televised Black youth culture in its various forms. Black popular cultures and diaspora aesthetics confront us with the need for a critical distinction *between* 'good' or 'bad' examples of Black cultural pro-duction, instead of allowing us to assume that it all has to be one thing or another, which, in any case, presumes that there is such a thing as an authen-tic or essential (good/bad) Black subject.

I am concerned with the relationship between how, selectively, British television representations draw on (and refuse) these lived cultures. There are, in a sense, two separate stories here and I am loath to reduce one (the 'lived' cultures where some of the most exciting modern cultural transformations have been produced) to the other (television's selective inter-pretation or misreckoning of them) – as if to say that the former has been outmanoeuvred or resignedly inhibited by the latter, or that the 'lived' cul-tures have spent all their creative energies 'waiting to be represented' by tele-vision. In fact, as I go on to argue, the new hybridized forms and dialogic manoeuvres – or the diaspora aesthetics – produced by young 'Black Britons' today, have largely developed outside of and without the support of the broader mainstream, and are ever more liberated from it. While we can agree that television itself is a form of popular culture, this does not mean that it always works in seamless harmony with other systems of the popular (e.g. film, fashion, records, advertising, cinema). Television defines its own normative ground as well as mediating how it treats other cultural forms. It sets its own parameters of what it regards as fashionable/popular, high/low, mainstream/marginal, serious/trivial, and so on. As well as taking on Hall's question 'What is this 'black' in black popular culture', I also want to consider how the 'popular' of 'Black popular culture' has been defined against the grain of more middling and mainstream television forms of populism (the Beadle, Barrymore and Black cartel). How does television act out this cultural politics of representation? And given the structures of dominance and subordination which the stereotypical image of the Black performer threatens to hold in place, what does the permanence and naturalization of the image say about Blackness and to what degree has this enabled it to sustain itself in a broader sense?

If the fact of ambiguity (of text, representation and address) was established in our discussion of comedy, then the story continues here, for Black popular culture is a verifiably contradictory space which cannot be understood through binary oppositions – 'high and low; resistance versus incorporation; authentic versus unauthentic; experiential versus formal; opposition versus homogenization' (Hall in Morley and Chen, 1996: 470). Like all forms of culture, Black popular cultures are always changing, usually dependent, sometimes more, sometimes less commercially appealing and always with varying degrees of 'authenticity'. The new diaspora aesthetics are never one thing, do not always deny their own versions of racial authenticity (as in the case of hip-hop) and are more than the sum of the diasporas of their past; they both extend and respond to Black and Asian cultural trajectories and are never passive or extricable from other forms of public space. Nor are they extricable from the tension between authenticity and exploitation, culture and commerce, liberation and constraint, since 'popular culture' is always the tension between the two. One question which arises here, as it did in relation to comedy and as it will in relation to sport, is to what extent Black entertainers themselves trade on, act up or play back the essentialist stereotypes of 'typical Blackness'; whether they are beneficiaries of White racism or victims of it; whether 'sending up' is an 'endorsement of'. In looking at the force of style in shaping political and cultural ideologies and working cultural patterns (language, social trends), we must also ask whether we can build anti-racist strategies around the arena of popular culture or accept it as an essentially shallow space.

variety in the early years   I want to use this first section to briefly address early television versions of light entertainment and 'variety', and the record of Black people's engagement with aural and performance traditions outside of current conceptions of 'youth culture'. Despite certain resistance to the 'low art form' of music and dance within the elitist early BBC (John Reith, BBC Handbook, 1928: 14), the Corporation was launched with a variety show broadcast live from Alexandra Palace (Tx: 2.11.36) featuring the comic duo Buck and Bubbles. On the same day, the notorious British Guyanese-born variety star/'racing adviser', Ras Prince Monolulu, could be seen on the BBC's topical magazine show, *Picture Page*. For the next few decades, the variety show reigned as a key television event, denoting occasion (inaugurating television's first broadcast and its postwar relaunch), nostalgia (traditional acts) and community (diverse acts and audiences all working together), and often featuring Black variety performers, many of them American and many of them women (Fryer, 1984; Pines, 1992; Bourne, 1998; Green, 1987). These included Adelaide Hall who appeared in various live broadcasts such as *Harlem in Mayfair* (BBCTV, 1939), *Dark Sophistication* (BBCTV, 1939) and *Variety in Sepia* (BBCTV, 1947);[3] and Elisabeth Welch, a New-Yorker, who went on to make over 150 appearances as a singer in variety shows and live broadcasts from Alexandra Palace in the late 1930s, including the BBC's postwar relaunch, *Television is Here Again* (see Pines, 1992, for extensive interviews with Henriques and Welch). Winifred Atwell, a Trinidadian-born pianist who came to Britain in 1946, made a number of television, radio, live and film appearances, and was, unprecedently given her own self-named series on the newly-formed ITV, *The Winfred Atwell Show* (1956) and then on the BBC in the next year. Paul Robeson, first seen on British television on 23 August 1939 in a ten-minute live broadcast of songs performed at Alexandra Palace, made various appearances in British films, television drama and variety programmes including *Val Parnell's Sunday Night at the London Palladium* (ITV, 1958) and *Paul Robeson Sings* (ATV/ITV, 1958). Behind these phenomenal achievements, and others led by Lena Horne and Josephine Baker, there was also a legacy of discrimination, racially-coded pressure and the actuality of hard labour and inequity (see Dyer, 1987).

One effect of the newly-formed commercial Independent Television (ITV) from 1955 was that the whole tone of (light entertainment) programming soon began to shift towards a more populist, modern and leisure-oriented approach and attract a new generation of viewers. Regular variety slots such as *Sunday Night at the London Palladium* (ATV/ITV, 1955–67, 1973–74) and *Chelsea at Nine* (Granada TV/ITV, 1957–60) often featured Black (many of them jazz) performers such as Sammy Davis Jr, Ella Fitzgerald, Duke Ellington, Cleo Laine, Robert Adams and Winifred Atwell. What many of these stars (and others such as Scott and Whaller and Harry Belafonte) reflected was a more general trend and taste for Black American performers. Pearl Connor who was an actress at the time says, 'we learnt early on that to be American Black or to have that American gimmick worked' (cited from *Black and White in Colour*, BBC2, Tx: 27.6.92). The emergence of the African-American star system was boosted by the rising independent Black media in the USA (such as *Ebony* magazine), while Black-Britons were still dependent on a largely disinterested White media. In order to support, motivate and promote Black talent in Britain, Pearl Connor, together with her Trinidadian folk singer husband, Edric Connor,[4] set up an agency in 1956 called 'The Edric Connor Agency' (later to become known as 'The Afro-Asian Caribbean Agency'). The agency, which operated until 1976, aimed to promote Black representation and handle practical matters such as rates, repeat fees, Equity and artists rights, but sometimes also helped artists to find lodgings and get drama training (see p. 137). Pearl later recalled how Edric (who died in 1968) 'had a strong sense of national identity which made him a pioneer of our folk arts in England. He was constantly promoting our songs, music and folklore, and trying to get people interested in our culture' (quoted in Pines, 1992: 33).

The fact remained, that the spaces where Black people were involved in television variety were always restricted to the level of performance. Cy Grant was the first Black light entertainment television star to be brought to the public's attention within a distinctly British context. Between 1957 and 1960, Grant made regular appearances on the topical-affairs BBC programme, *Tonight*, presenting a calypso interpretation of the news. Grant had previously been a serious dramatic actor and, although he appeared on peak-time television on and off for three years, he later recalled, 'I don't think if I had asked to be an interviewer, that they would have entertained that suggestion. I don't think anyone saw me as anything other than a calypso singer, someone singing something that was very trivial and expendable . . . while *Tonight* was great fun to do, there was a terrible price to pay' (quoted in Pines, 1992: 47). The circumscription of Black artists in (selected) performance roles reflected the broader patterns of regulated access at this time, and requests to be more actively involved in decision-making and creative control were continually turned down. Following the 1958 Notting Hill riots, Edric Connor put forward a proposal to produce a series about Caribbean music and culture (*Edric Connor Sings*) for the BBC, but this was rejected on the grounds of being 'economically unsound' (letter to Edric Connor from Ronald Waldman, Business Manager of BBC Television Programmes, 21.5.59). There are many such examples.

Perhaps the most offensive example of how potential Black-British talent was being overlooked in favour of more caricatured images of 'Blackness', was *The Black and White Minstrel Show* (BBC, 1958–78). The Saturday night television phenomena had its antecedents in the tradition of minstrelsy, which symbolized an essentially pro-slavery and anti-emancipatory politics; the days of the American Deep South when the good

Black slaves would serenade innocent White roses. Black entertainment, a key facet of slavery, was built on European theories (reified from as early as the eighteenth century) of Black people's natural 'happy-go-lucky' mirth and musical ability. Jolly, singing slaves were generally preferred to discontented, silent ones, so 'dancing the slaves' to see the 'merry nigger' was common practice. For the slave-owner this could be used as a justification for slavery but it also served Westerners' natural curiosity and interest in African dance and music (Pieterse, 1992). The minstrel, a new spin on the Black entertainer role, described by Kenneth Lynn as 'a white imitation of a black imitation of a contented slave' (quoted in Pieterse, 1992: 132), became one of the most popular early images of 'Blackness' and was absorbed in Britain in music hall, revue and radio. White performers would blacken their faces with burned cork to mimic the music and dance of Black slaves. Minstrel mimicry became even more pronounced after the Civil War, and when slavery itself threatened to be abolished (see Pieterse, 1992: 132). Following the minstrels' popularity on the stage and in 'Swannee River' style radio shows, George Inns' production of *The 1957 Television Minstrels* (BBC, Tx: 2.9.57) soon developed into a regular series with a 45-minute non-stop format of slickly choreographed Mississippi tunes and Country and Western Songs. Kenneth Connor and Ike Hatch, described in the *Radio Times* in 1961 as 'the two black looks' and G.H. Elliott as 'the original chocolate coloured coon', got star-billing. *The Black and White Minstrel Show* won the Golden Rose of Montreux Prize in 1961 and while on television, could guarantee audiences of at least 12 million – but frequently topped 18 million (matching *Till Death*), thus gaining a massive audience-share. The novelty-factor of the visually striking blacked-up faces (the programme enjoyed a revival after the extension of colour television to BBC1 and ITV in 1969) was the twist that made the programme work (Malik in Newcomb, 1997: 185–6).

The inappropriateness of the caricature of White people 'blacking up' to imitate Blackness in a multi-ethnic, post-colonial Britain (particularly when there were so few alternative media images of Black people) was not acknowledged by the BBC, or at least shelved because of the programme's vast ratings-success. In the early 1960s, *The Black and White Minstrel Show* began to emerge amongst liberal commentators as a public point of criticism directed at the BBC's racial insensitivity and in 1967 the Campaign Against Racial Discrimination delivered a petition to the BBC signed by both Blacks and Whites who requested that the show be taken off-screen. Clive West, the organizer, argued that the programme 'causes distress to coloured people by showing them as a race who cannot be supported as serious-minded citizens, but as singing, dancing, idiotic people' (*The Times*, 18.5.67). The BBC disregarded these moral arguments and continued to broadcast *The Black and White Minstrel Show* on peak-time British television for a further ten years, although as Bob Woffinden noted, the tide had turned, and for the BBC it had developed into a matter of competing embarrassments: the embarrassment of continuing to support the show weighed against the embarrassment of taking it off, which would mean both depriving millions of licence-payers of what appeared to be their favourite programme and also implicitly admitting that if it was wrong at the point that it was taken off, then it must have been wrong all along. (Woffinden, 1988: 11)

the development of black british youth culture and its impact on british television   These institutional modes of variety paid little attention to the ways in which Britain's youth were developing their own forms of popular music and dance culture. Early British television, still overshadowed by strong Reithian definitions of high and low cultural art forms, was hesitant about providing for a teen-exclusive audience, so the domestic, 'family-oriented' variety programmes (see Hill in Corner, 1991) – a blend of international crooners, variety acts and show-business personalities (Chambers, 1986) – persisted. The youth phenomenon (inaugurated by Rock and Roll) was increasingly being seen and regarded as a threat to safe, conventional societal values. The 'moral panics' (see Cohen, 1972) about teen violence and hooliganism, the rhetoric around 'permissiveness' and the threat to dominant mores and 'culture' of adult White society, and the concern about the 'Americanization' and 'levelling down process' (or 'dumbing down') of British culture, language and tastes (Hebdige in Waites et al., 1981: 194–218), reached their peak at around the time of the 1958 Notting Hill riots. The bulk of the new music was picked up by mostly working-class youth, and drew on black African-American musical roots, marking the beginning of a long history of White artists working with and co-opting 'Black' music traditions, and bringing new fears about the infusion of Black cultures into White society. As such, what were widely regarded as the 'negative' or 'delinquent' dimensions of new popular teen tastes and trends were fundamentally related to aspects of race/'race relations' (i.e. Teddy Boys vs. Blacks) and class (working-class youth). The more positive, clean side, or what Andy Medhurst has called the 'scrubbed and sexless' aspects of British youth, seen in movies such as *It's Great To Be Young* (Dir. Cyril Frankel, GB, 1956), was depicted as 'whiter-than-white' (Medhurst in Romney and Wootton, 1995: 62). The overriding image of British youth was double-edged (see Frith, 1988), and structured around what Dick Hebdige describes as the duality of 'youth as fun' and 'youth as trouble' (Hebdige, 1988:19); convenient scapegoats located, at different times, at the heart of the best and worst of the nation, stimulating both imagination and fear. In time, armed with the fresh concept of the 'teenager', and the fact of their spending powers since the immediate postwar years, British television began to target youth-exclusive programmes. *Cool For Cats* (A-R/ITV, 1956–61), *Six-Five Special* (BBC, 1957–58), *Oh Boy!* (ABC/ITV, 1958–59), *Drumbeat* (BBC, 1959), *Juke Box Jury* (BBC, 1959–67, 1979, 1989, 1990) and *Colour Me Pop* (BBC2, 1968–69) were just some examples. But British (and for that matter American) television was generally resistant to profiling Black artists and the newly emerging cross-cultural forms (Blues and beat scene, Black all-girl groups, ska music, Northern Soul clubs), so that Black (often jazz) acts would make brief guest appearances, but rarely took centre stage in any other capacity. Kenny Lynch (see p. 95), a rare Black-British-born example, made regular appearances in 1960s youth-oriented shows such as *The Beat Room*, *Thank Your Lucky Stars* and *Ready Steady Go*.

With the odd exception and apart from a cluster of BBC2 jazz programmes (the nearest equivalent to dance music on television), access to Black-originated music forms from outside Britain (Latin America, the USA, Africa and the Caribbean), such as Jamaican reggae and American soul, was frustratingly blocked within 'official' spaces. During the 1970s, it became increasingly apparent that 'the resistance and oppositional symbols provided by Afro-Caribbean political culture' were 'central reference-points for the struggles of other young people' (Gilroy, 1981–82: 218–19). Henry Martin, whose film *Big George Is Dead* (1986), paid tribute to this moment recounts, 'the mixture of sleaze and art and culture' that existed in areas such as Soho in the late-1960s and 1970s, in clubs such as the Flamingo, the 77 Club and the Sunset, and the influence of styles such as the Jamaican 'rude boys' on White British bands such as The Beatles and Dave Clarke Five, were a sign of emerging cross-cultural forms (Martin, interview with author, 16.5.96). Although broadly enacted within the context of music, dance, clubs, youth and the metropolis, these forms had deep, historic threads of continuity also influenced by the arts, literature, religion and religious spaces, the media, politics (in Britain and elsewhere), policing, Carnival, schooling and so on (Harris in Owusu, 2000: 395–404). For filmmaker, Isaac Julien, 1977 (the year of the Queen's Silver Jubilee and the setting of his film *Young Soul Rebels*) represented the emergence of 'very powerful counter narratives that outlined new kinds of national possibilities' (Julien in Julien and MacCabe, 1991: 1). As Gilroy notes, 'the seemingly trivial forms of youth sub-culture point to the opening up of a self-consciously post-colonial space in which the affirmation of difference points forward to a more pluralistic conception of nationality and perhaps beyond that to its transcendence' (Gilroy, 1993b: 62). The popular hold of the new sounds of disco, soul and funk jazz which pertained to the formation of specifically Black-British popular subcultures and to the birth of the British soul movement by the late 1970s, was not broadly picked up by television apart from a mandatory inclusion on music chart shows. Interestingly, the fascist Right did understand the 'dangers' of the allure and renewed persistency of Black popular music forms (and acknowledge its exclusion from television). A 1979 edition of the National Front magazine, *Bulldog*, forewarned: 'The record and the cassette is more powerful than television or the newspapers where youth is concerned. Disco and its melting-pot pseudo-philosophy must be fought or Britain's streets will be full of black worshipping soul boys.'

There were many routes to this cultural divergence. First, there was the empowering effect of Black Pride, the Black Panthers and the US Black Power movement since the 1960s, led by key Black figures such as Malcolm X, Angela Davis and Stokeley Carmichael.[5] The battle played out by the Black Power activists and the American Government became a particular source of interest and fascination for many Black people in Britain, who watched the drama unfold on their television screens (see Phillips and Phillips, 1998: 231–3; Egbuna in Owusu, 2000: 58–69). Secondly, there was the unifying impact of Jamaican reggae and its leading icon, Bob Marley, which now began to draw in younger Black-Britons who saw Rastafarianism as a symbolic form of identification and were attracted, in particular, to its music, culture and style. Thirdly, there was great interest in the sounds and consolatory role of gospel and American soul music. Fourthly, a new set of assertive Black political and style icons was emerging, including James Brown, Ray Charles, Muhammad Ali, George Clinton and Isaac Hayes. Within these distinct yet imbricating contexts, new forms of identification, style and subversion, and a unique, if marginalized, Black-British popular scene began to develop – the Soul II Soul sound-system, a spate of 'pirate' radio stations in the early 1980s playing Black music (Dread Broadcasting Corporation, Horizon, JFM and LWR), Benjamin Zephaniah and Linton Kwesi Johnson's fusion of reggae music with voice, poetry and political commentary to produce 'dub poetry', the emerging work of Black-British independent filmmakers (see Chapter 9) – these all formed an alternative space and 'anti-language' to the publicly dominant youth discourses (BBC Radio 1, *Top of The Pops* (BBC1, 1963–)) of the late 1970s and early 1980s. They were largely expressed outside mainstream television – in marginalized spaces such as in low-budget independent film, late-night scheduled slots, the early experimental 'multicultural' series – and in general, were not perceived as representative or central to the British experience. Despite the popularization of new Black cultures and their broad and marketable appeal, questions of commerce (or the racially-coded fear that White viewers would switch off and sponsorship would slacken) determined that they would operate in accordance with perceived 'commercial needs' in the 'official' public sphere.

The greater integration and interaction between young British Whites and Blacks in the formation of new youth subcultures such as house music in the late 1980s, and a new wave of interest in emerging US-based Black sounds and styles (for example, rap, hip-hop, sampling, cut 'n scratching), positioned Black youth at the cutting-edge of 'street-credibility' and resistance, and parts of television were struggling to tap into this. There were various structural, economic and technological factors involved here: the increase of videocassette recorders and the number of television sets per household; a shift from family-focused to individually targeted audiences (Morley, 1992); a new trend for narrowcasting, an expansion into new 'lifestyle' -markets and a differentiated sense of 'public service' (see Chapter 3); attempts to increase advertising revenue; more young Black people working in television; deregulation; and the prospect of satellite and digital cable technologies. Mainstream television was still not in tune with the younger audience in general; in the mid-1980s, the youth audience (16–24 year olds) constituted 15 per cent of the population, but only made up 9 per cent of the television audience (Frith et al., 1993). There were some groundbreaking attempts to capture a youth audience, including Channel 4's *Club Mix*, the anarchic *The Tube* (Tyne Tees/Channel 4, 1982–87), and magazine/discussion programmes such as *Reportage* (BBC2) and *Open To Question* (which was presented by the British-Asian news presenter, Krishnan Guru-Murthy when he was 18). *Network 7* (Channel 4, 1987), a technically innovative so-called 'yoof' current affairs programme roughly set the generic style for future youth programmes and acted as a launchpad for young British-Asian talent such as Sankha Guha and Jaswinder Bancil. The *Def II* (BBC2, 1988) zone, executively produced by Janet Street-Porter (Head of BBC Youth and Entertainment Features between 1991 and 1993), included *Dance Energy* (a live music show hosted by Black DJ/presenter, Normski), and *Behind The Beat* (1987–91), a Black music magazine programme created, produced and directed by Black-British media entertainment entrepreneur, Terry Jervis. For all his vast media success, Jervis reminisces that his most rewarding television experience was prompted when he caught a glimpse of the Second World War commemorations on television, and realized that the Asians, West Indians and Africans who had fought for Britain were nowhere to be seen (approximately 10,000 Black men and women had been part of the British Armed Forces, see Fryer, 1984; Phillips and Phillips, 1998). He decided to collect archive material of their involvement, and include it in the regular *Behind The Beat* 'Respect Due' slot. Jervis takes up the story:

When I put it in, it was Janet Street-Porter at the time who wanted me to take it out. She said it had nothing to do with music. I said, 'It doesn't have to, it's just "respect due", that's what we say in Black popular culture.' I was trying to relay that part of the culture and I won because it was my show. So I put it out, and when people called up from all over the world who had never seen that footage, it made me realize the power you have. (Jervis, interview with author, 20.3.96)

The *Behind The Beat* and *Dance Energy* era marked the beginning of a more extensive sea-change in terms of British television's generic style of presentation. 'Style' itself, the manner in which things looked and sounded in relation to the fashionable, had become increasingly influential in the design, targeting and exhibitionism of programming, and by the early 1990s, the overall 'look' of television (in terms of visuals, tone and modes of address and across the board from rap-inspired beer and building society advertisements, to 'funky' graphics, 'street' presentational-style and popular music interjecting serious commentary in factual programmes) had begun to appear a lot 'younger' and, for that matter, a lot more 'multicultural'. 'Black youth' had moved from simply being a symbolic form of resistance (Hall and Jefferson, 1976) to being a major form of commodity (Osgerby in Briggs and Cobley, 1998: 322–34).

hybrid formations and television's neglectful eye

The new cultural formations signalled how instead of shying away from or not drawing too much attention to ethnic distinctions, the young culturally active were now beginning to revel in them; proudly and playfully enunciating the difference of the Black subject, whilst also insisting that there are, equally, many different ways of being Black – and for that matter, Black-British. As Hall puts it, this 'led to linguistic innovations in rhetorical stylization of the body, forms of occupying an alien social space, heightened expressions, hairstyles, ways of walking, standing and talking, and a means of constituting and sustaining camaraderie and community' (Hall in Morley and Chen, 1996: 471). Such manoeuvres represented a novel twist on the 'anxiety', 'friction' and cultural pathology of being 'in-between' as narrated in the social problem television discourse, because it was precisely this 'in-betweenness' of cultural hybridity that was being used to emphasize the logic of fusion over the logic of friction. The new ethnicities were not so much *between* two cultures as something new arising from both; occupying hybrid spaces rather than being excluded from both – Black and British, a 'third space' (Bhabha in Pines and Willemen, 1989). The rise of darkcore, jungle, goa trance, garage and drum and bass in the 1990s, was a sign of the kind of fusion that was to emerge. On the commercial front, although the more usual story for Black-Britons was one of social *exclusion*, these were important signs that, through various acts of style, some Blacks were also becoming more *exclusive*, many of them emerging as part of a newly-affluent working class under the ideological aspirations of Thatcherism. By the late 1980s, Britain's Black artists were at last beginning to sell to the Americans, who were now getting a response to the commonly-posed question, 'Are there any Black people in England?' in the shape of *My Beautiful Laundrette*, *Looking for Langston*, Soul II Soul, Des'ree, Seal, Salman Rushdie, Naomi Campbell, Paul Gilroy and Stuart Hall. Later, the entrepreneurial thrust of style gurus such as couturier Oswald Boateng, street-style businessman Shami Ahmed, the Turner prize-winning art of Chris Ofili and Steve McQueen, the crossover mastery of musicians such as Tricky, Goldie and Nitin Sawhney, the diversity-edged literature of Zadie Smith, continued to sustain Black culture in the style ranking.[6] Specifically, the visibility of British-Asian hybrid expressive cultures was something which only began to reach national level in the 1990s, with films such as *Wild West*, the 'crossover' work of Gurinder Chadha, the bhangra-reggae fusion of Bally Sagoo, singer/DJ/presenter Apache Indian, the Mercury Music Prize winning Talvin Singh, and the cast of *Goodness Gracious Me*. Their reappropriation of the vernacular, cultural signs and music from the USA, the Caribbean and the Indian sub-continent drew on different sources, politics and experiences, and was refusing to be pinned down in any simple or definitive way.[7] Contemporary expressive forms are partly drawing on tradition/ heritage/roots and partly on new influences/the multicultural/the diasporic condition, and thus always producing themselves anew (see Hall in Morley and Chen, 1996: 465–75; Gilroy, 1993b: 1–15).

What we are describing constitutes something of a 'revolution' in popular culture. But in failing to acknowledge or significantly be part of many of these shifts at the time, television has looked unfashionably late or 'obvious' in terms of responding to the popular. Of course, this is the fundamental strain in trying to make the genuinely 'alternative' part of the mainstream. 'Real Cool' (as Tony Blair's brief but fundamentally doomed affair with the rebranding of 'Cool Britannia' in the late 1990s beautifully demonstrated), can never simply or completely be co-opted or universally owned. Just like British parliamentary politics, television's 'misfiring' or lagging response to 'lived' popular cultures is partly a result of its typical White, middle-class personnel, but also because of the medium's lengthy and sluggish production process and its ongoing submission to the print media's green light as to what is 'cutting edge'. The 1990s media frenzy over 'BritPop' (and BritLit and BritArt), although declared 'British', was principally focused on White artists. The fact is that many of the defining Black-British styles and trends have working-class, hybrid roots that are worlds apart from the middle-class perspectives and cultural lifestyles that govern television's 'house style' of production, management-approach and terms of access. This misfired call and downgrading of the popular is exemplified in the ongoing trend for zoning where Black entertainment culture is contained in specific slots (for example BBC2's *The A Force*, 1996–97), serving as a reminder that Black popular cultural expression is still remarkably perceived by some television-executives as a minority-based 'folk-culture' (Bennett, 1981: 77–86). Black-British musicians still rarely get onto the covers of the parochial music press and the manufacturing of limited modalities of Blackness is, in general terms, rife. Television, by selecting what is presumed to be far more spectacular and representative – usually the most sexy and outlandish views and images such as the violent, gun-carrying, gangsta-rapper from the ghetto – mediates, manages and translates those notions of 'Black popular culture' that are expedient, and preferred. Heavily-coded racism (predominantly Black women as animalistic and Black men as violent and sexually rapacious) still exists, and the old associations between the Black body, sexuality, primitivism and Nature remain strong and persistent (see Gilroy, 1993a on the sexualization of Jimi Hendrix's image). Think for example of the marketing around Black female entertainers (Ruth 'Miss Rhythm' Brown in the 1950s, 'Captured live . . . Tina Turner' draped in animal fur, Grace Jones pictured caged, on all fours, Naomi Campbell tagged 'the Black panther', and the Black Spice Girl better known as 'Scary Spice').

Cogent analysis of the complex moves and shifts around Black cultural expression are very rarely seen (exceptions might include Isaac Julien's *The Darker Side of Black*, *Arena*, BBC2, 1994, Julian Henriques' *We The Ragamuffin* (Channel 4, 1992), or BBC2's *Soul Night*, 1998). Such absences can also be found in the serious business of analysis and criticism, which rarely sees Black people occupy positions of authority, as commentators, writers or judges (notable exceptions here are journalist Ekow Eshun, writer Mike Phillips and Black American academic, Bonnie Greer). Remarkably, it is only since the mid-1990s that we have begun to see young Black presenters on music shows – Rajesh Mirchandani (BBC2, *The O Zone*), Margherita Taylor (*Videoteque*, Carlton, *T4*, Channel 4), Josie D'Arby (*Top of the Pops*, BBC1), Julie Sarpong (*T4*, Channel 4) and Richard Blackwood (*Top of the Pops*, BBC1). Broader 'symbolic exclusion' in terms of the personnel working on these programmes remains a problem (Andi Peters, presenter and Channel 4 commissioner of youth programmes is an exception to the rule). Terry Jervis suggests that 'Black music to White people is not esoteric. They're the biggest buyers of Black music . . . so they don't feel it necessary to have Black people producing a Black music show. They feel that they know' (Jervis, interview with author, 20.3.96). And so, typically, alternative spaces have to be set up to counter this marginalization: the televised MOBO Awards (an annual celebration of music of Black origin which accounted by the late 1990s for something like 40 per cent of all UK British music sales) recognizes artists that are largely ignored in 'mainstream' music awards.

Bearing some of these shortcomings in mind, let us briefly consider the specific example of the irreverent Black popular culture show, *Baadasss TV* (Channel 4, 1995–96), which was screened in a late-night Friday slot and targeted at a young, lost Black audience.[8] There were three main problems with the series: first, the focus on the bizarre aspects of Black culture laid the text open to criticisms that it was, in fact, inviting people to revel, once again, in Black people's supposed peculiarities. Terry Jervis, who produced and directed the first series, explained how, 'They didn't have another Black producer after me, so the only people pushing out those images were White males who thought that was popular hip Black culture, but it was only really their kind of fetishes' (Jervis, interview with author, 20.3.96). Second, *Baadasss TV*'s American bias in terms of content and presenter (American rapper, Ice T) marked a general and longstanding assumption, that it is African-American popular culture that is *the* 'hip' and 'trendy' element of Black popular culture, thus deflecting a focus once again from the specificities of Black-British popular cultures. Third, on a workforce level, former *Baadasss TV* Associate Producer, David Akinsanya, rightly draws attention to the inequitable schematic production arrangement (inexperienced Black researchers, decision-making executives, producers and editors), thus highlighting the ongoing problem of White editorial control in Black television output (Akinsanya, *The Voice*, 28.5.96: 10). Peter Stuart, *Baadasss TV*'s executive producer (and Managing Director of Rapido TV), argued that, 'In all the shows here I make the decisions. I'm White. If you do not like it then do not work here that is the tone and attitude of the company. I am not prepared to put a Black person above me just to appease other people' (Stuart, *The Voice*, 28.5.96: 3). Stuart's autocratic attitude and contemptuousness begs the question of how much we really can say that things have changed in television (and despite Channel 4's minority-conscious remit), when the custodianship is still being given to those who appear to have no familiarity with or understanding of Black-British cultures?

This is a complex, rapidly shifting field, difficult to summarize in conclusion. Meanwhile, marginality notwithstanding, the lived cultures largely maintain themselves on their own terms by remaining external to the formal culture that is terrestrial television, reflecting an implicit understanding that there is simply more (negotiable) room elsewhere for cultural enterprise and production (the public and private spaces of the record store, the dance-floor, the designer market, the mobile lifestyle portal, the music concert, the internet, the digital channel, and so on). As the emphasis shifts from markets to networks, and the economies of today's artistic production offer the possibilities of virtually instant cultural turnover, the mainstream media as the 'site of privilege' has become less tenaciously invested in by the young culturally active who are *themselves* producing, organizing and popularizing these cultural practices. In short, many of them are not waiting to be 'represented' and thus pose a challenge to the classic power structure around popular culture, of those 'from above' (the industrial magnates) as the definers of culture and those 'from below' as passively absorbing or performing it. This is not to say that when they do appear, the same structures of access, dominance and economic inequity do not apply, but that they, at least superficially, appear to have been weakening rapidly in recent years. Many young Black-Britons do not now see traditional broadcasting as a key site of conflict, as a point of identification, at the centre of their public sphere or as even being capable of answering their representational needs. The pay-off for broadcasters is revealed in the sudden urgency with which they are now implementing a host of diversity initiatives to heighten product identification, in response to a burgeoning, 'spoilt for choice' young Black and Asian population, and the increasingly popular hold of Black-influenced youth cultures. In 2000, it was estimated that 10 per cent of under-thirties and 12 per cent of under-fives are ethnic minorities, putting them at the leading edge of the commercial threat posed to terrestrial television by alternative areas of popular cultural production.

notes

1   See Bourne (1998), Dyer (1995), Bogle (1991), McRobbie in Chambers and Curti (1996), and Gilroy (1993a, 1993b, 2000).
2   The original 'whassup' Budweiser ad won the Grand Prize for best advert at London's 2000 International Advertising Awards.
3   *Variety in Sepia*, unearthed by the BBC Archive in 1990, is the earliest known tele-recording.
4   Edric Connor appeared with Evelyn Dove in the popular weekly radio and television music series *Serenade in Sepia* (BBC, 1946–47) and *Music Makers* (BBC, 1946). In 1972, Pearl Connor was awarded the Humming Bird Silver Medal for 'outstanding service to the immigrant community in the United Kingdom' by the government of Trinidad and Tobago. In 1992, she received the National Black Women's Achievement Award in Britain.
5   Michael X (Michael de Freitas) was founder of the 1965-formed, Malcolm X-inspired Racial Action Adjustment Society. See Phillips and Phillips (1998: 230–41) on Michael X and his relationship with the British media.
6   Shami Ahmed presented a Channel 4 series, *Dosh* (1996), Oswald Boateng presented *Roots, Toots and Suits* as part of BBC2's *Soul Night* (Tx: 29.8.98) and Tricky (along with Salman Rushdie and others) was part of the BBC's promotion campaign for digital television (1998).
7   Note various programmes on Black artists and music forms from outside Britain: (Faris Kermani's *Qawali: The Sabri Brothers* (1986), Albert Bailey's *Shadow: The Bass Man* (1985) and Pervaiz Khan's *Utterance – The Music of Fateh Ali Khan* (1990).
8   By the mid-1990s, television youth audiences in general were declining (BARB figure in *The Sunday Times*, 5.2.95).

reflections on black masculinities and british sporting culture on television

As the 2000 Sydney Olympics demonstrated, we are now quite used to seeing the televisual image of Black-British gold-medal winning athletes draped in a Union Jack. On the one hand, this vision of success marks a public confirmation that we have explicitly arrived at being Black-British; on the other, it is a reminder of the stubborn forms of resistance which still deny Black people as 'authentic' members of the nation in other areas of public life and, moreover, often in the sporting arena itself. Televised sport, the first port of call where we watch sport as a nation, brings the contradictory and ambivalent relations of Black representation to the fore: the popular, dominant media image of chaotic Black social life appears to be challenged here, where Black physical prowess is everywhere to be seen and is deemed perfectly natural. We have already seen the complicated ways in which naturalization can be central to the process of fixing racial difference. So how, and in what ways, are we invited to interpret the distinction between the visibility /treatment of Blacks in the 'mind' genres (documentary, drama, news) compared to the 'body' ones (light entertainment, sport)? What is being spoken about 'race' through these representations? Who mediates the look at the sporting body, why is the gaze licensed here and in what ways do we appear to be looking?

My focus in this briefer, discursive chapter is Black masculinity (and more specifically British African-Caribbean sportsmen) at the general level of representations within the television sports text. Television is able to combine its unique image-making and narrative properties with the voyeurism and dramatic pleasure of watching sport. Television sport, which tends to work alongside, rather than against other forms of sports media and promotion, is an elemental genre that binds race and nation together (it appertains to the liberal optimism of the immediate postwar years based around the inevitability of 'assimilation' and 'integration'), but also where contemporary racisms are articulated. Sport is a strangely respected yet denigrated space. Lord Tebbit, with his notorious 'cricket test' ('People who are cheering the country they came from rather than the country they came to are not integrated', 1990), used sport to play this race card based around reactionary definitions of 'in' and 'out' groups. The popular notion of a single, hermetically-sealed national identity and the assumption that the members of a team (be they players or fans), should never have split loyalties or mixed patriotism is based on the configuration of an unadulterated and essentialist British nationalism. This is a ludicrous hypothesis given the internationalization of sport, the countless national identities in translation and the multi-ethnic make-up of British sports teams, players and enthusiasts – these crossed loyalties and multiple identities do not, of course, only affect Black and Asian communities. When television brought us scenes of British-Asians watching the 1996 cricket Test Match between England and India at Lords and simultaneously cheering when news broke that the England football team had just qualified for the Euro '96 semi-finals (BBC, Tx: 22.6.96), it was clear that whilst they may have failed Norman Tebbit's 'cricket test', they would have passed a comparative 'football test' with flying colours. More than 50 years after the colonized accepted and learnt 'the sporting rules' strategically in order to master them, thus empowering themselves under the circumstances by which they were apparently being controlled (James, 1963), we have seen how the colonial traditions of the master/slave balance of sporting power and control, particularly in 'the gentleman's game' (cricket) and the 'game of the English' (football) have been transformed in modern, spectacular ways. A revision of England and Britishness is, whether we like it or not, necessarily taking place at the level of the sport text.

media economies and diversity at the level of image

Whilst sport exists independently of television, and television is not the sole carrier of images of Black people in sport, the medium functions as a key site in the making of sporting events and sports personalities by organizing them around dramatic structures and narratives that attract audience interest. Sport, a central tenet of mass consumer culture, has become increasingly TV-oriented over the years, and there has been a bigger investment in 'sporting icons' – many of them Black-British – who are promoted as athletes and general media stars with high profiles and bankable personalities. This alone speaks volumes about the kinds of legitimate spaces in which Black people (are permitted to) excel within a (representational) culture that has historicized itself so disparately – as discriminatory, resistant and yet liberal and assimilationist, often all at the same time. Sport culture is at the heart of these dramas around national identity, and television is particularly discriminatory in its system of indexing difference when it touches on 'racial' lines: in general, when it suits, there is an incontestable biological nexus between race and nation; Black people are deemed Other, alien, different; on other occasions, they are embraced as British. This dual reaction (as both 'inside' and 'outside') often overlaps – indicative of the racialized ambivalence at work in the media sporting text, and of the vulnerable (ideological) position of Black-British sports players. We have already addressed some of the issues at stake in simultaneously excluding and appropriating Black-Britons as part of the national experience, and seen how it plays upon the national psyche. Sport – as seen on television – leads us through some of these antithetic and unsure responses towards Black Britishness. As a principal carrier of notions such as loyalty, community and nationhood, it pushes forward these questions around belonging and exclusion, which are so fundamental to the mappings of racial difference. We can, as such, speak in terms of a British sporting culture.

The financial interdependency between sport and television is a key facet of their relationship, with television relying on sport coverage for revenue, and sport attracting sponsorship through television exposure. Recent battles between terrestrial television and cable/satellite channels over sporting rights, have set sport as a key site of contestation between public and private, generalist and theme-based, free-to-air and pay-TV models. It is the main area in which niche, extra-terrestrial channels (with revenue through subscription and pay-per-view systems) have usually managed to outbid the public, free-to-air broadcasters. But when leading Black-British boxing stars (Audley Harrison and Lennox Lewis) signed lucrative exclusive rights and promotion deals with the BBC in 2001 (thus bringing boxing back to terrestrial television after nearly a decade), it was a reminder that traditional broadcasters are still seen to have the edge when it comes to attracting bigger local audiences and in advancing the media careers of sports personalities. Black sports celebrities, a substantial part of media economies, are repeatedly seen on hybrid sports/light entertainment shows such as *Gladiators* (ITV), *They Think It's All Over* (BBC1) and *Fantasy Football* (BBC2), on chat-shows and quiz programmes, as presenters on anything from children's television to documentaries, and in advertisements for products ranging from trainers to Hi-energy drinks. Sport connects television with this local and global economy of cross-promotion in which fashion, style and sport increasingly feed off each other. Footballer, Ian Wright has presented *Top of The Pops* and his own chat-show *Friday Night's All Wright* (ITV, 1998–); athlete Du'aine Ladejo hosted the teenage chat-show, *Du'aine's World* (ITV, 1995); Jeremy Gusgott and John Fashanu were presenters on *Gladiators*; and Kriss Akabusi hosted the BBC's *Record Breakers* which, in 1998, became *Linford's Record Breakers*, presented by Linford Christie. Compare this to the dearth of non-sports Black entertainers with their own peak-time series in British television history (Winifred Atwell, Lenny Henry, Richard Blackwood). These media sports-stars and others such as Stan Collimore, Lennox Lewis, Colin Jackson, Audley Harrison and Prince Naseem (a rare Asian example) are in demand both for their traditional uses of the 'raced' body (physical, manual, performing), and as symbols of modernity (commercialism, style, consumption), rallying the dynamics between fixity and movement, tradition and modernity into a concoction of modern subcultural style. When the Utopian ethos of today's fully-fledged urban 'trainer culture' quite unreservedly uses anti-racism as a commercial logo and depends on the corporatization and capitalist buzz-words of freedom, unanimity and universality (think of Tiger Woods and the Nike® promotions), further questions are raised about the power of sport as a meaningful source of popular anti-racism.

the language of sportscasting   If Black-British sporting stars have proved to be inviolable on the economic front, then they have certainly not been invulnerable to attack – from sporting commentators, media representations and ugly opponents (both on and off the pitch) – revealing the thin line that exists between pride and prejudice, fear and fervour. The recruitment procedure for sports presenters, as with a lot of (broadcast) journalism, tends to work around informal recommendations and word of mouth.[1] Just as it is largely seen to be the preserve of White academics and journalists to engage in cultural criticism of 'the arts' (despite the huge grip of Black-led styles on popular culture), so Blacks, although highly visible as sporting performers, are rarely seen as television sports commentators (or for that matter as referees, coaches or managers). As such, the iconic representativeness of Black sportsmen still operates within a certain network of images and negotiated and socially dependent criteria. Sport depends on the cultural practices of actively looking and being looked at, so that we have (physically) active and (iconically) powerful 'trophy-men' who necessarily display their bodies for mass media consumption. Ultimately, the Black performer/athlete connotes, in Laura Mulvey's terms, 'to-be-looked-at-ness' (Mulvey, 1975: 214), but is very rarely allowed, at least in a professional capacity, to look. The exceptions to this rule who have 'crossed over' into the role of observation, such as Ian Wright, John Barnes, Garth Crooks and Ruud Gullit, are essentially 'guest commentators' who come from the specific experience of being sports performers (all footballers) rather than primarily being seen as professional commentators. The gap between sports performance and critical reflection, and across a range of sports (i.e. not just football, but also boxing, athletics, golf and horse-racing) remains huge.

Television represents itself as a reflective medium, appearing to innocently portray voluntarism, self-determination and the ordered categories of the 'real' sporting world, rather than being seen to negotiate and regulate where and how different racial types are seen (a pattern which is dependent on all sorts of complex issues around access, social exclusion, class, racial stacking procedures, unofficial segregation and the division of sports labour, see Coakley, 1994 and Jarvie, 1991). So the very real British traditions of hurling banana-skins at Black football players, racist jibing, and vile attacks by the extreme-Right targeted at various high-profile sports personalities in inter-racial couples occur, apparently without contradiction, alongside the salutation and branding of Black sports-players elsewhere. Sports commentary, the primary discourse which contextualizes lived sports activity and galvanizes viewers as part of the national sporting culture, makes no mention of equally lived forms of racism, once again self-positioning itself as a medium that does not intervene in such thorny matters. And whilst television brings us these glorified images of Black Britishness, the very language of sports coverage, implicitly lets negative ideologies around race and nation slip through virtually unnoticed. A television commentator's chuckle over Jonah Lomu's stature (the Tongan-born New Zealand rugby player), the conditioned use of the words 'chip on his shoulder', 'aggressive', 'hot-headed' (and even 'savagery' in the case of Mike Tyson following the Holyfield ear-biting incident in 1997),[2] the incredulity at displays of a Black athlete's 'power' – these are television's polite responses which never quite dare speak the name of 'race'. Television sport then, is a classic zone which relies heavily on observation of the body (a 'spectator sport') but shifts between not explicitly acknowledging that 'Blackness' exists, to not letting its subjects 'transcend race' (biology controlling all). It links quite nicely to what Gilroy has identified as the two key approaches to Black experiences in cultural representation: on the one hand, the commodification approach which traffics Blackness while depoliticizing it and, on the other, the anti-marketeer approach which sees all Black cultures and manifestations of it as necessarily carrying essential and unchanging racial and thus political meaning (Gilroy, 1993b: 3–5). Despite these strained attempts at neutrality, the very language of sportscasting runs through a supremely White, English and male discourse, hinged upon these 'in-jokes', nods and winks, soliciting identification with notions of the 'superhuman' and biologized Black body and therefore positioning it at a point of ambivalence.

As with the early television variety tradition, the most prominent Black figures that British television viewers were likely to see in the medium's embryonic years, were American – although there were, in fact, a number of Black sports players in Britain (a fact left undocumented in the major sports retrospectives). When sport did become more racially integrated, the competitive racial element was often exploited by the dramatic spectacle of Blacks and Whites being posited against each other, and physical power was often indicated by racial catchphrases. For example, in the 1930s and 1940s, heavyweight American boxer Joe Louis (who was up against the Aryan idol, Max Schmeling in 1936), was often referred to as 'The Dark Destroyer' or 'The Brown Bomber'. Following Joe Louis' win against Primo Carnera in

1935, US news stated, 'Something sly and sinister and perhaps not quite human came out of the African jungle last night to strike down and utterly demolish . . .' (Quoted in Mead, 1985). In Britain, wrestling Heavyweight Champion of the British Empire turned actor, Robert Adams, was called 'The Black Eagle'. Footballer, Albert Johanssen who faced a vast amount of racism on and off the pitch, was referred to by his Leeds United colleagues and fans as 'The Black Flash'.[3] Thus, 'Blackness' was often associated with the physical and primeval (which linked to manual roles during slavery and further back still), and with being 'superhuman' (i.e. more-than/less-than human).

popular tropes of black-british masculinity   The mid-1990s saw a rise in debates around the rudiments of racial science and genetics as a general explanation of social behaviour, IQ and bodily structures (Murray's *The Bell Curve*, 1994; Christopher Brand's *The g Factor*, 1996; *Rushton's Race, Evolution and Behaviour*, 1994; Roger Bannister's speech at Edinburgh University in 1995). We know of course that these approaches serve the dual function of both reintroducing conceptual hierarchies of humanity as well as questioning the so-called meritocracy of sporting success. For our concerns, this is not just a question of whether Blacks are rendered as inferior to Whites (e.g. in the intellectual stakes, as was suggested by Murray and Rushton for example), but also about where they are permitted to excel and exhibit themselves as superior to the White man which, in any case, maintains a sense of out-group difference (see Marekh Kohn, 1995). Either way, the black man is biologized. It is precisely the assumptions that underpin the popular law of racial biology, which spill over into the area of televised sport and sports-related commentary.

Let us take the obvious example of a tabloid newspaper headline, 'Why Can Blacks Run Faster Than Whites? . . . It's all in the genes say experts' (*Sun*, 7.8.93). This story, printed in direct reference to Linford Christie, one of Britain's most outstanding Black athletes, and more specifically to his win in the 100 metres World Championship the previous day, had more to do with Christie's 'race' than the race he won. As Fanon discussed in his seminal book *Black Skin, White Masks* (1986), the image of the Black man is dependent not just on his 'Blackness', but he must also be Black in relation to the needs (and desires) of the White man. Such needs dictate that race is bestowed upon the Black body to produce a set of visual and verbal codes around all that the White man is not – the Black man's image depends therefore on his racial contrariety. The unfolding of Linford Christie's public persona has depended on such notions of ethnic difference, particularly in relation to the supposed constitutive principle of the Black man – his penis. Christie's so-called 'lunch-box', a term inaugurated by the *Sun* (and later to be added to the *New Oxford Dictionary of English* in 1998) in reference to Christie on the day following his gold-medal win at the 1992 World Olympics, has since become a popular racist cultural reference point, whilst simultaneously, functioning as a 'key ethnic signifier' (Mercer, 1994: 103). Despite widespread Othering by the national media, Christie's position as Olympic, World, European and Commonwealth 100 metres champion was accompanied by his unquestioned deference to the Union Jack (during his laps of honour following the 1986 European title and his 1992 success in Barcelona for example – the brief representational moments when Christie was 'nationalized') (see Figure 5). Christie had no doubt that, 'When I win, I win for my country. . . . I can't be anything other than British' (Christie quoted in the *Guardian*, 11.11.95). When he appeared on the sports talk-show's *Sport in Question* (ITV, June 1995), Christie, at the point of breakdown, spoke about 'stereotyping the Black man' in direct reference to the media's treatment of him. Thus in response to the shameful question posed by the co-presenter of the programme, Jimmy Greaves, 'why do you wear shorts then, why don't you wear something more suitable?', Christie explained, 'I go out there to run, you should be watching my form when I'm running, the fact that I'm winning, not what's in my shorts!' If there was ever an example of the onlooker's impulses of envy, fear and desire, then it was highlighted in Greaves' response to Christie:

Figure 5

Linford Christie holding the Union Jack
at the 1992 Barcelona Olympic Games
Source: Copyright Mark Shearman

Greaves: Well, well, a lot of women are fascinated by it for starters [*Grins*]

Christie: Stereotyping the Black man!

Greaves: No, no, no. I don't accept that, I won't accept that Linford. . . . I'm just saying that maybe there was a time when Linford might have changed the shorts that he was wearing, if he's been offended by it. He's never offended me with it, I can tell you!

What this exchange suggested, was that the Black body functions as the agent of fascination and desire. And that fear often accompanies desire (see Stern, 1982 on desire). If the gratification of desire comes from the act of desiring itself, then television can play an active part in focusing on Black men and aspects of their bodies as an invitation to the scopophilic gaze (Freud uses the term 'scopophilia' to refer to 'pleasure in looking', 1977: 70). Laura Mulvey, in her development of Freudian psychoanalysis, argued that women are positioned as the image (the passive object to be looked at), and men as the bearers of the look (the active eye), and that the male figure cannot bear the burden of sexual objectification (Mulvey, 1975). In overlooking the differences *within* gendered categories, Mulvey neglected the fact that looking relations, as well as being dependent on gender, are also racially (and sexually) constructed (see 'Reading Racial Fetishism' in Mercer, 1994: 173–85; Hall, 1997: 223–90; Nixon in Hall, 1997: 291–336). The sport text is a primary example of where the picturing of Black men moves away from the dominant systems of imaging men and women in culture – a system which otherwise depends on the dichotomies of active/passive, masculine/feminine, desire/narcissism. Christie, in this instance, was responding to how the media was incessantly treating him as a passive object-to-be-looked-at. These processes of 'fixity', containment *and* ambivalence touch at the heart of the symbolically charged zone of sport, shedding light on the contradictions around sameness and difference, envy and loathing. Kobena Mercer argues:

As a major public arena, sport is a key site of white male ambivalence, fear and fantasy. The spectacle of black bodies triumphant in rituals of masculine competition reinforces the fixed idea that black men are 'all brawn and no brains,' and yet because the white man is beaten at his own game – football, boxing, cricket, athletics – the Other is idolized to the point of envy. (Mercer, 1994: 178)

On a later appearance on the sports chat show, *On Side*, Christie once again talked about the media's ceaseless obsession with his penis, second-guessing that, 'It's the fantasies in people's minds. All the people who write about it, just wish it was them' (Christie talking to John Inverdale, *On Side*,

BBC1, Tx: 1.12.97), thus deducing that he was being treated as a masculine, yet objectified, agent of desire. As Hall explains, 'stereotypes refer as much to what is imagined in fantasy as to what is perceived as "real". And, what is visually produced, by the practices of representation, is only half the story. The other half – the deeper meaning – lies in *what is not being said, but is being fantasized, what is implied but cannot be shown*' (Hall, 1997: 263 [Hall's emphasis]). The marking and overemphasis, the 'freakishness' and 'difference' of Black male physicality is deeply grounded in the visual, unable to transcend the body in which it is seen, whereas 'spirit' (the unseen) remains a White preserve (see Dyer, 1997 for more on this in relation to White masculinity).[4] Despite these varied attempts to use the television forum to denounce such racism, the media continued this simultaneous fascination with and denigration of Christie, and further still, attributed Christie's critical response to his inability to take 'a joke'. On a 1996 edition of the popular sports quiz, *They Think It's All Over* (BBC1, 1995–), a blind-folded celebrity guest had to identify a sporting figure of Christie in the 'Feel the Sportsman' round. This part of the programme usually has a live sportsperson on it, but in Christie's case, it was a waxwork model, giving Christie no right of reply and further positioning him outside the laddish tone through which the humour of the programme operates. On touching the dummy's lower half, 'team-captain' Gary Linekar said, 'It's bigger than me' and his sidekick Rory Bremner retorted, 'Well down here there's a wax Ronnie Corbett',[5] much to the studio audience's delight.

In a similar laddish vein, the Nottingham Forest footballer, Jason Lee, was heavily mocked in the British media, and on television in particular, for his long, dread-locked hair. The initial trigger (for laughter, copycat taunting and Lee's subsequent removal to a transfer-list) was David Baddiel and Frank Skinner's popular television comedy, *Fantasy Football League* (BBC2, 1996), which simultaneously ridiculed Lee's missed goal opportunities and his display of 'indiscreet', 'natural' Black hair 'reconstructed' by Baddiel and Skinner using a pineapple (thus playing on the joke that his locks weighed him down whilst playing football). This 'joke' inverted the notion of Black people's traditional physical prowess; instead of being blessed by excessive power or an elongated heel (or other such myths around Black physicality), Lee's sporting performance was shown to be *hindered* not *enhanced* by his Blackness. This inextricable measurement of Black athleticism in relation to the Black body in popular representations, is expected to be taken in good spirits, so when Frank Skinner heard that Lee was deeply upset about the programme, he defended his sense of humour by saying:

I think Jason has a great career ahead of him. The rumour here in LA is that the man from Del Monte is about to say yes to him. Anyway, we've taken the mickey out

That these public 'jokes' affected Lee and Christie, deemed them 'bad sports', unable to identify with the nation's taste in humour, unlike, according to Skinner, Andy Cole, another Black-British Premiership footballer. My point here, is that this racial taunting (the tabloids, in an attempt to sustain the joke, followed with pictures of bananas in the place of Lee's dreadlocks) was a direct reference to Lee's race and culture – 'Black hair' is a Black thing, and as Mercer reminds us, functions as a 'key sign of racial difference . . . the most visible stigmata of blackness, second only to the skin' (Mercer, 1994: 101). Of course, one of the ironies is that dreadlocks were 'stylistically *cultivated* and politically *constructed* in a particular historical moment as part of a strategic contestation of white dominance and the cultural power of whiteness' (Mercer, 1994: 108). These seemingly innocent, playful signs – 'the pineapple' and 'the lunch-box' – present themselves as innocuous and arbitrary and yet the connotative meanings are deeply entrenched in ideas of racial difference. The dual or multi-codification of Black sports personalities is also, of course, a key feature of representing the Other (Hall, 1997).[6] The racialization and objectification of these public images can be traced back, as can so many images of Black masculinity in the television sports or sports-related text, to scientific racism and/or a tabloid agenda.

One senses, in these exchanges I have been briefly looking at, that less 'sensitive' or 'quarrelsome' Black sportsmen and/or those who are willing to play up to the raced stereotype are, in fact, more likely to be included on this symbolic, national level, thus indicating the slippage that routinely occurs in, and between, representations of Black masculinity. For example, Paul Gilroy (1993b), Kobena Mercer (1994) and Ben Carrington (in Owusu, 2000) have all observed the very different structures of representation at work in the media treatment of Frank Bruno, the London-born boxer. Bruno, commonly referred to as 'Our Frank', is one of Britain's most famous personalities, making a television career out of appearing in chat shows, advertisements, quiz shows, the pantomime circuit, and in a number of 'light entertainment' programmes. Bruno, who acts as the very antithesis of the aggressive Black man (despite his heavyweight boxing background), entangles himself in a more obvious system of collusion, implicitly playing on and up to the affectionate responses to his histrionic simplicity, and to his sporting successes and failures. It is precisely this flawed, unthreatening spectacle, with his nationally-compatible South London roots, self-declared patriotism and pro-Conservatism, that allows Bruno to be paternalistically nationalized ('He's been adopted by fans as Britain's best sportsman' (*News At One*, Tx: 29.8.96)). By contrast, Chris Eubank, who unquestionably plays up to a different kind of caricature (that of an old-time Englishman with his plus fours, monocle and cane), is contrastingly packaged, as the ITN News put it, as 'the showman British fans love to hate' (ITV, Tx: 24.9.97). We can see then through Bruno, Eubank and other Black sportsmen such as 'Prince' Naseem Hamed, that they more wittingly support this arresting public profile in order to build their public image, performing or acting to fit the stereotype, thus illustrating how Black sportsmen are not always subject to or outside the process of stereotyping but are, in fact, often actively involved in its production. We can therefore make a distinction between involuntary structures of typing (Christie, Lee) and facilitated ones (Bruno, Eubank, Hamed); where the Black sportsman plays a sometimes lesser, sometimes greater role in colluding with the media in order to make themselves more telegenic. 'Pleasure in being looked at', or what Majors has called 'cool pose' (Majors, 1986: 184–5) makes the Black sporting star easily 'representable', upgrades his commodity-value and flavours the cult of personality.[7] Of course, the route that these public images take depends on many things, not least how the Black sports star is located or locates himself in relation to his respective 'imagined community' and the degree to which he/his 'community' is seen – or not seen – to integrate with the British temperament. But the discourse of corporate diversity in sport, just as that found in contemporary television youth cultures, often depends precisely on the kind of image-making which holds aspects of racial difference in place. This fascination with racial difference tends to represent a convoluted (rather than a simply negative) form of racism. Following Homi Bhabha's discussion of the stereotype in colonial discourse, it is useful to remind ourselves of the possible readings and contrary subjectivities which images of the Black body throw up, as 'always simultaneously inscribed in both the economy of pleasure and desire and the economy of discourse, domination and power' (Bhabha, 1983: 33). With its verbal and visual pervasiveness, television is pivotal in inscribing 'race' to the body of the Black subject through a range of ethnic markers and national criteria. The cultural practice of Othering involved here is the point at which we hit upon television's struggle over and deflection from truly coupling 'Black' with 'British'.

notes

1   At the 1996 CRE conference, Herman Ouseley stated that when the BBC *Sportsnight* anchorman, Bob Wilson, left for ITV and Britain's 'blue-eyed sporting hero', Gary Linekar, was considered a natural successor, he wrote to the BBC and suggested that they should have considered a woman or a Black person for the post.

2   For example, 'Tyson's moment of savagery', ITN *News at One*, ITV, Tx: 9.7.97.

3   Albert Johanssen was the first Black player in a Wembley Cup Final (1965). Note the BBC documentary profile of *Johanssen, Picture This: Remember Albert*, BBC2, Tx: 27.8.96.

4   See Dyer's analysis of 'White men's muscles', mainly in the context of cinema, 1997, 14–83.

5   Ronnie Corbett is a British comedian who is short in size.

6   Of course, there are also a number of distinct codes around which Black women have been represented in sport, often in relation to classic notions of Black femininity. For example, media representations of the late Florence Griffith-Joyner ('Flo Jo') and her sister, Jackie Joyner-Kersee (see *The Sunday Times*, 1988 Olympic Special, 9.10.88, and Stuart Hall's 'The Spectacle of the Other' in Hall, 1997: 225–90).

7   Laura Mulvey says in her discussion of scopophilia, 'There are circumstances in which looking itself is a source of pleasure, just as, in the reverse formation, there is pleasure in being looked at' (1975: 207).

casting the black subject in television drama

We have been looking at how television functions as a privileged site in translating and organizing the imagined needs and definitions of the nation. These imagined needs and definitions – with the emphasis on translation – are especially important in relation to drama, because it is here that we can speak more unequivocally about 'representation' rather than 'reflection' (or about 'the active labour of *making things mean*', Hall, 1982), compared to say sport, news and variety that depend in greater degrees on representing what is happening 'out there'. In broad terms, there is no pre-given reality to reproduce in dramatic form, only a set of choices to make about *whom, how* and *what* to represent. The lengthy and pre-meditative processes involved in drama production (deliberate decisions about scripting, casting, directing and scheduling), has positioned it at the heart of talks around multicultural content, integrated casting, narrative diversity and minority access, making it a potential space where considered alterations in 'racial typing' can be made. But drama is also expensive to produce and such 'risks ' therefore are arguably (increasingly) less likely to be taken.

the early phase of drama with a black presence

Given the live nature of the early medium, there were obvious links with theatre, and a set of stage productions such as *The Emperor Jones* (BBCTV, 1938, 1953 and ITV, 1958), *The Merchant of Venice* (BBCTV, 1947), Eugene O'Neill's *All God's Chillun Got Wings* (BBCTV, 1946) and *Deep are The Roots* (BBCTV, 1950), all featured Black actors and were adapted for television.[1] The Guyanese actor, Robert Adams, who founded the Negro Arts Movement in Britain in 1944, became Britain's first Black television actor when he appeared in *Theatre Parade: Scenes from Hassan* (BBCTV, 1937).[2] Important as these dramas were, they were usually linked to the variety tradition (a legitimate zone for early Black performers), and mostly had all-Black casts, thus providing no obvious sense of real integration. Besides, in the light of American competition (see Chapter 6), and broader discrimination and artistic expectations of Black actors, many Black performers had to take small parts or work as understudies. For example, Pauline Henriques (who came to Britain as a child in 1919), despite her training at the London Academy of Music and Dramatic Art, found herself 'playing a variety of American Coloured maids' (quoted in Pines, 1992: 26).[3] Realizing these obstacles and whilst understudying Georgia Burke in the American Negro Theatre Production of *Anna Lucasta* (1947–48), Henriques, together with other understudies such as Errol John, Earl Cameron and Rita Williams, formed 'The Negro Theatre Company', a Black British theatre production group which began to stage its own productions. If theatre work was scarce, television work was even harder to come by, and often meant playing 'undignified' bit parts, essentially based around the so-called 'Uncle Tom' and 'Aunt Jemima' server-roles (see Bogle, 1991), although they were usually better-paid than the more diverse theatre-parts. In any case, the climate of expectation was quite different at this time. As Colin Prescod, whose mother Pearl was an actress during the 1950s says:

> I didn't feel as though any one was making or being part of productions that they should feel ashamed of. One has to say about my mother and those that she worked with, that they were colonized people; they weren't looking to be too critical of the hands held out to them by liberal Whites who wanted to do Black stuff . . . what I mean by the colonized mind is that they just felt happy getting work in order to get seen and that was the job of the actor. My mother had to do lots and lots of work before she got recognized – a lot of bandana-head work and small parts – and as a consequence of that somebody actually saw her. (Prescod, interview with author, 19.11.96)

The uncoordinated institutional response meant that there was no organized financial backing or support for Black artists (see Pearl Connor in Pines, 1992: 39). Equity had no Black section to represent Black performers (this only emerged in 1974 with Equity's Coloured Artists Committee) and the impracticable Equity rule that an actor required 40 weeks' work experience in the West End to become a member, effectively blocked such access for most Black actors in Britain (with exceptions such as Lloyd Reckord and Horace James). In line with the 'official' *laissez-faire* approach to British race relations at this time, Equity maintained a 'colour-blind' approach, thus overlooking the problems affecting Black actors' chances of getting work and the racial basis by which they were cast and commissioned. To add insult to injury, there was still a common practice, carried on from the vaudeville minstrel days, of White actors 'blacking up' to play Asian or African-Caribbean characters. This was usually justified by casting directors on the grounds that Black actors 'lacked experience' or that their 'style' did not fit the production (see the experiences of two of Britain's finest classical actors, Zia Mohyeddin[4] in Pines, 1992 and Hugh Quarshie in Owusu, 2000).[5]

Far from being passive to these patterns of racialized omission, some Black people – and notably Pearl and Edric Connor, John La Rose[6] and Nigerian playwright Obi Egbuna (who had formed the Universal Coloured Peoples' Association in June 1967 and was subsequently imprisoned in Britain for police death-threats) – mounted a series of individual and collective strategic interventions to create alternative spaces, tackle institutional discrimination, and gain public recognition. From 1956, the Edric Connor Agency (see p. 112) was pivotal in securing Black artists' rights and in profiling and promoting their talents and helped many go on to develop careers in television (including Nina Baden-Semper, Oscar James, Cy Grant, Lloyd Reckord and Nadia Cattouse). Every available opportunity ranging from production tours, to the use of the Royal Court Theatre Upstairs on Sunday nights (with the help of Oscar Lewenstein and George Devine), to access of school/town halls was seized. The Caribbean Artists Movement (CAM) (1966–72) which began as a gathering of artists and intellectuals in Britain formed by writers Ed Braithwaite, John La Rose and Andrew Salkey, became a literary and visual international movement designed 'to reassert their own tradition in the face of the dominant tradition' (Walmsley, 1992: xvii). What this range of efforts represented was the obvious sense of community and network of support that had emerged, largely emanating from a shared history of colonialism and immigration, a sense of cultural marginalization in 'the host country' and a deep-seated passion for the arts. Just as the various clubs and dance-halls proved critical in forging alternative social arenas for cultural expression based around music and dance, so other spaces such as the newly-established Africa Centre, the Keskidee Centre (set up by former CARD member, Oscar Abrams, in order to encourage Black artists, playwrights and poets), the socialist Unity Theatre and the West Indian Students' Centre (where the West Indian Students' Drama Group would meet around 1957–58), were essential in building unions, relationships and solidarity amongst Black artists.[7]

When a 'Black story' was to be produced, it was up to the White (usually male and middle-class) writer to 'fight the Black corner' in the newly-emerging form of socially-conscious drama (a complement to the documentaries of the time). John Elliot's *A Man From The Sun* (BBC, 1956), a live production featuring a range of Black-British acting talent,[8] was the first drama about the lives of Caribbean settlers in Britain, or what Elliot described as 'the clash between this mythical Britain and the actual grotty Britain, which West Indians would face when they got here' (quoted in Pines, 1992: 86). A few years later, Ted Willis' *Hot Summer Night* (ABC/ITV, 1959), featuring Lloyd Reckord, dramatized the impact of a Black presence in Britain. When the BBC's second channel began in April 1964, it became a critical outlet for new single drama slots such as *Theatre 625* (BBC2, 1964–68) and *The Wednesday Play* (BBC2, 1964–70). Many of the single plays kept within the prevailing discourses of ethical humanism (addressing moral issues such as homelessness, single mothers, race relations and abortion), but also matched the criteria of topical, populist and hard-hitting scheduling under Hugh Carleton-Greene's management. Although these 'controversial' dramas were born out of a BBC environment that was still organized around notions of objectivity established by the Royal Charter and a conservative Board of Governors, many of them did inadvertently champion the need for, or critique the arbitrariness of, specific social and political legislation. One has to say of these productions, that they were real cultural events and a major talking-point for an entire nation and generation of television viewers, but also that 'race conscious' productions were exceptions amongst a larger set of plays that were generally notable, as were other anthologies such as ITV's *Play of The Week* (1956–67) and the BBC's *Play of the Month* (1965–83), for their lack of Black presence and themes.

Out of this context emerged John Hopkins' play, *Fable* (BBC1, Tx: 27.1.65, part of *The Wednesday Play* series)[9]. Although the play made oblique reference to continuing repressive legislation in South Africa and the establishment of Bantustans by the South African government, it was set in a fantasy Britain where the balance of apartheid was reversed, so that Blacks held political power and Whites were subjugated; Blacks were the master-majority and Whites the slave-minority. The screening was delayed by one week following concerns that *Fable* would 'stir up' racial tension (and threats of fire-bombs if the BBC decided to go ahead with the screening), largely because of its apparent correspondence and proximity to the 1965 Leyton by-election (MacMurraugh-Kavanagh, 1997). In envisaging a world in which the dominant racial power relations were transposed, *Fable* took the viewers on an imaginative voyage (thus breaking with the governing hallmark of documentary realism), inviting them to think through an illusory scenario in order to be reminded that racial discrimination is based on social, conceptual differentiations that manifest themselves in a political sense. Carmen Munroe, who starred in the play along with other Black actors such as Barbara Assoon, Dan Jackson, Thomas Baptiste and Bari Jonson, says that for the actors themselves, 'it was actually very frightening . . . because suddenly you were being asked to perform the sort of acts that were performed against you in real life' (quoted in Pines, 1992: 58).

At a time when Black characters were notable for their absence in 'serious' television drama and with Whiteness posed as a social norm in terms of address, content and looking relations, *Fable* unsettled otherwise taken-for-granted ideas of what Black and White ethnicities constitute (for example, in terms of casting – the murderers, pimps and prostitutes were White here). In this sense, it served as a unique early illustration of how television *could* reconceptualize (through shifts in tone, format and characterization) the typical ways of representing race and race relations. Unsurprisingly, *Fable* produced mixed responses (BBC Audience Research Report, WAC Ref:T5/1,348 – *Fable*, 12.2.65). Despite Hopkins' anti-racist agenda, for some White-British viewers who had, to date, only seen Black-British people on television as light entertainment stars, athletes or as the anthropological subjects of social documentaries (thus where they could be objectified and were assumed to be naturally placed), the image of themselves as subservient triggered fear not compassion. For many, the play intensified the 'swamping, overcrowding, racial tension' fears that were being encouraged elsewhere by 'numbercentric' documentary programmes, anti-immigration legislation, and panic-merchants such as Enoch Powell. Thomas Baptiste, who appeared in *Fable* as Mark Fellows (a liberal academic who was part of 'the movement' which did not believe in the oppression of White people), received a letter after the broadcast, warning, 'How dare you appear on our television screens, even as a friend or a liberal. Get back to your country! Hideous ape!' (Quoted in Pines, 1992: 67).

'Unofficial' dramatic representations of 'race' were often up against this kind of resistance or at least triggered certain nervousness both within the industry and amongst viewers. Let us take the example of ITV's first long-running series *Emergency – Ward 10* (ATV/ITV, 1956–67), a mainstream hospital drama which included a number of Black-British actors such as Frank Singuineau, Clifton Jones, Earl Cameron, Carmen Munroe and in 1959 featured Gloria Simpson, making her the first Black actor in a British soap. Joan Hooley[10] starred as Dr Louise Mahler, a trainee house-surgeon in Oxbridge General Hospital who had come to England from Africa. Her role was short-lived, largely because of a 'controversial' storyline in 1964 of the middle-class Mahler falling in love with her White working-class fellow doctor, Giles Farmer (John White). A proposed scene involving the couple's kiss in a bedroom caused a stir in the British press. In response, the Independent Television Authority (ITV's regulator), 'compromised' by reconstructing the 'delicate' scene as a gentle kiss in a garden, thus revealing their deep-seated fears about portraying 'miscegenation', although they always presented it as an issue around the sexual (not racial) nature of the exchange. (Inter-racial couples had been part of British social life for years – Hooley herself was married to a White man.) British television's self-image of moral, public responsibility and its perception that it was somehow more progressive or 'ahead' of its audience, meant a quick exit for Hooley who was soon written out of the serial after her character was bitten by a snake (Phillips in Givanni, 1995: 66). By the late 1960s, Black faces were more consciously being written into scripts, usually within the context of dramatic conflict because of the problems their 'colour' was assumed to bring, often with the stability of the White family nexus at stake (Pines, 1997) (e.g. the White girl bringing home a Black boyfriend, the problem of a mixed marriage, trouble with 'fitting in' or being accepted). Of course there were other stories to tell, but many White writers – who generally lacked familiarity with or understanding of Black and Asian lives – clearly had problems with creating 'a Black character' that was also dramatically engaging and not subject to White responses. A notable exception here was the first fully-fledged drama series with a central Black character, *Rainbow City* (BBC1, 1967), a six-part production based on the West Indian experience in Britain that was developed by Black actor/writer Horace James and John Elliot, and which starred Carmen Munroe, Horace James and Errol John (also a writer who had won the 'Observer Play of the Year' competition back in 1953; see Bourne, 1998: 210–22).

One key pattern (long familiar to us from American cinema) which began to emerge in the 1970s, was of Black characters in 'service' roles; as nurses, chauffeurs, waiters, hospital orderlies, and so on. Black people were often included, as Munroe puts it, to 'dress the set' (Munroe, speaking at the National Film Theatre, 20.2.96). Of course, within the political context of mounting pressure for more Black representation, this gave the *look* of multiculturalism. This shallow 'integrated casting' approach was also influenced by the new stream of integrationalist imports arriving in Britain from America (Bill Cosby in *I Spy*, 1965–68; Greg Morris in *Mission Impossible*, 1966–73; Nichelle Nichols in *Star Trek*, 1966–69). Filmmaker, Alrick Riley, who began his career as a television and theatre actor during the 1970s (*Grange Hill, Scum, Welcome Home Jacko)* recalls that, 'One of the reasons I got out of acting was because I was always playing muggers and thieves' (Riley, in Bailey, 1994), but as Riley goes on to acknowledge, in broad terms, the problem was not just one of stereotypes, but also of dull, superficial casting and lack of character development. For Black actors and aspiring writers, there was inevitably frustration. For example, Carmen Munroe, one of Britain's leading actresses had enjoyed a fruitful theatre career through the 1960s, and appeared in television dramas such as Barry Reckord's *In The Beautiful Caribbean* (1972), *Ted* (1972) and *Shakespeare Country* (1973), but considering her extensive background as a professional actress and the fact that she had been an Equity member since 1962, the rewards were scarce. She recalls, 'we [Black actors] were constantly trying to raise the levels of expectation … there was always this feeling that we were playing this catch-up game' (Munroe, speaking at the National Film Theatre, 20.2.96). She says, 'there was an emptiness, a feeling that I had come to a very, very low point. I thought if I'm not going to be able to work at what

I really want to do, then there's not much point even in living' (Munroe, quoted in Pines, 1992: 62).

One area where Black people were beginning to have a more mainstream presence during the 1970s was in soap opera. This was especially important because of the genre's wide appeal, patterns of familiarity and repetition, local realism (a feature of British drama in general) and the way in which it represents the nation to itself through strong and authentic national and social characteristics (for example, pub culture, class differentiations, regional dialects). In 1963, Thomas Baptiste had become the first Black actor to appear in Britain's favourite soap, *Coronation Street* (ITV, 1960–), when he was cast in a few episodes as a wrongfully-sacked bus conductor (see Baptiste in Pines, 1992 for criticisms of how he has been disregarded as part of the programme's history). Carmen Munroe later appeared as Sister Washington in *General Hospital* (ATV/ITV, 1972–79) and Cleo Sylvestre[11] starred as a factory worker in *Coronation Street* in 1966 and two years later, as Melanie Harper (Meg Richardson's adopted daughter) in *Crossroads* (ITV, 1964–88, 2001–). These were exceptions to a more general rule of White-exclusive soap operas. In 1974, the newly-formed Equity Coloured Artists Committee criticized the under presence of Black people in soap opera (*Coloured Artists on British Television*, August 1974). The usual defence by the programme-makers, was that a Black narrative presence did not 'reflect reality' or would disrupt the British reality being shown. For example, H.V. Kershaw, an early scriptwriter on *Coronation Street* argued that introducing Black characters would be controversial because, 'in keeping faith with our existing characters, we would again be forced to put unhelpful comments into the mouths of fictional men and women who command a wide following among the serial's millions of viewers, with potentially dangerous effect', and that it was, 'quite wrong . . . for an entertainment programme to run such risks and accept such responsibility' (Kershaw, 1981: 170–1). The fear that Black characters would represent a problem or make trouble in some form, and were somehow antithetical to the 'pleasure' of a narrative entertainment programme because they would unsettle its flow and familiarity, was a common racist fear that was excused with this kind of socially responsible morality rhetoric based around the perceived 'innocence' or 'needs' of the viewers. Apart from anything else, it was utterly dismissive of the ethnic diversity of soap opera viewers and failed to accept Black people as part of the British (television) nation.

Within this marginalized context, *Empire Road* (BBC, 1978–79) was a major breakthrough, despite being axed after two short series. It was the first British television series to be conceived and written by a Black writer (Michael Abbensetts) (see Malik in Newcomb, 1997: 1–2) for a Black cast and about the Black-British experience, and for many it was the first series which reflected Britain's Black community in a realistic light (Mike Phillips,

Guardian, 21.8.79). Set in the Birmingham suburb of Handsworth, it featured some powerful performances by a South Asian and West Indian cast including Nalini Moonasar, Wayne Laryea, Norman Beaton and Corinne Skinner-Carter. Horace Ove, by now an experienced filmmaker (see Chapter 9), directed three out of ten episodes in the second series, although he recounts how, 'people were always on my back, trying to tell me what I already knew. ... I constantly had to deal with those kinds of problems, and it came from my being the first West Indian director, which did and still does make people in the business nervous' (quoted in Pines, 1992: 125). It is difficult to imagine how much of a Black television drama presence there would have been at this time without Horace Ove and Michael Abbensetts, virtually the only two Black writers/directors in relatively frequent television work at this time (others included Mustapha Matura, Buchi Emecheta, Samuel Selvon).[12] Abbensetts' *The Museum Attendant* (BBC2, 1973), *Black Christmas* (BBC2, 1977) and *Roadrunner* (Thames/ITV, 1977) and Ove's *The Garland (Shai Mala Khani)* (*Play for Today*, BBC1, 1981), *When Love Dies* (1989) (starring Josette Simon and Brian Bovell), *The Orchid House* (1991) and *A Hole in Babylon* (*Play for Today*, BBC, 1979) were landmark productions during these years.

'multiculturalizing' british television drama in the face of change and tradition   The late 1970s/early 1980s brought a significant structural shift within the genre – the demise of the literary-based, classic, single play format and its replacement with the more populist, package-oriented continuous serial/series structure – triggered by the commercial need for ratings-maximization and the quest to hook viewers on long-running drama series. This had a dual effect on Black representation: on the one hand, Black people began to have an increased ongoing presence in contemporary drama on a weekly basis; on the other, this appeared to act as a substitution for the fact that they continued to be locked out of a whole tradition of 'quality', high-budget, often heritage-based drama (the effects of which span from on-screen representations, to cultural viewpoint, to restricted employment opportunities for Black actors). Commercial needs dictated that television was becoming increasingly closed off to those considered inexperienced in delivering popular television, to those programmes that did not feature high-profile stars, or to work that did not 'fit' with the identity of the series. The investment entailed in launching and producing a new series which would draw in as many viewers as possible, meant that few 'risks' were being taken (within the wider context of a now increasingly competitive and populist new four-channel system) so that drama largely continued as an exclusion zone for many Black artists and writes who were still dominantly viewed as ratings-risks or too narrow in their agendas or creative range. The BBC's *Play For Today* (1970–84) was taking its last gasp just as Channel 4 was coming to life, and soap operas were replacing the single play as the nation's theatre. Whilst Channel 4 was playing a key role in the development of Black-British film (see Chapter 9), and had a number of committed inside 'negotiators' such as David Rose (Head of Drama up to 1988 when David Aukin took over) and Peter Ansorge, its drama-specific policies and initiatives were random and, also it seemed, beyond the scope and budgetary demands of the Multicultural Department.[13] (This is an arrangement that continues today, both with Channel 4 and the BBC's multicultural units.) But BBC Drama did broadcast a number of specially-written, one-off dramas such as Farrukh Dhondy's *Good at Art* (BBC2, 1983), *King* (BBC1, 1984) starring Thomas Baptiste, Caryl Phillips' *The Hope and The Glory* (BBC1, 1984) and Mustapha Matura's *Playboy of the West Indies* (BBC2, 1985).

The more general situation, as indicated by Preethi Manuel's analysis of Black and Asian representation in more than 600 drama productions on British television in 1984, was that only 2.3 per cent of actors cast were Black and that the majority of Black characters were only seen in a narrow range of roles such as violent criminals, school pupils, garage-mechanics, nurses and almost always as working class. Meanwhile, the casting of Whites was found to be diverse in terms of background, age, class, occupation and so on. There were also few signs of meaningful integrated casting and Blacks were rarely depicted in caring relationships with each other, or in family situations and were usually characterized as violent, mixed-up, or hostile (Manuel, 1986). One drama that focused some of the emerging critical debates (around positive and negative images, realism, access, authorship, authenticity and continuing structures of television representation) was the four-part serial *King Of The Ghetto* (BBC2, 1986). Based within a topical political setting in London's East End, where a number of Bangladeshis live, the series worked within a framework of gritty realism, laying the text open to complaints of 'misrepresentation' and of creating a new set of stereotypes (e.g. corrupt Asian businessmen, dodgy community leaders). Many resented the British-Asian writer's (Farrukh Dhondy) assumption that he understood the politics of the East End community on which the serial was based and others were concerned that, as he was also Channel 4's Multicultural Programmes Editor, he held too much power in deciding which images of them to bring to screen (a criticism levelled at Channel 4 Commissioning Editors in general who have total licence to accept or reject a programme proposal according to their own preferences). The fundamental question of Black authorship was raised here. For years, Black people had been used to having their lives narrated, almost without exception, by White, middle-class men. The cruel recognition that Black authorship, in itself, carried no guarantees was now being made in drama, as it was in relation to Black magazine programmes and comedy (see Chapters 3 and 5). Black producers faced a new 'burden of representation', the sense that their work had to solve all the problems of Black representation at once and had to match up with a particular version of 'reality' against which all representations could be tested. Whilst the programme's publicity claimed that the series broke with traditional Asian stereotypes (*Radio Times*, 26.4–2.5.86), others felt that 'real life' Bangladeshi-initiated political movements such as those witnessed around the trials of the Newham 8 and Bradford 12 in the early 1980s had been overlooked, and 200 Bangladeshi's from London's Brick Lane protested about the serial outside BBC Television Centre in May 1986 (see Fatima Salaria's article in *Artrage*, Issue 17, 1987).

Two other major drama series that managed to avoid this level of criticism were *Black Silk* (BBC2, 1985) and *South of The Border* (BBC1, 1988). With the majority of the eight-part *Black Silk* series written by different Black writers (including Rudy Narayan, Mustapha Matura, Edgar White and Tunde Ikoli), its themes were heavily focused, not on reinstating law and order (as in the conventional crime genre, see pp. 149–51), but on exposing it as routinely unjust; an early public acknowledgment of 'institutional racism'. Storylines included a critique of British Immigration Laws through the fictional experience of an Asian couple, the problems involved in Black self-defence in the British courts, and the Prevention of Terrorism Acts (Gardner, *Listener*, 31.10.85). The mainstream-targeted *South of the Border* meanwhile, starring Buki Armstrong as Pearl Parker, an ordinary Deptford citizen turned detective, brought a touch of contemporary realism to the adventure/crime series while also subverting its traditional White, male dominance. These varying discourses – multicultural, social-conscience, politically divisive, crossover – emerged out of the divergent 1980s context of public anti-racist struggle, ethnic-minority cultural politics, targeted programming and mounting commercial pressure.

This was arguably the innermost strain within the 1980s epic, heritage (read English) text, a series of nostalgic enterprises which also appeared philanthropic in their nod to the inequities of the colonial dominance of the past. From Waris Hussein's television adaptation of E.M. Forster's *A Passage To India* (BBC, 1965) to Ruth Prawer Jhabvala's *Heat and Dust* (Dir. James Ivory, 1983), from *Gandhi* (Dir. Richard Attenborough, 1983) to M.M. Kaye's *The Far Pavilions* (Channel 4, 1984), a recurrent preoccupation of these quintessentially English colonial adventures was the demise of Empire and the days of the British Raj. *The Jewel In The Crown* (Granada/ITV, 1984), the focus of our attention here, was a 14-part series that purported to give a 'realistic' representation (through its use of Pathé newsreels, period costumes, and 'authentic' colonial mise en scène) of the melancholic twilight years of the British Raj (1935–60). General responses to the series were of praise, discussing the drama in terms of authenticity, quality and 'fairness', and seeing it as anti-imperialist, and reflective of a modern, liberal approach which was keen to 'show the other side'.[14] *Jewel* was indeed classically liberal (appearing to address a moral race issue and include Black characters), but like the social-conscience discourses of the 1950s and 1960s, it also dominantly excluded a significant Black narrative presence (that is, it spoke on behalf of 'the Other'). This was arguably a difficult gap to bridge within the recreated setting of colonialism where Black people were silenced 'in real life', but the trick of the series was in how it managed to locate itself within the ideologies of broad-mindedness, nonconformism and anti-Thatcherism (see Dyer, 1997), whilst also doing virtually nothing to tell us anything oppositional, challenging, or otherwise about a silenced colonial experience. In fact, through its extreme nostalgia, *Jewel* facilitated a rearticulation of the discourse of colonialism, English nationalism and social Whiteness and as such, acted as sedation prescribed to move but not, in any real sense, disturb its very multi-racial audience. In terms of *Jewel*'s liberal effect then, it is worth asking liberal to whom, by whose standards and in comparison to what? *Jewel* was certainly hooked up in these liberal complexities.

The series' prevailing liberal effect was partially put in place by its depiction of the crueller side of colonial rule through the juxtaposition of Hari (Art Malik) as the good Indian with Ronald Merrick (Tim Pigott-Smith), the bad Briton, a powerful endeavour to sustain *Jewel* as a critique of British colonialism. In any case, Hari was characterized in relation to his complex sameness and difference with Britishness, epitomized in his declaration, 'I hate it – India. I hate all the beggars and the heat and the bugs, and most of all myself for being Black and English. . . . I'm Indian, incapable of being anything except an Indian, something totally alien to me' (Hari, Episode 1). By empathetically drawing us towards its central White female characters, Daphne Manners and Sarah Layton, the series also upheld female Whiteness as the benevolent (albeit powerless) voice of narrative authority. As Richard Dyer explains in his detailed analysis of the series, these women, the symbolic bearers of the civilizing mission, 'express disapproval of British practice in India, though always at the level of how Indians are treated rather than whether they should be treated at all; they criticize the conduct of empire, not the enterprise itself' (Dyer, 1997: 186). This shifting of subject positions within *Jewel* (where the Western woman character is atypically granted the active (colonial) gaze and becomes the conveyor of Western civilization (Shohat, 1991)), allowed the traditional gender balance to be inverted, but the dominant race relations were sustained (Blacks as the silenced objects and unable to see the workings of the powerful). For example, Daphne, the heroine of *Jewel In The Crown*, functioned as the archetypal face of colonial benevolence; she was constantly filmed smiling at servants, eating Indian food and educating others (including Hari) about

Indian history. Moreover, our heroine 'crossed the boundary' with Hari, her racial Other, a fatal move for which she was to be sharply reprimanded in the form of gang rape by nameless Indian peasants. The subtext of this double violation of race and class signposted the inequity and sensible distance that needed to be preserved between the British and the Indians, or what Winston Churchill had called the 'primitive' Indians and the 'Indian danger'. The compassionate 'struggle' of British imperial rule was best exhibited in the overwhelming sense of emptiness, stasis and hopelessness that characterized the series and, it followed, the colonial project at large. Guy Perron articulated this most clearly in the final episode; 'What else could we have done?' to which Sarah replied, 'Nothing – nothing we could do. It's like Daphne Manners – like Hari Kumar. After three hundred bloody years of India we've made this whole, damn, bloody, senseless mess.' *Jewel* spoke through a language of unashamed and exclusive Whiteness, never once interrupting the gaze of White viewers and always working within the narrative pattern of historical truth. Television, as we know, is actively involved in this process of cultural selection and exclusion, and narrative meaning is shaped as much by absences, as by what is represented. So whilst *Jewel* appeared to be striving towards redressing the imbalance of other 'return to empire' texts which more explicitly privileged the White viewpoint, the majority of Indians in the serial actually served as little more than 'atmosphere artistes', as native backdrop to White privilege, opulence and order, a narrative approach it shared with the early set of Empire films in the 1930s and 1940s.

Fundamentally, what we are talking about again is telling a story from an uncontested White British viewpoint, and always within the boundaries of admissible leniency. If we compare *Jewel* to the major landmark slavery series *Roots* (ABC, 1977), we can see that it is possible to create a historical drama that can access alternative perspectives and unsettle a culture's dominant assumptions, instead of one which more or less judges history in terms of its own times.[15] This naïve/nostalgic mythology when it comes to representations of history, and the repeatedly undiscerning television adaptation of literary work, was echoed over a decade later in *Rhodes* (BBC1, 1996), a lavish eight-part 'bio-series' claiming to chart the life and times of British imperialist, Cecil J. Rhodes (played by Martin Shaw). Rhodes was presented simply as an adventurer, a pioneer of modern Africa, as a tolerant rather than ruthless colonizer. This heroization simply reproduced national mythologies in sympathy with the glorified colonial project (it contained all the formal costume-drama clichés such as flashbacks, dusty settings, silent Blacks, and a cursory princess), and showed virtually nothing about 'native' opposition to Rhodes or of *how* he shaped Africa. As Colin Clark argued, 'Antony Thomas's script takes a *Boys Own* view of *Rhodes*, lacking both objectivity, and any trace of modern thinking ... it is astonishing that the

BBC should gloss over his disgusting and often unethical behaviour' (Clark, *Punch*, 14–20.9.96: 83).

diversity as modernity   The supposed modernity of 'industrial-ized Blackness' – as something new, cosmopolitan and different – meant that Black actors in the 1980s and 1990s were more generally being character-ized in modern British settings. This kind of mimetic harmonizing of sup-posed 'real life' and the aesthetic of dramatic realism (that is, Black people as silenced in the colonized past and thus also in the colonially-based text, and politicized/more visible in the Western metropolis and thus in the con-temporary staged situation) was ingrained in the very structure of television drama. This pull between the past and present, the heritage-based and the ultra-modern was, in any case, the national agenda set under the terms of Thatcherism and later to be continued by Tony Blair, with his emphasis on a modern Britain with an eye on the past (a mollifying response to the dual processes of devolution and European federalism). Accordingly, we began to see Black characters positioned within present-day, multiculturalist narra-tives, and depicted as part of the fabric of everyday institutional British life in integrated workspaces (in hospitals, the fire brigade, schools, the legal sec-tor, the army, the police), particularly in long-running mainstream dramas such as the BBC's *Casualty*, *Cardiac Arrest*, *Holby City*, *Grange Hill* and *This Life* and ITV's *London's Burning* and *Soldier, Soldier*. Given Black people's long-standing physical presence in Britain, these were welcome, if late, acknowledgements. Treva Etienne,[16] commenting on his role as a fire-man (Tony Sanderson) in the long-running series *London's Burning* (LWT/ITV, 1988–), says that whilst the series gave him mass exposure and was a valuable learning experience, he also felt that some writers found it difficult to negotiate giving his character both a home and work life. He recalls, 'They got a little bit weary about how far they could go with it . . . if a Black person doesn't fit, then they become the afterthought. . . . They try to write something which they think is correct but without any real type of research' (Etienne, interview with author, 24.11.95).

This grappling with formal equality, cultural difference, perceived commercial needs and cultural demands, was a major problem in drama, particularly in soap opera which relies on both ratings and local realism. During the 1980s, the genre became a key source of competition between the broadcasters, with new soaps created or the existing ones 'spiced up'. The diversification of characters and settings through the inclusion of more 'minority' characters, became an important supply of multicultural regular-ization, and was hoped to potentially draw in minority audiences, boost the multicultural realism of the drama, meet the needs of an ethnically-conscious political climate and renew and innovate existing storylines. *Albion Market* (Granada/ITV, 1986), *Family Pride* (Channel 4, 1991–3), *Brothers and Sisters* (BBC2, 1996), *Tiger Bay* (BBC1, 1996) and *London Bridge* (Carlton/ITV, 1996–99) all took a racially integrated or Black-centred approach, but few of these series managed to pick up the momentum of the 'mainstream' soaps (some inevitably suffering because of poor scheduling, selected regional airings, or insufficient promotion).

The ways in which the mainstream soaps have largely failed to 'manage race' have been detailed elsewhere (Daniels and Gerson, 1989; Pines, 1992; Ross, 1996). The genre needs to be noted as one which has attracted severe criticism both by minority viewers and Black soap actors themselves for their tokenistic, politically correct and undeveloped characterization. For example Shreela Ghosh, who played shopkeeper Naima Jeffrey in the BBC's leading soap opera *Eastenders* (BBC1, 1985–), complained, 'I keep playing scenes week in, week out which have no substance. . . .We're a political football . . . a trump card over all the soaps' (Ghosh in Daniels and Gerson, 1989: 128; see also the *Guardian*, 24.10.91). Tellingly, most of the soaps feature at least one Black character at any given time, as though they are working to a quota-system (i.e. that x amount of Black characters is 'enough'). *Brookside*'s (Channel 4, 1982–) Mick Johnson (an 'ethical', hard-working, single father) has been in the popular drama since 1989 and stands out as an exception to the more typical soap rule of federation Whiteness best exemplified by *Emmerdale* (Yorkshire TV/ITV, 1972; *Emmerdale Farm* until 1989) and *Coronation Street* which wittingly present us with a more 'traditional' (Black-free) slice of British life. There is an ongoing problem with writing engaging, realistic and ethnically plausible Black characters, instead of, to use Montgomery's term, 'narrative donors', who solely function to help the 'real action' of the central characters come to fruition (Montgomery et al., 1992: 181). Take for example, two of *Eastenders'* longest-running and most central Asian characters, Sanjay (Deepak Verma) and Geeta (Shobhu Kapoor), who were often seen in the pub or chatting in the market, but rarely depicted in the 'private' space of their home, or more importantly as Indian (in terms of language, food or dress for example) – except when there was a racist attack, and even this story disappeared without trace (August, 1994). This home/work, private/public dichotomy, as hinted at by Etienne in relation to his *London's Burning* character (see p. 147), is a familiar pattern with Black characters in television drama: it is as though the Black character's personalized sphere is too intimate, too close, too 'real' for the writers. I am not suggesting that the ethnicity of a Black character has to be calculatingly signposted, but such lack of attention to cultural and individual detail marks a broader and prevailing fear of alienating the majority mainstream drama audience because of 'ethnic distinctiveness' or 'too much difference' (so that often the only 'Black' aspect of the character is that they look Black). When Sanjay and Geeta were scripted to exit the serial, there was no dramatic car crash and no salacious revelations; just a quiet petering out after years of living in Walford, as though Albert Square had never noticed their arrival. This assimilationist, 'colour-blind', 'narrative donor' approach to Black characters not only enables the discourse of universalism and tolerance to prevail, but it is especially interesting in the case of soaps, because elsewhere the genre tends to accentuate and work through differences (gender, regional and class distinctions for example). With race however, there seems to be a problem with balancing the fact that Black people are both the same and different, and also perhaps an inherent backlog of guilt about a legacy of poor Black characterization; as if ignoring the fact of cultural difference, will correspondingly avoid all criticisms of 'negative stereotyping'. This awkwardness and indifference to Black characters reflects itself and is extended by the para-texts around soap operas (magazines, tie-ins, trailers and chat shows), which rarely feature the few Black soap actors in any significant way. In today's culture of marketing and celebrity magazines, this plays an integral role in how viewer interest and pleasure is developed (or not), and further sustains Black actors as low-profile which, in turn, is seen to limit their ratings-appeal. These specific examples that we are looking at, add up to a bigger mainstream culture of Black exclusion.

The crime series is another dramatic space that has struggled over managing the needs of equality and difference. Early crime series (*Dixon of Dock Green*, BBCTV, 1955–76; *Z Cars*, BBCTV, 1962–78) had rarely featured Black people. By the 1980s however, the genre was being reworked as one which could effectively update and extend the topicality and realism of the medium, largely through the vexed questions of morality, society, 'law and order' and citizenship, the dominant public narratives of Thatcherite Britain (see Chapter 4). The reproduction of 'gritty realism' is of course a generic convention of British television crime fiction and a classic form of race relations discourse. As such, where Black people are and are not seen in crime drama tends to tally with broader (expectations of) public images of Black and White crime (the Black as mugger, pimp or drug dealer, the White as racist thug or crime-hatcher, the Asian as victim of male oppression, racist attacks (usually in their shops) or shady businessmen). Thus the Pakistani children-snatcher (Art Malik in *Stolen*, ITV, 1990), the West Indian prostitute and pimp (Bella in *Widows*, Ria in *The Sweeney*, Carol in *Band of Gold*), and the Black mugger (*The Gentle Touch*) serve the visual and ideological effect of realism. The dramatic realism of the (fictional) crime genre works alongside the dominant sense of realism, or what Neale has called the 'generic verisimilitude' (Neale, 1981), constructed in other (factual) television genres and cultural sources. The race-dependent effects (that is, to cast Black people as villains, criminals or social deviants) serve the dominant sense of 'authenticity' of the crime genre (and make such characterizations defensible because they are 'realistic' according to what the news media tells us). This of course, is not dependent on an 'external' pre-given truth (i.e. that Blacks are more likely to be villains), but on the 'internal' sense of realism produced amongst television's dominant narratives, both in other crime series and television genres (Brunsdon in Baehr and Dyer 1987: 192). This inter-textual network of realist imagery, produced by the medium itself, helps us understand how whilst each television genre constructs its own distinct codes, conventions and sense of realism, each is also continually engaged in dialogue with the realist discourses and stereotypical tendencies of other television genres. This is how 'truth' is enacted through inter-textuality, and how a meta-discourse of 'law and order' is constructed.

Given the more run-of-the-mill, positive/negative framework and narrow character types through which the crime series operates (the good cop, bad cop, victim, criminal), Black characters are often switched from the 'wrong' to the 'right' side of the law, so that television's dominant sense of truth around Black criminality is bypassed. But these anti-stereotypes, because they break with racial axioms, are usually drawn as *exceptional* and atypical; the novelty is to be found in their non-criminality (thus the *good Black cop* (*Wolcott*, ATV/ITV, 1981), the *Chinese detective* (*The Chinese Detective*, BBC1, 1981–82) and the *successful Black lawyer* (*Black Silk*, BBC2, 1985)).[17] We often see this character used to serve the genre's over-riding need to reinstate moral order, to liaise with 'the Black community', to be juxtaposed with a more typical (villainous) Black character or community (characterized by authentic markers such as urban setting, muggers, drugs, disaffected Black youth). From the Pakistani hero (undercover agent Khan/Ahmed Khalil) in *Gangsters* (BBC1, 1976, 1978), to G.F. Newman's *Black and Blue* (BBC1, 1992), to the Glaswegian cop Shan Khan (Tarun Dev) in *Bombay Blue* (Channel 4, 1997), to David Harewood as Sgt Joe Robinson in *The Vice* (Carlton/ITV, 1999–), these are 'alternative' codes with which we are now familiar.

Let us briefly use the example of *Prime Suspect* (Granada/ITV, 1991–96), one of Britain's most popular crime series and a defining influence on subsequent 'Black-inclusive' crime dramas such as *Cracker* (ITV, 1994–96), *The Cops* (BBC2, 1999–2001), *The Bill* (ITV, 1983–) and *Prime Suspect 5* (*Errors of Judgment*) (ITV, 1996). The increasingly edgy and urban feel of 1990s television (crime) drama (the BBC's *Undercover Heart* and *Holding On* and ITV's *The Knock*, *The Vice* and *Trial and Retribution* for example), began to reflect both the multiracial actuality of 1990s Britain, and feed into contemporary and reimagined notions of Black people within the stylized context of 'Cool Britannia'. With television as a whole beginning to feel the commercial pressures at this time, television drama (along with documentary, light entertainment and comedy), had grasped the appeal of style, violence and sexuality, something nicely complemented by notions of Blackness.

These narratives were also influenced by the 'urban' style and multi-culturalist discourses of popular US-produced 1990s urban drama series such as *ER*, *Homicide: Life On The Streets*, *NYPD Blue* and *Oz* (see Gray, 1995) (all screened on Channel 4). *Prime Suspect 2* (ITV, 1992) introduced an assertive Black detective, Bob Oswalde (Colin Salmon), to an otherwise institutionally White police-force (as marked by the absence of Black characters in the original *Prime Suspect*). Because the lead role of DCI Jane Tennison (Helen Mirren) was a woman in a male police culture, this dispersed the sociological emphasis between gender (Tennison) and race (Oswalde), thus creating more than one institutional 'Other'. Together with the complex premise of their respective characters – Tennison as privately vulnerable but professionally tough, and Oswalde as a hybrid of stylish, hard Black male and sensitive 'New Man', the viewer was encouraged to take on a negotiated and complex reading of the text. Interestingly, Oswalde also acted as Tennison's lover, thus functioning as a device to cross over into Tennison's private sphere. This I would suggest, secured the essential modernity and liberalism of the text and of its leading female icon. For example, the sexual encounter, although initially given narrative precedence, never substantially evolved. It disappeared in place of other plot developments, making it a 'story hole'; an unresolved part of the narrative, curiously incomplete in a text otherwise directed towards narrative closure (solving the crime). Of course such carefully crafted narratives are (un)developed for a purpose and, to this end, the symbolic inclusion of the encounter cemented, amongst other things, Tennison's liberalism (sexually involved with her racial Other) and thus ensured that Tennison continued to sustain her narrative image (fair-minded, empathetic, tolerant, reputable) which was so central to the success of the first *Prime Suspect*. The affair also signified Tennison's femininity, her heterosexuality and the fact that she was both open to, yet needed no man. Oswalde, although a central, relatively developed, and complex character, functioned, in this instance, as a 'narrative donor' (see p. 148), enhancing the defining aspects of Tennison's characterization. Whilst Oswalde added these race-dependent meanings to the text, he was also juxtaposed against other Black characters in the series with the effect of highlighting 'the Black community's' heterogeneity. In this case, Oswalde as a representative of the law was positioned against Tony Allen (a Black suspect who eventually hanged himself in a police-cell), to represent ideologically opposed racial positions and, as such, demonstrated how Blackness does not homogenize police and 'street' positions. I am suggesting here that it is perfectly possible for antithetical, mould-breaking racial representations to work alongside more racially typical, expedient ones, and further still, that these meanings are capable of arising from the same characterization; a Black character can send out various signals and can carry a number of apparently conflicting meanings.

What we have been outlining is how television drama experienced an important turn during the 1980s; a more natural sense of multiculturalism and diversity substantiated at the level of text, 'lifestyle' and the unifying image. Since then, we have seen signs of a greater ease of presence ascribed to signs of Blackness, where Black characters more legitimately share the narrative space with their White counterparts and where there is a more obvious sense of 'Black-Britishness'. This has signalled broader strategies of inclusion and multiculturalism that facilitate a visual modernization and expansion of ideas about nation, and which, in turn, serve to authenticate and update the dramatic text. The television adaptations of Hanif Kureishi's Whitbread Prize-winning novel, *The Buddha Of Suburbia* (Dir. Roger Michell, BBC2, 1993), *Turning World* (Channel 4, 1997), *Peacock Spring* (1996), *Little Napoleans* (Channel 4, 1994), and Caryl Phillips' *The Final Passage* (Channel 4, 1996), have been exciting pieces of drama profiling lead Black characters. Four years after the broadcast of *The Final Passage*, a rare Black heritage-text, tracing the experience of a young 'Windrush generation' couple as they came to Britain, Caryl Phillips criticized the Black presence in drama since its screening, explaining, 'it wasn't meant to be something in isolation' (Phillips, 2000: 2). The difference of some of the multiculturalist discourses to have emerged, such as *This Life* (BBC2, 1996–97) and *Holding On* (BBC2, 1997), is that they have not set themselves up as 'Black dramas' *per se,* and never organized a perfunctory (Black) storyline around a more dramatically engaging (White) one. *Holding On* (which received a BAFTA in 1998 for Best TV serial) established a number of interweaving (but at first seemingly unconnected) storylines, resulting in a convoluted narrative structure designed to 'reflect life at breaking-point' in contemporary London. The inescapable connections between 'Blackness', 'Asianness' and 'Whiteness' were built into the very structure of the series, which started out in its opening episodes separating the Black and White fictional worlds, only to see them gradually connect in rich, emotional and sometimes tragic ways. Similarly, *This Life*, based on a group of young twenty-something lawyers and flatmates,[18] offered a genuine notion of unity across difference (the sexual preferences, class, and ethnicity of each of the characters varied). *This Life* moved its leading Black characters, Milly (Amita Dhiri) and Ferdy (Ramon Tikaram), beyond mere tokenism and broke with the obligatory pattern of 'racial problems' (thus no bricks were thrown through windows, no arranged marriages happened and none of the obvious problems were created by inter-racial relationships). The pay-off was fully-rounded, credible, Black characters – facilitated, precisely because of the only-occasional reference to race and because no one Black character was expected to be 'representative', 'three-dimensional' or signposted as 'a Black character'. *Holding On* and *This Life* both stand as rare examples, but later dramas such as *Never Never* (Channel 4, 2000), *Metrosexuality*

(Channel 4, 2001), *Attachments* (BBC2, 2000) and *Storm Damage* (BBC2, 1999) (featuring some outstanding Black-British talent in Sophie Okonedo, Ricky Beadle Blair, Justin Pierre and Lennie James respectively), also succeeded in varying degrees, in creating dramatically engaging and politically astute Black characters.

Television drama continues with two key racialized discourses. The first is the modern multiculturalist discourse (gritty, 'realistic', set in the metropolitan present) that we have just been describing; and the second is the historical traditional heritage-centred text, or one that is set in a contemporary, idealized, antiquated White rural England. There are many example of this, ranging from classic 1990s popular television series such as *Heartbeat*, *Wycliffe*, *Peak Practice*, *Inspector Morse*, to historical costume dramas such as *And The Beat Goes On* (Channel 4, 1996), *Pride and Prejudice* (BBC1, 1995), *Middlemarch* (BBC2, 1994), *Jane Eyre* (ITV, 1997) and *Our Mutual Friend* (BBC2, 1998). But there is also a third kind which perhaps indicates a growing trend for the future under the force of globalization. This is the kind of socially White drama of which we have a constant supply today; the kind of productions that the industry literally buys in, predominantly from the USA. We cannot fail to notice for example, that the most watched and sought-after imports on British television – *Friends*, *Frasier*, *Dawsons's Creek*, *Ally McBeal* and *Neighbours* and before that *Roseanne*, *Cheers*, *Home and Away* and *Beverly Hills 90210* – are all notable for their displacement of multicultural reality and for their absence or tokenistic inclusion of Black characters. Like so many of the liberal texts of the 1960s and 1970s, when a Black person does make a rare appearance in these productions, they are usually brought in to teach the White characters some important life lessons about integration and to make them question their attitudes towards Black people (a 'quick-fix' anti-racism), only to be speedily excised from the series and characters' lives. Bruce Gyngell suggests that the UK's penchant for White-exclusive Australian soaps such as *Neighbours* and *Home and Away*, which have been screened on British television since the 1980s, depends on the fact that they 'represent a society which existed in Britain . . . before people began arriving from the Caribbean and Africa. The Poms delve into it to get their quiet little racism fix' (Gyngell in Andrew Culf, *Guardian*, 21.11.93). Whilst there is no doubt that these unequivocally White discourses offer a certain cultural reassurance, this complicates the whole question of why so many Black people also engage with these programmes. As Mike Phillips reminds us:

We are all multicultural in our homes and on the streets so we have a private multi-culturalism which isn't reflected in the media. When I watch *Inspector Morse* I don't think of it as not belonging to me and there is no reason why a white person shoudn't feel the same about our programmes except that they are never given the chance to because those kind of programmes are very rarely made. (Phillips, *Impact*, 2, 1992: 27)

notes

1 Notable for their absence in the archives are Errol John's *Moon on a Rainbow Shawl* (1960), Jan Carew's *Drama '61: The Day of The Fox* (1961), the Negro Theatre Workshop's *The Dark Disciples* (1966), Evan Jones' *Go Tell It On Table Mountain* (1967), Obi Egbuna's *Wind Versus Polygamy* (1968), and Alfred Fagon's *Shakespeare Country* (1973).

2 Robert Adams was also the first Black actor to play a Shakespearian role on television, (the Prince of Morocco in *The Merchant of Venice* (1947)). He also appeared in W.B. Yeats' *Deirdre* (BBC, 1938) and *The Emperor Jones* (1938).

3 During the 1930s, many working-class Black-Britons from areas such as Cardiff, London's East End and Liverpool would travel to Shepperton and Beaconsfield to earn money playing bit-parts and extras in films such as *The Thief of Bagdad* (1940), *Sanders of the River* (1934), *Black Narcissus* (1947) and in all of Robeson's films with the exception of *The Proud Valley* (1940) (see Bourne, 1998: 43–63).

4 Following his appearance as Dr Aziz in Santha Rama Rau's adaptation of E.M. Forster's *A Passage To India*, Zia Mohyeddin went on to star in the television version (as part of BBCTV's 'Play Of The Month', 1965) directed by Waris Hussein. Meanwhile, fellow Asian actor Saeed Jaffrey had set up his own English theatre company (Unity Theatre) in Delhi in the early 1950s and has since gone on to become one of Britain's most popular Asian actors (his main television work has included *Gangsters* (1975–76), *Tandoori Nights* (1985–87), *Little Napoleons* (1994) and *Coronation Street* (1999)).

5 In 1938, Ralph Richardson blacked up in the Old Vic's production of Othello, and Laurence Olivier did this for the same role in 1964. Despite a heavy Asian cast in Channel 4's *The Far Pavilions* (1984), Amy Irving blacked-up to play the lead part of Princess Anjuli. Meanwhile, Michael Bates blacked-up to play Rangi Ram in *It Ain't Half Hot Mum* (BBC, 1974–81).

6 Along with the Black Parents Movement, La Rose had been a key player in a 'supplementary' Black education centre, the George Padmore School.

7 Theatre companies and spaces such as the Temba Theatre Company, the Drum Centre, The Dark and Light Theatre Company and The Black Theatre of Brixton were also important here.

8 Cy Grant, Earl Cameron, Gloria Simpson, Errol John, Nadia Cattouse and Sonny McKenzie.

9 Hopkins had written a dramatic episode of *Z Cars, A Place of Safety*, focusing on police racism in the previous year.

10 Joan Hooley later became a scriptwriter on *Desmond's* and from August, 1998, made appearances in *Eastenders*.

11 Cleo Sylvestre also appeared in Ken Loach's *Up The Junction* (1965) and *Cathy Come Home* (1966).

12 Other exceptional television dramas of the time included Mustapha Matura's *Nice* (Channel 4, 1984), featuring an award-winning dramatic monologue by Norman Beaton; Abbensetts' *Black Christmas* (BBC2, 1977) based on a Black woman's (Carmen Munroe as Gertrude) attempt to make her family's Christmas run smoothly; Nigerian writer, Buchi Emecheta's *The Ju-Ju Landlord* (Granada TV/ITV, 1976; part of *Crown Court*) and *Nigeria* (*A Kind of Marriage*) (BBC2, 1976; part of *Centre Play: Commonwealth Season*).

13 Alon Reich, Assistant Editor at Channel 4 Drama (with specific emphasis on development) admitted, 'In terms of Channel 4 drama, we have no specific initiative to bring on black and Asian talent' (ICA 'Black and White in Colour' conference notes, 1992).

14 See Salman Rushdie's article 'Outside The Whale' (1991: 87–101), and Dyer for a detailed analysis of Whiteness in relation to *Jewel* (Dyer, 1997: 184–206).

15 The historical slavery saga, *Roots* (1977) became the most watched entertainment programme in American broadcasting history, but was first seen as a potential risk by US networks. Many Black-British cultural practitioners have cited Alex Haley's story of Kunta Kinte (La Var Burton) and Black slavery as a key cultural moment (for example, Kobena Mercer and Linton Kwesi Johnson in 'Black and White in Colour' archive interviews).

16 Etienne subsequently became a member of the government's Film Policy Review Action Committee.

17 For more on the very interesting case study of *Wolcott*, see Pines in Daniels and Gerson, 1989: 63–70.

18 *This Life* also brought in relatively new television writers such as Ian Iqbal Rashid (who was chosen for the BBC's Black Screen script-writing scheme) to script individual episodes.

pounds, policy and pressure:
black-british filmmaking –
'as seen on tv'

British film has a long-standing relationship with television; personnel, funds, genres, the state, companies, points of exhibition, distribution and a commercially-based sensibility link the two industries and mediums. It is, in fact, impossible to speak of (Black) British film without acknowledging its connections to British television, and most obviously to Channel 4 which has played a critical role in boosting a Black-British film practice and an independent commissioning structure, which, broadly speaking, expanded the number of Black film and television producers in the 1980s. By acting as a 'publisher-contractor', Channel 4 combined the public service and free market models and became a negotiated site between cultural practitioners, filmmakers and the state. For our concerns, we are focusing here on the institutional context of Black-produced films, most of which have had a theatrical release, but all of which have an obvious television link (meaning they have been supported by television money through grants, pre-sales, equity finance and/or television rights). There is a whole other story – from *Sanders of The River* (Dir. Alexander Korda, 1935), to *Sapphire* (Dir. Basil Deardon, 1959), to *Secrets and Lies* (Dir. Mike Leigh, 1996) – about the ways in which Black people have been represented in White, mainstream film texts (Pines, 1975; Young, 1996) and some valuable textual analysis in this area that goes into more detail than I am able to here (Mercer, 1988; Young, 1996; Bakari in Owusu, 2000). By focusing on the specific production contexts of Black-British film, I want to lay out some of the institutional questions which will lead us towards our conclusion and summary in the next chapter.

Our story really begins in the late 1970s and mainly focuses on the 1980s, because it was during this time that the relationship between the two mediums and industries became more intrinsically connected. Up to the 1980s, British broadcasting companies (unlike European public-sector television) were relatively uninvolved in film production intended for theatrical release. Channel 4's first Chief Executive, Jeremy Isaacs, announced plans for the *Film on Four* strand on the first day of its transmission in November 1982. This was a major initiative, made up of mostly feature-length, fictional, independent productions with the chance of subsequent cinematic distribution. The emphasis was on funding 'art house' productions and on broadcasting rarely seen film seasons from around the world (African and South Asian cinema for example), which, in turn, supported a new-found interest in (alternative kinds of) British and global film. Channel 4's unique publishing commissioning model, its commitment to backing British cinema, and its remit of distinctiveness and multiculturalism led to the creation of a unique environment in which the low-budget independent sector became a feasible and fundable option. Black-British films, most of which emerged from the context of grant-aided collective practice, generated a set of critical debates in relation to diaspora aesthetics, identity, 'third cinema' and hybridity, advanced by a number of Britain's leading Black academics (Hall, Pines, Mercer, Gilroy, Bhabha). In fact, this was one of the primary aims of the Black workshops – to develop as a resource-base and access-point with an emphasis on 'integrated practice' in which production was linked to education, training and documentation, rather than designed to attract large audiences.

In line with escalating commercial pressure during the 1990s, Channel 4 and the BBC (now with its commercial arm, BBC Enterprises Ltd) began to reinterpret their distinct 'public service' ideals as the need to attract as many cinema-goers and, ultimately, television viewers as possible to the films they were helping finance. As David Aukin, then Head of Drama at Channel 4 (which operated as a co-producer of a lot of Channel 4's *Film on Four* productions) said in a discussion about Channel 4 and British cinema in 1995, 'we had to re-establish a pact with our audience' (Aukin, Vancouver Film Festival, August 1995). Interestingly, this did not necessarily mean revisiting the channel's original remit, but rather that they wanted to see bigger audiences for films with a Channel 4 connection. This deduction was based on the commercial logic that the basis of a healthy film industry and successful channel was more 'bums on seats', a reasoning which many Black-British filmmakers also began to take their cue from. But such changes also had an obvious impact on those lower-budget, non commercially-driven, smaller-profile ideas, companies and films that had made some headway in the 1980s, and raised further criticism that Channel 4 had 'gone commercial'. This was essentially what the demise of the Black independent workshop sector was about, and what conjunctively gave rise to the more 'crossover', commercially-geared Black-British films we began to see in the 1990s. Significantly perhaps, since 1995, this new populist direction was also being encouraged and tied to a new source of major funding, the National Lottery, although how this was to benefit a Black-British film practice was still uncertain, and remains so, both because of the absence of inscribed policy/strategy about specifically supporting under-represented filmmakers, and because of the emphasis on 'commercial franchises'. What is clear is that the new commercialism (which also impacts on where the distribution of lottery funds is directed) has not successfully assimilated or encouraged Black-produced work within a broader sense of British film culture, leaving it once again at the hands of reverberated 'diversity action-plans' and 'special funds'. In base terms, Black-British film today remains under-capitalized, poorly-distributed, selectively-exhibited and widely unknown, a criticism of course which could be levelled at a large proportion of British film. Moreover, for those Black filmmakers who are concerned with producing politically-committed, avant-garde, non-profit motivated, or more 'art house' films (characteristics of the bulk of the 1980s Black-produced films), the growing crisis in terms of distribution and the closed doors that a lot of Black producers still face from television and film decision-makers, make the future look even bleaker. Whilst convergence has meant that the means of production have become cheaper and more accessible, the political context and business emphasis have also shifted; thus it may be easier for a Black amateur producer to make a film aided by the new digital technologies, but the chances of getting it commissioned have not correspondingly broadened.

the formation of black-british film and notions of independence   Prior to the late 1970s, there were, as we have seen, a few Black audiovisual practitioners in Britain that were involved in television production as directors or writers (Michael Abbensetts, Edric Connor, Horace Ove, Lloyd Reckord, Barry Reckord). As we know, they had to face a discriminatory dominant culture and its associated narrow criteria in relation to the institutional race narratives of television drama and documentary. Besides, if there were programmes/films to be made about 'race', then there were also plenty of professional White practitioners around to make them, who were well-versed in telling Black stories 'realistically' within the context of the social-realist tradition, the privileged aesthetic form in which the 'problem' of Blackness was addressed (for example in television documentaries, drama, press journalism and photography) (see Bailey and Hall, 1992: 18). On the rare occasion when Black people were more actively involved in the creative process, the production would also often trigger a disproportionate level of criticism, anxiety or depreciation (*Pressure, A Hole in Babylon, Blacks Britannica, Grove Music, The People's Account*). In basic terms, the tight expectations and lack of possibilities in television for Black people had a generative effect on openings in film, so that those who went on to become some of Britain's most prolific filmmakers were usually White, male and had a background in 'social realist' television where the really serious 'filmmaking' was done (for example, Stephen Frears, Ken Loach and Mike Leigh).

During the 1960s and 1970s, there were only a handful of 'practising' Black filmmakers who, with little public funding and support, managed to get their films made. In general, aspiring Black filmmakers found it virtually impossible to organize independently, given the comparatively expensive nature of the medium. Against the odds, some inspiring Black-produced films emerged, including *Jemima and Johnny* (Dir. Lionel Ngakane, 1963), *Ten Bob in Winter* (Dir. Lloyd Reckord, 1963), *Dream A40* (Dir. Lloyd Reckord, 1965), *Baldwin's Nigger* (Dir. Horace Ove, 1969) and *Reggae* (Dir. Horace Ove, 1970). Since these films were virtually totally self-financed by single filmmakers (with the exception of *Ten Bob in Winter* which was funded by the BFI), they had no immediate dependency on or relationship with other cultural institutions, although this too ensured that they remained further marginalized in terms of exhibition and general support, and thus operated on the sidelines of both mainstream and independent film and television practice. One of the early producers of Black-British film, Lloyd Reckord, says that his primary purpose in directing two experimental films was, in fact, to get into television. He thought, 'this was the way to do it – a way of showing the television companies that I could direct a film. But it didn't work. I showed them the first film, then the second . . . but they just weren't interested. I got the impression that they weren't interested at that time in hiring black directors' (Reckord in Pines, 1992: 54–5). Similarly, Lionel Ngakane, who only made one film as a British director (*Jemima and Johnny*), left England to enjoy a more fulfilling career working with African cinema (see Givanni, 1994: 13). In the late 1960s, Ngakane said, 'the trouble in this country is that people in theatre and films simply can't visualize a coloured man as a director. . . . I have been here for eighteen years now and am still considered incapable of handling British subjects' (quoted in *The Times*, 15.11.68). Ove remained the only practising filmmaker and television director (with documentaries such as *Colherne Jazz* (1972), *Keskidee Blues* (1972) and *Skateboarding Kings* (1978) and various dramas outlined in the last chapter), although in the 1990s, he followed many of his counterparts and relocated to the Caribbean (highlighting perhaps that, in practice, 'voluntary repatriation' does exist, at least amongst some Black artists).

The first set of Black themed and/or Black-produced feature films to emerge were *A Private Enterprise* (Dir. Peter K. Smith, 1974; co-written by Dilip Hiro), a BFI-funded feature examining the British-Asian experience, *Black Joy*[1] (Dir. Anthony Simmons, 1977), based on an idea taken from Jamal Ali's play *Dark Days and Light Nights* and *Pressure* (Dir. Horace Ove, 1975), the first Black-British feature-length film to be funded by the BFI[2] (see Figure 6). These exemplified the drama-documentary, realist, social-issue genre, and attempted to recode and 'answer back' to what Jim Pines has

Figure 6
Pressure (1975) Dir: Horace Ove

BFI Stills, Posters and Designs

called the 'official race relations narrative' (Pines, 1988: 29), which set them within a canon that can be described as the 'cinema of duty' films (Malik, 1996). The 'official' 'master narratives' of race relations had, as Mercer reminds us, 'positioned Black subjects as "problems" or "victims", always as some intractable and unassimilable Other on the margins of British society and its collective consciousness' (Mercer, 1994: 82). In this new set of narratives, the Black Subject became the Black British Subject, located *within* Black and British communities/settings so that 'Whiteness' was no longer the dramatic or narrative centre around which 'Blackness' was based. Whilst these films did not have a production collaboration with television, they used the space of film to set in motion alternative narratives and perspectives and break with the authoritative 'cultural verisimilitude' of the racialized discourses which had, to date, characterized the television race relations documentary, drama and news story. This is not to infer that these films were just a contrary response to television, but they can usefully be read within the context of the medium, because this had reigned as the privileged knowledge portal through which the nation's racialized common sense or accumulation of prejudices had developed. To use Mercer's phrase, 'the problems of representation created by the hegemony of documentary realism in racial discourse' (Mercer, 1988: 11) had an important bearing on the terms by which these films were received, acclaimed and analysed – as oppositional, subcultural and contentious or alternative, heterogeneous and revised.

During this time and within the context of various Black political movements and the general Black arts movement which had taken root in Britain since the 1950s (see pp. 135–8), there arose a specific drive towards developing a more mainstream awareness of 'Black arts' (for example, Naseem Khan's 1976 report, *The Arts Britain Ignores* and the establishment of the Minority Arts Advisory Service). As filmmaker Imruh Bakari says of the situation prior to the 1980s:

> There was no notion about Black people being able to make films . . . or anything that was BBC standard or meritorious as cinema. When we started making films, we made films because we were going to make films by any means necessary. There was no promise of finance, there was no promise of support or access even to the BFI. (Bakari, interview with author, 10.12.96)

Furthermore, what became apparent through the first 'Black Film Festival' in 1982 (presented at the Commonwealth Institute jointly with the British Film Institute), the follow-up GLC 'Third Eye: London's Festival of Third World Cinema' (1983) (see GLC, 1986) and the 'Anti-Racist Film Programme Cinema Circuit' (1985), was that there was an audience who were interested in (debating) these sidelined (in all corners, from *Screen*-type film criticism to marketing) representations. Black independent film collectives such as Black Audio Film Collective (BAFC), Star Productions, Retake Film and Video Collective, Sankofa and Ceddo began to organize themselves around particular agendas, issues and genres of filmmaking. In order to get financial support, the self-organized collectives subsequently established links with various public institutions such as the British Film Institute, the Arts Council, the newly-formed Channel 4, and the Greater London Council.

Essentially though, these belated new forms of cultural 'assistance' had been stridently fought for and demanded as a cultural right (through various Black-led organizations such as CARM and BMWA, by certain individuals, and obliquely via the 'riots' of the 1970s and 1980s). The 1982 Workshop Declaration was an industrial agreement signed by the BFI, the Association of Cinematograph, Television and Allied Technicians (ACTT), television companies such as Channel 4, and English Regional Arts Associations, which included the GLC and the Welsh Arts Council. General agreements about pay and conditions were negotiated so that a British independent film and video sector (six of the collectives were Black) could materialize and develop (see Lambert, 1982 for funding details). Channel 4 (and particularly the Multicultural Department and the Independent Film and Video Department where Alan Fountain was the commissioning editor for grant-aided film and video work) was to become the main supporter of the workshops, not only in terms of financial backing, but also in exhibiting a number of so-called 'programmes of work', primarily in its two 'experimental' film slots *Eleventh Hour* and *People To People*.[3] In the early 1980s, Alan Fountain (replaced by Stuart Cosgrove in 1994 and then by Adam Barker) stressed that he wanted 'the look' of Channel 4 to be less slick, thus 'breaking up the sameness of current television' (Fountain, quoted in Lambert, 1982: 150). Given the legacy of blocked cultural access, Black independent film workers were now being offered the chance of television exposure while themselves remaining within the tradition of film independence.

The term 'independent' or notion of 'ideological freedom' could not be taken literally, since all 'independents' were *dependent* in varying degrees for sources of funding, distribution and exhibition on local or central government and on television (which had its own limited agendas and institutional narratives around 'race'). The workshops, widely regarded as the most obvious form of independent Black filmmaking – because of their collective practice (workshops), their aesthetic preference (anti-narrative) and their relation to audience (i.e. not being ratings-driven) – were inescapably signing into a culture of dependency. The non-industrial, grant-assisted premise of the workshop arrangement generally meant that those involved could, to an extent, avoid the constraints of commercialism and the logic of the marketplace, but others felt pressurized to produce what funding bodies considered to be 'a *black* film' (Pines, 1988) or, for that matter, a prototypal-diaspora cinema ('experimental', 'avant-garde', rejecting Hollywood's story-telling conventions) (see O'Pray in Higson, 1996). Although 'independent creatives' was the common term used to describe these new cultural workers, the category actually contained a diverse range of practitioners with different aims and areas of operation. As well as the grant-aided or subsidized workshop sector, a space in which the collectives could produce relatively small-scale, micro-budget, innovative and experimental films, there were many Black filmmakers who could not get in to the workshops or who had separate goals or were self-financed. Independent production companies such as Kuumba Productions, Anancy Films, Penumbra Productions and Social Film and Video were commissioned by the mainstream television industry to make individual films. There was also the occasional, low to medium budget (roughly between £0.5 and £3 million), relatively mainstream Black feature. One such example was the partially Channel 4-funded *Playing Away* (Dir. Horace Ove, 1986), a light-hearted dramatic comedy based on a Brixton cricket team in a rural English setting, representing a shift from the 'heavy', social-realist approach of the majority of earlier Black features.[4] Another was Menelik Shabazz's 1981 BFI-funded feature *Burning An Illusion*, which was unique in its central positioning of a Black female protagonist, but as Shabazz recalls, the film faced problems in terms of marketing and distribution: 'BFI marketing were not in tune with how to market the film . . . they didn't really have a clue' (Shabazz, *Black on Screen*, Radio 4, 15.01.01). There was also evidence of some emerging innovative short film work by British-Asian directors, most notably Suri Krishnamma's *Mohammed's Daughter* (1986) in association with the BBC, and Gurinder Chadha's BFI-funded first film, *I'm British But . . .* (1989). Both directors went on to direct popular television dramas and mainstream film features; Krishnamma with the BBC-funded *A Man of No Importance*, and Chadha with *Bhaji On The Beach* (both films were produced in 1994 and transmitted on Channel 4 in 1996).

Films such as *My Beautiful Laundrette* (Dir. Stephen Frears, 1985), Sankofa's *The Passion of Remembrance* (Dir. Isaac Julien and Maureen Blackwood, 1986), *Dreaming Rivers* (Dir. Martine Attille, 1988, Channel 4), *Territories* (Dir. Isaac Julien, 1984), *Testament* (Dir. John Akomfrah, 1989) and *Looking For Langston* (Dir. Isaac Julien, 1989), with their art-house feel, signalled a radical departure from the formal realist aesthetics and ideological constraints and conventions of dramatic or documentary realism(s), from the 'cinema of duty' films of the 1970s and from what mainstream British cinema was doing at this time. For example, *Handsworth Songs* (Dir. John Akomfrah/Black Audio Film Collective, 1986), Black Audio's first film, explicitly broke from the passive notion in the tradition of

British actuality programming of the camera as a tool of authority which was simply there to tell an objective truth. It shared many characteristics with a Third Cinema style: formal innovation, a break with an individual protagonist and conventional narrative, its connection to active liberation struggles, its invitation to the spectator/viewer as participant or comrade, its collective production process, and its opening up of dialogue between film-makers and theorists (see Pines and Willemen, 1989). *Handsworth Songs* unhinged the traditional race relations narrative by using a non-linear, layered texture with interweaving news footage from the 1985 Handsworth riots, archival newsreels of Black historiography and a general 'cut 'n' mix' style. In 'the struggle . . . to find a new language' (Hall in Mercer, 1988: 17), it developed various non-linear paths and alternative viewpoints, thus dislodging the central and marginal positions of subject and viewer, and offering a decisive change for audiences reared on monotone riot television documentaries.[5] For these reasons, and because of its dual exhibition space and redefinition of traditional racialized narratives, *Handsworth Songs* might be considered not just as 'Third Cinema', but also as 'Third Television'.

Although most of these films had both cinematic and television screenings, they also marked a shift from television to film as the key enunciator, as it had been for over four decades, of discourses around 'race'. Most Black independent filmmakers' working practices, thematic preoccupations and aesthetic approaches were now overwhelmingly different from those of the medium (television) that they now found themselves organizationally and materially bound to. The paradoxical circumstances involved here were obvious: not least that many Black filmmakers were clearly 'biting the hand that fed them', 'collaborating' with the ideologies of Thatcherism by fulfilling its enterprising needs, whilst also explicitly registering a critique of a Thatcherite Britain and, indeed, its impact on British culture (see Kureishi, 1988: 72–3). Kureishi's *My Beautiful Laundrette* (commissioned by Channel 4's Film Four International with a budget of £650,000), had been pivotal in foregrounding some of these debates around British national cinema,[6] and in addressing issues such as class, race, homosexuality, miscegenation and racism within a comi-tragic framework. Kureishi, in characteristic style, insisted that, 'At the moment, everything is so horrific that if you wrote straight social realism people wouldn't be able to watch it' (Kureishi, *Sight and Sound*, 1985/6: 67). In fact, the majority of 'practising' British-Asian filmmakers at this time were working in the documentary or social-realist tradition, highlighting just one of the many critical differences and similarities between and amongst the aesthetics of Asian and African-Caribbean film practitioners (*Living In Danger*, Dir. Ahmed A. Jamal/ Retake; screened on Channel 4/*Eleventh Hour*, 1984; *Hotel London*, Dir. Ahmed A. Jamal, BBC2, 1989; and *Majdhar*, Dir. Ahmed A. Jamal/Retake, Channel 4/ *Eleventh Hour*, 1985). Retake, as the first Asian film and video collective, became a fully franchized workshop in 1984 and defined itself as a group of Asians, 'who felt that there was an urgent need to challenge the stereotyped images of black people in the media' (*Majdhar* publicity leaflet), although, as I have argued elsewhere in direct reference to the assimilationist text of *Majdhar*, some of this 'oppositional' work was not exempt from reproducing orthodox stereotypes (see *Black Film Bulletin*: Navigations – Asian Diaspora Issue, Autumn 1994 Vol. 2, Issue 3 and Malik, 1996)

In a culture where diverse visual images of Blackness are so rare, many Black filmmakers did indeed find themselves weighed down by new pressures to accurately reflect 'the Black experience', or for not 'coming to any concrete solutions as to the way forward' (a criticism levelled at *Handsworth Songs* by a *Caribbean Times* critic, quoted in Petley, 1989: 261). In particular, realism was proving to be a particularly messy, 'can't live with/can't live without' exercise within the context of Black-produced work, highlighting how what was dominantly referred to as 'the realist aesthetic', also held its own limitations, contradictions and indeed, differences.[7] Many Black audiences were critical of being 'misrepresented', whilst also resenting that they could be represented in any one way. As John Akomfrah of Black Audio argued:

We knew that you can't just 'tell it like it is', that it wasn't just an ethnographic issue of finding hidden stories and making them available. That's what television had mainly done – to see race as the dark continent of our media culture, so that anything about black people becomes like a voyage of anthropological discovery. From the word go, there was always this tension between the desire to make a progressive cultural and political statement about race, and the desire to delineate a mode of practice which wasn't one anchored in conventional documentary or social-realist film-making. (Akomfrah in Petley, 1989: 261)

The 1988 'Black Film, British Cinema' Conference at London's Institute for Contemporary Arts was instrumental in highlighting some of the responses to the 'new wave' of Black-British film, a diverse and often contradictory critical reception that revealed four main things: first, that Black audiences were heterogeneous, active and sometimes resistant to formal innovation; secondly, 'the recognition of the extraordinary diversity of subjective positions, social experiences and cultural identities which compose the category 'black' (Hall in Mercer, 1988: 28); thirdly, that we had transcended the 'siege mentality which says that anything we do must be good' (Henriques in Mercer, 1988: 18); and finally, that the cinema had become, in Mercer's words, ' a crucial arena of cultural contestation' (Mercer, 1994: 73).[8] If we think about what was happening concurrently in terms of television-specific access, funding and anti-racist strategies during the 1980s, Black cinematic activity was being activated on two fronts: the first, was on the material side in relation to funding, distribution and exhibition; and the second, was over the question of aesthetics itself – of how new paradigms, languages and agendas could be formed through and within the new Black diasporic arts. Channel 4 also broadcast specific Black film seasons such as its Multicultural Film Season in November 1993, which screened non-British Asian films such as *Mississippi Masala* (Dir. Mira Nair, 1991) which had in fact been funded by Channel 4's Multicultural Department, *Electric Moon* (Dir. Pradip Krishens, 1990) and *Masala* (Dir. Srinivas Krishna, 1991). Many of these films would have often been missed at the cinema (often for distribution reasons or simply because they had only been granted a fleeting cinematic release), but were now being brought to viewers via television, making this an exciting opportunity for viewers and for Black film in general (which had always faced the problem of mainstream exhibition and audience-building) (see Fountain in Mercer, 1988: 42–4).

the demise of institutional backing   By the late 1980s, a number of public arts institutions had begun to feel the financial strain, and the 'cultural enterprise' was under threat from the commercial one. The knock-on effects of the Conservative Government's overriding hostility towards the public sector and its increasing stranglehold on public expenditure in general and on subsidies for the arts in particular (see pp. 16–21), led Channel 4, the BFI and other public institutions to reassess their commitment to the independent film and video sector. The very low-budget films (under about £1 million) which were usually those made by first-time directors and producers, now had to struggle to get meaningful distribution and thus, funders were less likely to recoup their investments and saw them as implicitly lacking in value. By 1990, the revenue funding of the film and video workshops had virtually ceased. Some workshops subsequently closed and others began to operate a mixed economy, relying partly on public grants, partly on earned commercial income. Nadine Marsh-Edwards describes how the Channel 4 bubble burst; ending the support that Sankofa had received from the Channel 4 Independent Film and Video Department:

> We were determined to make the best of it we could for as long as it lasted. We just didn't realise how quickly it was going to be over. . . .We suddenly kept being told about a 'mixed economy' and we had to learn a new 'Thatcher-speak' language.

> Funding for our infrastructure became less and less by the late 1980s. First the GLC funding stopped and then Channel 4 funding stopped around 1990. (Marsh-Edwards in Hood, 1994: 202–3).

The complex reasons for the demise of the Black workshops, and their partial continuation in updated forms, need to take account of wider cultural, political and economic shifts that led to the fragmentation of the independent workshop structure *in general*.[9] As such, they need to be considered as befitting and a success *for their time*, and for the critical momentum they triggered, the landmark theatrical releases (particularly *Handsworth Songs* and *The Passion of Remembrance*) they initiated, and for the avenues they opened for many of the practitioners involved in them (John Akomfrah, Isaac Julien and Nadine Marsh-Edwards for example).

The cultural, technological and economic impact in the 1990s of Britain's first explicitly commercial (satellite) broadcaster, BskyB, and cable (with entire channels dedicated to movies and pay-per-view systems), the growth of video retail, a fifth terrestrial channel with a film-heavy schedule, non-linear programming, video on demand and a general increase in the sophistication of visual home entertainment, posed vast competition to terrestrial television at large, and specifically to Channel 4's position as a core financier and exhibitor of film to British audiences. Meanwhile, in terms of the daily nuts-and-bolts of getting funding, the core financiers began to invest in more 'obvious' theatrical releases that would potentially reach an international audience (hence Film on Four International), and have a terrestrial and digital presence (Channel 4 set up its own pay-TV digital film company, the Film Four Channel in 1998). By the early 1990s, the cheaper (to produce and screen) short film format had become the dominant and most accessible form of film-making for Black-British practitioners (showcased in *He-Play/She-Play* (Channel 4), *Short and Curlies* (Channel 4), *10X10* (BBC2) and the late-night themed short-film zone *The Shooting Gallery* (Channel 4)) and various schemes such as *Black Screen/Siren Spirits* (BBC/BFI), *Synchro Projects* (Carlton Television/Arts Council) and Crucial Films' *Funky Black Shorts* and *Crucial Tales*, were specifically set up for Black-British filmmakers to work on short films for television. Alongside the television developments (and setbacks) of the 1990s, and despite the fact that Black-British films were still broadly perceived to be locked into the enemy of commercialism – culture – films such as *Who Needs A Heart* (Dir. John Akomfrah, 1991), *Welcome to the Terrordome* (Dir. Ngozi Onwurah, 1996, Channel 4), *Wild West* (Dir. David Attwood/1992; Scr. Harwant Baines, Channel 4, 1994), *Speak Like A Child* (Dir. John Akomfrah, 1998), *Babymother* (Dir. Julian Henriques/Parminder Vir, 1998), *Blue Notes and Exiled Voices* (Dir. Imruh Bakari, 1991), *Franz Fanon: Black Skin White*

Masks (Dir. Isaac Julien, 1997) and *Rage* (Dir. Newton L. Aduaka, 1999), did get made and the majority had a television connection. A handful of Channel 4 funded and screened features – *Young Soul Rebels* (Dir. Isaac Julien, Channel 4/BFI, 1991), *Bhaji On The Beach* (Dir. Gurinder Chadha, 1994, Scr. Meera Syal), and *East is East* (Dir. Damien O'Donnell, 1998, Scr. Ayub Khan Din) – became the first Black-British features since *My Beautiful Laundrette* to 'cross over' from relatively selective, small-scale, art-house audiences to larger, more varied, commercial and international ones (see Figures 7 and 8). But the resistance was often strong before the universal appeal of these films was proved. *East is East* for example, was rejected by the BBC on the grounds that it was 'too specific' in terms of style, content and address. David Thompson, Head of Films at the BBC who replaced Mark Shivas during negotiations over the BBC's investment in the project, said, 'this was a very risky project. It was set in the Seventies, it had uncertain international appeal and it had no stars' (quoted in the *London Evening Standard*, 2.12.99). *Bhaji* made Chadha the first British-Asian woman to direct a feature film in Britain, but years after its vast success, she was still

Figure 7

A scene from *Bhaji on The Beach* with Asha
(Lalita Ahmed) and Ambrose (Peter Cellier)

Courtesy of Channel 4 Picture Publicity

Figure 8

East is East, a shot of the cast

Courtesy of Channel 4 Picture Publicity

being sent 'things with Asians in or films about young girls being abused' (Chadha in Wambu and Arnold, 1999: 41).[10] Chadha looked towards the USA to fund her next feature, *What's Cooking?* (2000). Other British-Asian features such as *Brothers in Trouble,* (Dir. Udayan Prasad, 1995; in collaboration with BBC), *My Son, The Fanatic* (Dir. Udayan Prasad, 1997, Scr. Hanif Kureishi; in collaboration with BBC) and *Guru in Seven* (Dir. Shani Grewal, 1997; privately funded), also worked towards heightening the interest in British-Asian film, moderately helping to demarginalize (both critically and institutionally) a neglected area of cinema within an already culturally marginalized Black-British film sector.

In any case, the impact of these pivotal socio-economic shifts during the 1990s signalled something more general about the changing cultural politics of the time, and about where (and where not) financial and other institutional support was likely to be channelled in the future. The whole language of cultural representation was shifting towards institutionalizing 'manageable' levels of cultural diversity, whilst getting on with the really pressing matter of making money. Thus, the closure in September 1996 of the British Film Institute's African-Caribbean Unit headed by June Givanni, marked, in a sense, the end of an important phase, because it had been one of the few remaining institutional spaces specifically geared towards supporting the exhibition and production of Black-British and diaspora film.[11] The focus, as Givanni went on to observe, began to shift to the 'New Technology', as if 'black concerns are simply part of a pre-modern "politically-correct" world and therefore do not feature in the Future' (Givanni, 1996: 2). In fact, it was precisely those relegated to the margins who were beginning to make intelligent use of the new 'acultural' means of production and who now have the most to gain from the new digital technologies that offer the possibility of more complex representations of reality and narrative. As the penetration of new broadband technologies advances in the UK, as it has in the USA, the revolutionized modes of production, access and viewing, hold all kinds of prodigious opportunities for the viewer and the 'independent' producer. Besides, this arrogation identified by Givanni, was also to be directly contradicted by the end of the decade in the reinscription of 'cultural diversity' strategies by those same organizations that had abated Black-arts support just a few years earlier (BFI, Channel 4, BBC for example). It was now being acknowledged that the social is in fact, deeply tied to the economic; hurrying the need to remanage and reincorporate diversity into the global marketing plan and brand identity of corporate arts manifestos – the BFI with its Towards Visibility campaign, Channel 4 with its pan-channel multicultural remit, the BBC with its various diversity 'champions' and accompanying strategies, and collectively with the Cultural Diversity Network (see pp. 10–11). In April 2000, the Film Council, a National Lottery and Treasury-funded organization (which has amalgamated the Arts Council of England, the British Film Commission, British Screen and funds BFI production) was established. It has a responsibility to encourage both commercial and cultural film activity, and has a declared commitment to cultural diversity and directly targeting under-represented groups. Parminder Vir, who began her media career in 1978 as an Arts Administrator with the Minority Arts Advisory Service and who now sits on the Film Council Board of Members, insists that the Film Council's New Cinema and Development Funds will be critical in supporting the future of Black British film (Vir at 'What's Cooking in the UK Film Industry', National Film Theatre, 4.11.00). One hopes that these moves will prove to be committed beyond the level of unifying image and multicultural conventionalism and will differ from the 'exposure to new cultures' ethos behind many of the multicultural manifestos of the 1970s and 1980s which often only cared to elevate the kinds of difference that didn't really make a difference.

Black filmmakers today are still considered as 'minority artists', not an easy position from which to negotiate when trying to survive in the free market, a US-dominated marketplace and alongside notions of 'typical' British cinema. The major question today is 'Who is going to watch these films?' – a question with direct reference to audience-size, ratings and box-office success and directly related to the vexed issue of distribution. It would appear that we have come full circle in relation to film; without public funds, many of today's Black-British filmmakers are being forced to subsidize their own productions or move beyond Britain's shores, just as the Black-British filmmakers of the 1960s and 1970s were inclined to do. There is a legacy of Black-British talent, from Errol John to Calvin Lockhart through to Thandie Newton, Adrian Lester and Gurinder Chadha, who have turned their sights to the US for recognition. As Lester, who as a virtual unknown starred in Mike Nichol's *Primary Colors* (1998) alongside John Travolta puts it, 'It's a shame that in order to get a career, I had to go to America' (Lester, *Black on Screen*, Radio 4, 15.01.01). Where big money is involved, there still remains a deep-seated anxiety about the presence of Blackness, particularly when it comes to globally marketing this as part of the national story: the thought of an all-Black *The Full Monty* (Dir. Peter Cattaneo, 1997) (written about a group of Black male strippers but ended up including only one) was too much to bear for Britain's film executives; Channel 4's *Notting Hill* (Dir. Roger Michell, 1999) was set in a highly-populated Black area but hardly a Black person was seen. It is now well known that in 1997, Marianne Jean-Baptiste, who had just been nominated for an Oscar, BAFTA and Golden Globe for her performance as Hortense in Mike Leigh's *Secrets and Lies* (1996), spoke out about the White bias of the industry when she was excluded from a 'networking' trip to Cannes organized by *British Screen*. No other Black actors were invited. At the time she said, 'If you think about it, I made history. Not only was I the first black British woman to be nominated for an Oscar, I was the first black British person.' Simon Perry, the chief executive of British Screen commented, 'There were people who in terms of credits had the edge. Everybody has their *pet omission*' (quoted in *Guardian*, 15.5.97; my emphasis). If these 'pet omissions' continue, we will keep seeing these patterns of exclusion (see Jean-Baptiste interview in *Independent on Sunday*, 14.2.99), and if you don't make Black people into stars or sought-after directors, there will be an ongoing absence of Black people involved in the star-dependent projects which dominate the schedules and cinemas today.

notes

1 Norman Beaton was named Best Actor by the Variety Cub of Great Britain for his performance in *Black Joy*.

2 According to Imruh Bakari *Pressure* 'was considered to be a bad representative of Britain or unrepresentative of Black life in Britain or a British response to Black life. . . . Then Notting Hill happened and everybody else said "Oh, we'd better look at *Pressure* then, *Pressure* is mild considering what happened down in The Grove in those few years"' (Bakari, interview with author, 10.12.96).

3 Black-British films screened in these two strands, included *On Duty* (Cassie McFarlane, 1984), the four-part *Struggles For Black Community* (Colin Prescod, 1982), *I Am Not Two Islands* (Milton Bryan, 1984), *Flame in my Heart* (Ruhul Amin, 1984) and *They Haven't Done Nothing* (Liverpool Black Media Group, 1985).

4 Despite this, Barry Norman on reviewing the film argued that Horace Ove, 'is black and he knows about black people but he does not know about white people' (quoted by Ove in Mercer, 1988: 57). If nothing else, this comment revealed the level of White, mainstream arts criticism.

5 For a range of responses to the film see Mercer (1988: 16–18) and particularly the debate between Rushdie and Hall in the *Guardian*.

6 Stephen Frears has argued that by allowing Channel 4 to fund *My Beautiful Laundrette*, more people got a chance to see it (Howkins, 'Edinburgh Television' *Sight and Sound* 54, 4, 1985, 238–9).

7 For more on conventions of realism, see Comolli and Narboni in Nichols (1976: 23–30), and Colin MacCabe 'Realism and the Cinema: Notes on some Brechtian Theses' in Bennett et al., 1981, 216–35).

8 Black-British film continues to be a central focal point in a number of conferences, special seasons and festivals including the Bristol-based Black Pyramid Festival, the Bite The Mango Festival in Bradford and at selected forums in the Birmingham International Film and Video Festival. In December 1995, the ICA screened a retrospective of Black-British film and video entitled 'From Pressure to Terrordome'. *See London Film and Video News* (Issue 5: Nov/Jan 96), a report by the LFVDA which is supported by the BFI, Channel 4 and Carlton Television and operates the London Production Fund.

9 Some of the original workshops such as Black Audio Film Collective, Sankofa Film and Video and Star Productions continued to operate as production companies.

10 In 1995, Chadha received the acclaimed *Evening Standard* award for 'Best Newcomer' for *Bhaji*. Channel 4's screening of *Bhaji on the Beach* got 2.1 million viewers (source: BARB/BFI) and ran for an unprecedented (for a British-Asian film) number of weeks (approx 15) in cinemas across London's West End.

11 The BFI's African-Caribbean Unit was formed in 1991, with an initial brief to organize the 1992 'Black and White in Colour' conference. *The Black Film Bulletin* which was launched in 1993 by June Givanni and Gaylene Gould, and which has been a vital source of information, debate and exchange for those interested in British and international Black film, continues today (under different editorship).

the struggle for meanings of 'blackness': summary and conclusion

It is too late in the day to get worked up about it or to blame others, much as they deserve such blame and condemnation. What we need to do is to look back and try to find out where we went wrong, where the rain began to beat us. (Achebe in Killam, 1977)

Nigerian writer, Chinua Achebe, speaking here about the postcolonial enterprise, notes the potential value of historical work. Whilst all 'looking back' is essentially interpretative, it seems clear to me that television, far from being 'free' and independent, actively racially organizes, constructs a reality and 'neutrality' of its own, and always makes active choices and judgements about who, what and how to represent. We can as such speak of a racialized cultural politics that functions through television as a significant form of public pedagogy. These race narratives are polysemous in nature, but when coupled with ideas of Blackness, signify key moments in the 'racialization' of British society; moments when the presence of 'race' itself has been realized. When we 'unpack' this history, we can see how the pervasiveness of this racial binding (Blackness) and exnomination (Whiteness) has also allowed such racial 'common sense' to largely go unquestioned.[1] Television, as a powerful conveyor of the imagined community of the nation, fluctuates between two models – a comforting realm of social Whiteness, and more recently, a unified cultural diversity in which multiculturalism seems perfectly well 'reflected'. These two trajectories mark a broader confusion when addressing ethnic difference and sameness, and when faced with competing economic (commercial pressure) and cultural (ethnic-minority cultural politics, public service) demands. I want to use this final chapter to draw some overall conclusions.

As we have seen, these meanings around 'race' are never fixed and are always changing, but then 'culture' itself is always in motion and is always a potential site of struggle. This makes it difficult to identify a simple progress model in representations of 'Blackness' on British television. We are not talking about a television society that is more or less racist now compared to then; we are experiencing different approaches, languages and ideologies around race, but ones, as I have been arguing, that are still governed by television's 'official' public service needs as dictated by conservative and neoliberal ideologies. Whilst we may now live in a media society that will no longer comfortably tolerate Alf Garnett, *Love Thy Neighbour* or outright racist casting, we are also in one that continues to accommodate anti-Black political party television campaigns, a hugely disproportionate level of White decision-makers, a fervent and unchallenged investment in Black-free heritage texts, and poorly marketed, scheduled and funded Black-based production. Given the changing notions of 'acceptability', in 20 years' time one hopes that our contemporary media society will be seen as antiquated and objectionable, or at least as confused and contradictory, as was the one which allowed *The Black and White Minstrel Show*, *Mind Your Language* and poorly-disguised institutional disregard. It becomes easier to identify how such public racisms work in hindsight. Whilst today's systematic televisual multiculturalism might make it impossible to speak of a 'colour-line' as identified by Du Bois in 1903 as *the* problem of the twentieth century, the fact of these ongoing racial patterns and the struggle over signs of Blackness in the public sphere, signal that we are yet to see the genuine and effortless ideological acceptance and no-nonsense delivery of cultural diversity for us all. The seemingly broad and racially-free range of Black images that television offers us today – the verifiably multicultural *Top of the Pops*; the nation's favourite newsreader, Sir Trevor McDonald; Trisha Goddard, a Black British-born presenter on her morning confessional show; Frank Bruno, the quintessence of pantomimic television light entertainment; Ainsley Harriott, the ubiquitous TV chef – all these characters appear to confirm us as a media society based around acceptance and meritocracy. But behind this panorama of ever more normalized multiculturalism lies a cycle of racial codes, preferred readings, blocked access, and a profoundly uneven multiculturalism, laced with a liberal claim to 'show it like it is'. The incontestability has intensified over the years, making new racist meanings increasingly difficult to pin down, as television confronts us with progressively more coded and yet seemingly neutral patterns of raced representation.

If we were to stand back from the detail, we can draw some overall conclusions. The first, is that African-Caribbeans are mostly seen in social issue discourses, music and light entertainment, sports and comedy. The second, is that Black people in general are less often seen in one-off dramas, major roles, big-budget landmark productions, British films, and non-'race-related' documentaries and news stories, or in positions of expertise (as sports, lifestyle, financial, cultural or political analysts) (see Cumberbatch et al., 2000). And the third, is that Asians, on the whole, are more usually marked by their absence. A Broadcasting Standards Commission report in

2000, found that 32 per cent of Asian representation on ITV was accounted for by one Asian newsreader (Shulie Ghosh) and one Asian character in *Coronation Street* (Vikram Desai). Even on BBC2, one of the two 'alternative channels', it was found that 97 per cent of speaking parts were White and only one per cent was Asian. Similar results were found across all the terrestrial channels (Patrick Younge, *Media Guardian*, 20.10.00). What is clear, is that Asians have largely been understood and characterized by way of 'ethnicity' and through its associated connotations of religion, customs and culture (immigrant Other, culturally alien, religious fundamentalist). If Asians have attracted more culturalist forms of thinking, African-Caribbeans have tended to bring out and reinforce the biological racism in the popular imagination (although of course, these biological and culturalist racisms often cross each other's paths; for example, biological assumptions about Asian athleticism and defensive ability, pathologized notions of Black culture). The excess representation of African-Caribbeans in sport, light entertainment and to an extent, comedy, supports the very idea of 'race' which hinges on the biological notion of 'advantage' as inscribed through signs of the ultra-Black body. The 'disadvantage' comes forth in the discourses of truth such as news, documentary and certain kinds of drama and film. It is precisely this split between body and mind, superiority and inferiority, excess and lack, which positions and maintains 'Blackness' as 'different', exceptional, and as poles apart in either direction from the White norm. These doubly-codified, mutually-compatible expectations of Blackness in relation to its 'advantages' and 'disadvantages', run deep through the very centre of British television, and are perfectly capable of emerging out of the same/different historical moments, using the same/ different representational language and of operating within and across different genres and discourses. We can note that the body genres depend more on the mechanical processes of reflecting 'lived cultures' (dancefloor trends, the music charts, sports and fashion, subcultural style) and actual performance (albeit extremely mediated and often Americanized), compared with news, documentary and drama (which, as we know, more vigorously mediate and set the agenda themselves and in ways that *they* consider appropriate). So when more deliberate, conscious, boardroom decisions have to be made about presenting or reflecting Black people in less obvious spaces, where they play less definite roles and where they are assumed to be unnaturally placed, there still remains a certain amount of restraint, awkwardness or ratings-anxiety. Or we witness attempts, particularly in integrationalist films and dramas, to 'smooth out' difference, to the extent where the writers or directors have been so preoccupied with making their Black characters 'noble', 'proud', 'good' or 'non-stereotypical', that they forgot to make them into characters or avoid making them 'too Black' (either culturally or physically). It is no surprise then, that emanating from the entrenched tolerant centre of these typically White boardrooms, there has be en a strong tendency to avoid the subject of race altogether; this has been the polite liberal response underpinning a prevailing discomfort over the apparently difficult matter of 'race'. This is precisely how ideas of racial difference manifest themselves on screen; through the dual strategies of stereotyping and exclusion, or what James Snead, in his discussion of Black representation in film termed, *marking* and *omission* (Snead, 1994). The struggle over these meanings of 'race', participated in by Blacks and Whites, viewers and producers, can be seen in the various assimilationist, ethnically-idealized pluralist tolerant White-exclusive and multiculturalist discourses that dominate racialized narratives on television.

We can compare the main stereotypes of Asian femininity (oppressed, passive, exotic), with those of African-Caribbean femininity (sexual, aggressive, predatory) and the main stereotypes of Asian masculinity (patriarchal, timid, assiduous, orthodox), with those of African-Caribbean (hyper) masculinity (criminal, violent, feckless, sexual). The recurrence of these 'raced' and indeed 'gendered' motifs, although they often vary from their modern and traditional forms, do not always depend on the 'negative' and each 'type' can contain apparently contradictory and opposing qualities. Representation, and for that matter, stereotypes, is the making of someone into something unreal – good or bad; it is quite possible to be adored *and* violated, excluded *and* objectified, to be treated as inclusive *and* Other, *and* for these processes to work contiguously both in a multiracial society and within representation. Racisms then, are not always about stereotyping, marking and abjecting; they are also about omitting (heritage texts), excluding (public debates) and misrecognizing (Black-British youth cultures). In terms of Black representation, it is often an either/or game, so that, for example, the premium placed on Black-British youth today (in adverts, sports-style, youth presenters, music chart shows), is expected to serve as a substitute (for it is always one thing *or* another) for an extreme and prevailing ageism (and classism and sexism) that exists towards Britain's older Black communities who, after all, probably have the biggest backlog of stories to tell and views to express not least about the Black-British experience (see Beryl Gilroy in Owusu, 2000: 122–132). My basic point here is that it is necessary to talk of multiple, varied Black representations, but also to trace their connections. The *timing* of the intensified use and production of the raced stereotype is of particular importance. Discourses around Otherness and difference often become increasingly intensified in moments of crisis, anxiety or when the concept of White nationhood itself appears to be under threat (culturally different 'outsiders' during the 1960s anti-immigration period; Islamaphobia during and after the Rushdie affair; Linford Christie following his 1992 Olympic Gold success; Black youth during the 1981 Brixton riots coverage; reaffirmations of nationhood and

Euroscepticism in the midst of refugees seeking asylum at the turn of this century; a re-emphasis on Black (racist) crime in the post-Macpherson period). Such responses converge and project society's fears and fantasies onto the racial Other at times when it is perceived that there is 'the most to lose', which adds to the complexity of how 'Blackness' is 'Other-ed' because it casts doubt on the supposition that Black stereotypes are unconscious, causeless and unintentional.

the liberal impulse   Having said that, conspiracy theories cannot explain so systematic a pattern. As I have been arguing, the schemes of Black categorization that we find in British television are both arbitrary and imposed, and the influences of patterns of choice around ideologies of 'race' are not a one-way process – they are certainly not simply the reinforcing of pre-existing views, images or ideologies into a passive culture by the image-makers. We have in fact seen that the medium is a significant site of struggle, conflict, and sometimes even agreement between those with often wildly differing viewpoints. Culture itself, the individuals who 'inhabit' it and the cultural industries which shape it, are all caught up in a complex 'feed-back loop', with no visible beginning or end, no part of which itself can be con-sidered in isolation. Thus, the circulation of racist discourses – or discourses which open themselves up to racist readings – are not necessarily the result of racist-minded producers, although they can be directed by a lack of indi-vidual and institutional racial awareness, by the medium's intercommunica-tion with other élite groups in society, by positioning the national audience as White, and by racially-based assumptions and fears. (Racist) meaning, like (racist) ideology, is a complex of ideas, facts and explanations and is part of this complicated signifying system of representation. Since it is not reducible to the overt intentions of its producers, nor to any simple or singular set of audience effects, ideological production and circulation can-not be considered solely in terms of a monolithic, static White 'ruling-class' (although in respect to British television, it is mostly staffed by an 'élite' of White, English, middle-class, men), dominating 'the rest'. (In any case, White middle-class masculinity, like racisms, Britishness and Blackness, is a continuing social formation that also struggles over meanings of Blackness.) There have also been a number of non-Black cultural insiders – John Hopkins, John Elliot, Peter Ansorge, David Rose, Tony Garnett, Tony Marchant, Charlie Hanson and Humphrey Barclay, to name but a few – who have worked against the grain and invested in Black stories and talent. The questions we need to keep asking are: Who has the power within the text to be liberal or tolerant? Who has the power to choose the object of discussion? Who has the power to look? Whose common sense is followed? What kinds of (alternative) images are tolerated? Who is signified as the racial Other? And more obviously, who is the narrator, the interviewer, the central character, the writer, the policy-maker and so on? In short, who holds the symbolic power and how is ethnicity used?

The main ground for this struggle has been 'liberalism'. 'Good, liberal intentions', the dominant paradigm through which British broadcasting works (institutionalized in terms of regulation, personnel, policy, structure, modes of address, subject-matter), can be shared by apparently disparate thinkers: racists, anti-racists, conservatives, assimilationists, social pluralists, and so on. It says, 'we have Black people living in Britain and we need to consider what impact they are having on our society'. Behind this liberal voice, there is usually a well-meaning impetus, driven by inclusionary notions based around solidarity, communality and welfarism, as seen for example in the social documentaries and dramas of the 1960s by the likes of John Elliot, Philip Donnellan and John Hopkins. But the powers and pleasures of liberal intent do not assure a definite anti-racist reading – and we have seen this in some detail in relation to *Fable, The Negro Next Door, Jewel In The Crown* and *Till Death Us Do Part*. The tricky issue here is that the sentimental, nostalgic and parochial uses and effects of this liberalism can, in fact, work to sustain more discriminatory and individualistic sensibilities by shaping and policing the grounds of tolerability, community and expediency. Classic liberal thinking allows extreme Right broadcasts, but not Prolife ones (see pp. 81–3); it commissions diversity manifestos that are also usually drawn, overseen and delivered by Whites; it has a moral objection to 'strong' religious beliefs and aspects of minority cultures (notably British Muslims by way of the Rushdie affair and other popular images of Islam) when they do not coincide with Western freedom and 'tolerance'; it locates the extreme-Right and anti-racists on the same racist plane; it embarks on anthropological enquiries which dominantly position Black people as objects not subjects; it is discursive and speaks on behalf of 'the victims'; it positions television as the middle ground between what *it* defines as 'the extremes'; it is sometimes too polite to say 'race' and 'Black'. In 'dealing with' 'race problems' and in roughly the same way, mainstream television heightens its self-image of moral integrity and fair-mindedness, which is central to its public service obligations. Liberalism is concerned with optimism and the belief that tolerance will prevail, and works *through* notions of impartiality and independence in order to support itself. Liberalism never *seems* to interfere, but always shapes the underlying agenda and defines the limits of 'the normal' in such a way as to confirm its democratic status: it does what we might colloquially call 'sitting on the fence', teetering between overemphasizing to ignoring the presence of race. As Parekh and Bhabha argue, 'Liberalism has always remained assimilationist: others must becomelike us, my present is your future. It has always remained profoundly fundamentalist' (Parekh and Bhabha, 1989). According to Stuart Hall, the liberal consensus is, 'the linch-pin of . . . "inferential racism". It is what keeps active and organized racism in place' (Hall, 1981: 48). This is not to collapse a racialized regime underpinned by liberalism into one occupied by the radical or racist Right, nor to collapse reformism into racism, but simply to say that liberalism, by definition, is neither defiantly radical nor effectively anti-racist – this is neither its achievement, nor its goal, but it can be its limitation.

social whiteness   Like other areas of public and political life such as the press, education, arts and science, early British television took on the heritage of what I have been describing as cultural and social Whiteness, based around the presumption that the racial characteristics of Whiteness are unobvious and thus 'belong' unproblematically (at least in terms of race) to society. We have, throughout this study, encountered how this hegemonic racialized structure sustains itself predominantly through the medium's iterative discourses of family, nation and citizenship. This is so important, because it is how televisualization mobilizes and presents itself as a united 'we'; it is how it speaks to the nation as part of that unifying cultural project. One of the ways this discourse of Whiteness hegemonizes itself, is by assuming the racial (White) homogeneity of the British television nation, which goes far to explain the racially specific, exclusionary and binary (either White or not) logic of its modes of address (as seen in separatist discourses such as traditional multicultural programmes for example). This is what I mean by 'when the presence of "race" itself has been realized', because the normalizing of Whiteness and the projection of 'difference' onto Black communities alone has made television an active player in the development of 'race' as a trope relevant, in the main, to non-White groups – wherever Blackness is not, is where Whiteness, its imaginary opposite, takes its place. Whilst Black people have been racialized in representation, White people have been shown to have no obvious race to represent, rarely been directed to think of themselves as also having a racial identity, or as helping to construct 'the problem'. They have simply been asked to acknowledge the newest 'racial situation', try to understand it, and then come to terms with the growing crisis that is presumed to accompany it (think for example, about the response to 'inner city riots', or the public rhetoric around Kosovar asylum-seekers since 1999 which has largely failed to connect the situation to Britain's role in the Balkan crisis). Whiteness, after all, is to be found everywhere and nowhere. It is all and nothing: all, because it is everywhere to be found and assumed to be the norm; nothing, because it is presumed to be nowhere in particular, inconspicuous by its presence and not requiring to be 'marked'. It follows then, that 'the Black presence' has been aligned with 'race relations' and, in turn, racial tension, race rows, race riots, and now, allegedly, racial sensitivity, racial political correctness, racial preference and racial rights. These have been seen to be directly *caused* by the presence of 'Blackness' – not by historical context, structural inequality or racist attitudes, but by Others' ethnic specificity.

This collective and individual sociological burden of 'race' manifests itself in all kinds of ways – in White people's expectations of the types of programmes a Black person can and should make, in the agendas of cultural workers, in the way a text is received and contested, in how Black characters are drawn, and of course in how 'Blackness', 'Britishness' and 'Whiteness' are known. Struggles to reinforce, break or negotiate this prevailing logic, has characterized the ongoing dialogue around race and representation, and seen new interventions and deliberate reconfigurations of the proverbial 'negative Black stereotype'. That it is to say, it has been reverberated, worked through, troped and challenged. I have in mind productions and characters such as *Fable, Empire Road, Goodness Gracious Me, Ali G, Prime Suspect 2, Bhaji on the Beach* and *This Life* which, in vastly different ways, visually rework official race narratives and thus manage to keep the representation open, allowing more than one way of knowing and visualizing 'Blackness', 'Asianness' and for that matter, Britishness. But we also know that the processes of cultural negotiation involved in reading 'dominant' and 'alternative' texts demand more or lesser degrees of 'work', perhaps more when we read a comedy character like Ali G or watch *Goodness Gracious Me*, than when we watch the news coverage of inner-city riots. If we are raised on an ideological and inter-textual diet of television drama, documentaries and news reports showing us Black people as dysfunctional, reactive and/or bordering on criminality within the language of a 'reality text' and across genres, we are left with less space to contest the representation or the way in which the image has been racialized. This becomes the grand narrative and the backdrop of 'truth' which all other representations (even if they are more pertinent or representative) are read against. The power of decades of reductionist images of Blackness represented as and taken as 'truth', although often based on little more than easily palatable myths, serves to locate the majority of alternative representations and/or anti-racist strategies not only as transgressive but as essentially preferential, provocative and unrepresentative. Think for example of the nervous institutional responses to *Pressure, Grove Music, The People's Account* or *Blacks Britannica*, or the perceived 'bias' of *It Ain't Half Racist, Mum* or *Southall On Trial* (or of the later public reactions to the Commission for Racial Equality's anti-racist publicity campaigns in the 1990s or the Runnymede Trust's Report in 2000). The active role of the television institutions themselves via its key decision-makers, in determining what is deemed expedient, too provocative or unacceptably opinionated has a profound effect on how the perceptions and prejudices of what is 'central' and what is 'marginal' are organized within our society.

If this cultural territory of Whiteness maintains itself through this universalization and naturalization (Gabriel in Cottle, 2000: 67–82), then it processes Others' 'racial difference' through assorted cultural and ideological practices such as spectacle, objectification, desire, envy, fantasy, exclusion, nostalgia and selection. Nostalgia for example is everywhere to be found on British television: in heritage-texts, in historical reviews, in television retrospectives, in rural-based dramas, in law and order discourses, in social problem narratives, and so on. It attempts to summon an irretrievable past as catharsis and solicit an undiluted condition before 'race' became an issue, when we know of course that Britain's past was racially-divided and imbued with identity struggles and cultural diversity well before the postwar years when the more obvious Black presence was accredited with 'dividing' Britishness. The pretence of pre-Black cultural homogeneity is an evocative central part of the British national story. This social Whiteness also has real, lived effects on where talent is nurtured (see Chapters 8 and 9). The BBC's TV60 celebrations (BBC1, 1996), which commemorated the sixtieth year of British television, acclaimed almost without exception, the work of White (mostly male) BBC stars and programmes, with only a cursory and awkwardly-placed acknowledgement of the work of Lenny Henry – the only Black star it could boast in its 60-year history. Similarly, the results of the BFI's industry-wide poll of favourite television programmes, BFITV100 (announced in 2000) saw virtually no programmes with a Black presence (www.bfi.org.uk). We are talking here about very prolific and unnatural absences and silences in television history.

If we think through 'social Whiteness' chronologically, we can roughly identify three phases. The formative years of television (up to the 1970s) saw the erasure of points of views that were not White and television adopt an inclusionary notion of White nationhood in which the Black subject was posed in relation to and a social referent to be explained to 'White society' (for example, a victim of a menace to/reacting against/unassimilable within). This double marginalization of the Black social subject – as: one, the 'victim' of bigotry, racism and intolerance; and two, of their own alienation and marginalization within the race-related narrative – was a key feature and central strain of early Black representation. The ideological trope of the Black 'social problem' was, often with the best liberal intentions, seen as a predicament that needed to be reformed or 'solved' in order to make society and 'race relations' 'better'. White characters and settings were often depicted as 'put upon', agitated or unnerved by an alien, disturbing or forced Black presence (a Black neighbour, or Black son-in-law, or Black employee), or by an attack on the senses (new musical sounds, new odours, new foods, new languages, new colours). When racism was identified, it was usually emptied out of its political meaning by being focused on the personal dynamics of discrimination (*A Man From The Sun* (1956), *Hot Summer Night* (1959) and *The Negro Next Door* (1965) for example). It was generally depicted as violent or explicit, typically in a working-class, uneducated, ignorant form, but seldom as institutional, referential, subtle or middle class. Thus the working-class neighbours' open racism, the 'working man's' humour of Bernard Manning and his ilk, the unsubtle bigotry of Alf Garnett, became easy and obvious targets and spaces where we could pinpoint British racism, whilst the customary inferential racism of the middle-of-the-road, middle-class presenter would slip by virtually unnoticed.

The second shift in the cultural leadership of 'social Whiteness', although not totally unsettled by the emerging forces of 'multiculturalism', did see important challenges posed to it. The battle for access and funding during the 1970s and 1980s, in order to mobilize shifts from a third to first person position, from the object to the subject – to become an accessed voice – helped to forge important alternative spaces such as specialist multicultural programming and Channel 4. These advances also produced new challenges over the question of individualism versus collectivism; of whether one can actually represent (speak of/for) a lot of essentially different people with some overlapping interests/experiences at any one time. From how we should label ourselves, to what we should expect from Black creative artists, to how Black communities should be represented, to whether we should have specialist units (and if so what they should be called and whom they should address), the dialogical interplay between aspects of heterogeneity and homogeneity had become *the* bone of contention in debates around race, representation and political action during the 1980s. Whilst some of these counterhegemonic responses were critical for repositioning the Black subject, for recycling knowledge, for highlighting that meaning is never fixed and has the power to be renegotiated and 'trans-coded', much of the output had limited circulation and did not, in a broad sense, attract attention beyond the cultural critic, the 'minority viewer', and the already 'converted'. 'Alternative representations', as I have argued, were always battling against general 'mainstream' public opinions, and positioned as an add-on to the more general consensus and to a supposedly neutral flow of programming.

The third, most recent phase, has seen on the one hand, the unsettling of social Whiteness and some important signs of new, confident Black-British ethnicities playing out their influence on the nation, but on the other, the resurgence of new forms of nationalist discourse which call upon the 'authenticity' of Britain as an 'essentially' White nation. Today we can probably speak of heightened awareness and agree that there is *more* Black representation and that, broadly speaking, the types of image we now see are more diverse and not solely based on the folklore of the Black problematic.

By the late 1980s, we began to see the general look of mainstream British television become more pluralist and the medium increasingly narrating itself as 'multi this-and-that', with social acceptability becoming broader within 'ordinary' public life. Three main factors – the critical turn raised by the new debates around Black representation, diaspora art and realism; the new commercialism triggered by advanced technologies, globalization and deregulation; and the more obvious and permanent sense of Britain as a multiracial society (advanced by all kinds of changes related to demographics, economic power and an increasingly style-based culture) – amalgamated into what we could call 'the commercialization of multiculturalism', a badge of honour and innovation which is celebrated in the manifestos and by the culturecrats of all arts organizations today. There are two additional points to reiterate here: the first, is that there still remains a Black exceptionalism factor, with the individual successes of Black personalities as exceptions to the more general rule of Black absence and marginalization; the second, is that these signs of Black achievement are mutually developing alongside continuing forms of everyday racism. This is the basis of the widening chasm between those Black-Britons reaching positions of exclusivity (through public acts of style and celebrity), and those that continue to be excluded at a more grass-roots level within British society and, for that matter, within television's representational hierarchy.

Besides, in characteristically capricious style, we have also seen British popular culture since the 1990s (drama, documentaries, chat/game shows and British cinema) develop a new tolerance and taste for visions of Whiteness. The emphasis on bankable stars, high-profile personalities and on accessible, unchallenging and risk-free programming has, in other senses, narrowed the scope for representing cultural diversity. The rise of the cult of the White, masculine, 'ordinary', cloned personality in the form of 'the new laddism' for example, is respectabilized and feted by a certain middle-class populism and assented precisely because 'he' appears to 'balance out' the supposed gains of 'minority groups'. This new, persistent, sociocultural discourse (*The Full Monty, loaded* magazine, Frank Skinner, Chris Evans, Guy Ritchie, football hooliganism, Euro 1996 and 2000 as random examples), has overtones of racism and sexism cloaked as traditionalism, and relays important messages about inclusion, citizenship and about the imagined mappings of nationhood. It also satisfies the growing 'tabloidization' and 'lifestyling' by successfully drawing in the viewers, appealing to popular sensibilities and verifiably encapsulating as big a niche market as possible.[2] We have seen this 'new laddism' in Chris Evans' recurrent lampooning of Black people in his weekly show, *TFI Friday* (Channel 4) ('Cedric's Comment from the Café', 'Asian Lookalikes', 'The Plunging Asian Shopkeepers of Britain'); in Richard Littlejohn's[3] populist vitriol against all who are not White, male or heterosexual; in Jeremy Clarkson (*Clarkson*, BBC2, 1999–), who earns simultaneous support and affectionate disdain for his chauvinistic comments; in Gary Bushell's constant derision of 'loony leftism' and 'multiculturalism' as a threat to 'good old British values' (*The Trial of Enoch Powell, Bushell on the Box*); and in sports quizzes which boyishly poke fun at the physique of Black athletes.[4] This backlash phenomenon, securely positioned in the mainstream, reflects a new thirst to speak 'uncut', for the supposed majority, and outside 'the new conformism': that is, to produce anything that is antithetical to 'political correctness' whilst also daring the 'thought-police' to back-up any evidence of 'racism'. The convergence of this kind of middle ground entertainment-focused culture across the channels has reduced the range of spaces where 'alternative' voices can be heard.

television, power and industry needs   These are broad conclusions in a history that has accommodated further deep contradictions, but they do help us to locate and think through the kinds of complicated issues we are up against here. In this moment of frantic diversity-conscious policy, the past (and its various 'integrationalist', 'multicultural', 'anti-racist' strategies) serves as a useful reminder that paper-driven directives cannot simply be taken at face-value or singularly eliminate other burdens – of representation, audience-response, subject-matter, ratings and cultural value. Most broadcasting policies on race, although well meaning, are not just often difficult to implement, but also easy to dodge. Just as the interests and agendas of (Black and White) programme-makers do not always correspond with those of the viewing public, so the concerns of the power-brokers and the policy-makers do not guarantee appropriate or meaningful intervention in representing cultural diversity. Of course, you cannot 'solve' racism in a manifesto any more than you can in a television programme, but those involved in the sector who have sat through dozens of conferences, seminars and 'special events' on 'Black representation', 'Black intervention' and the newest industry-commissioned reports, know how little the subject of discussion (training, funds, access) and source of discontent (racist attitudes and expectations, few Black decision-makers, poor funding) has progressed. We are so uncertain about the future, because we are so used to seeing a lack of, or a sluggish pace of change. As the former Chairman of the law-enforcing CRE, Herman Ouseley, stated in his frustrated address to a number of influential broadcasters in 1996:

At the end of the day the CRE cannot do anything: it is down to you, the people in television that make the decisions . . . but I am making it quite clear to you today, and

> this is a promise, that the CRE will be coming after some of you. I am told by some of my advisors you cannot formally investigate television companies and their casting practices. But we *can* investigate the way in which contracts are given out, we *can* investigate the way in which deals are being done. (CRE, 1996: 31–2)

The question of how global cultural flows are likely to 'work with' and have an impact on differences, national-identities, nation-states and Black diasporic communities is now of foremost concern. For everyone who argues that a global media future will dismantle space and disrupt time, connect nations and their peoples, and celebrate diversity and difference (McNeill, 1994; Young, 1996; CRE, 1996), there is someone else ready to argue that it will merely bring about an erosion of that which distinguishes the local, global and national (Ross, 1996: 172). The main issue, with respect to our concerns, is whether or not these changes will encourage a homogenizing global postmodern shift towards and within cultural representations and organizations, and a 'downgrading of cultural specificity in themes and settings and a preference for formats and genres which are thought to be more universal' (McQuail, 1994: 112). We are already witnessing how the new cultural scene is facilitating what Schlesinger terms 'identity by choice' (Schlesinger, 1991), where communal values related to ethnicity or religion are being reflected in and forged out of and across diverse TV channel options, posing further questions about whether, 'with greater transnational communication, the identities of individuals may be determined more by economic, political and cultural communities, than by nations' (Richards and French, 1996: 36–7).

We are left with some more specific questions. What impact will current technological, economic and global/local shifts have on what we might call the cultural and sociological state-regulated aspects of the media, on the future of 'public service broadcasting', and on the importance of television *per se*? To what extent can 'generalist' terrestrial, free-to-air channels remain committed to addressing diverse and distinct local audiences? How local can local channels be to still gain profit from advertising? And what chance do Black media practitioners have of developing a powerful counter-force in a rapidly metamorphosizing marketplace preoccupied with aggressive global marketing strategies? There is a bigger question about what national image we are choosing to project not just locally, to ourselves, but also now to the rest of the world as the marketplace expands itself globally. Perhaps these are nostalgic concerns when we reflect on a terrestrial, 'public-service' based history which has also seen piecemeal offering after smokescreen solution used to harness discontent, subsume community activism, quiet radical ventures and contain talent in powerless spaces (or lack of talent in powerful spaces).

Whilst Britain's public service ethos has proved to be important for holding certain 'minority-sensitive' regulatory ideals in place and for maintaining a degree of regard for classic forms of public service programming (education, news, multicultural strands, regional programming), to date, it has also been unable to resolve – in consistent ways – the acute conceptual incongruities between universality of citizenship (intrinsically based on the notion of an 'ideal citizen') and the actual differences of and multiplicity within ethnic and other diversities.

If the overall tone of this conclusion sounds pessimistic at worst, or sceptical at best, then it is not supposed to, for my overriding argument is that television has the power to change and 'work' in a number of different ways, and that the best evidence of this is in its past. We have encountered, en route, the ways in which the medium's core ideals have constructed certain important 'ethical' parameters around the structure of race representation. We need not aspire towards more 'truthful' representations of Blackness, but towards ones that are more diverse, aesthetically innovative, informative, respectful and sometimes more accurate – although of course, much of the problem lies in the fact that these are arguably terms as ambiguous and subjective as early Reithian ones. We need to boost resources in order to invest in better, more diverse kinds of programming; open up the image to new kinds of knowledge; rethink our national heritage; invest in Black on and off-screen talent; and support the new forms of culture as much as the new forms of commercialism. 'Public service' television has its own responsibilities and indeed, powers, to generate important, radical and influential notions of 'race', identity and difference for us all, and as such, the industry is arguably too important to leave to the industry alone. The future could further erode even these fragile defences.

notes

1 See Hoare and Nowell-Smith, 1971: 326 for important arguments about how 'common-sense' produces 'the folklore of the future'.

2 When Craig Phillips, a White working-class northern male, won the UK version of the reality TV show, *Big Brother* (Channel 4, 2000), it was widely agreed that the public liked him because he was 'just an ordinary person' – unlike, one presumes, the two runners-up, Darren, a young Black Londoner and Anna, a lesbian former-nun.

3 Littlejohn presented ITV's *Thursday Night Live*, appeared as a regular panel-guest on the topical discussion programme *The Sundays* (Channel 4, 1998) and had his own satellite show *Littlejohn: Live and Unleashed* (Sky 1, 1998).

4 See interview with Bushell in Phillips and Phillips (1998: 268–9).

bibliography

Ainley, Beulah (1998) *Black Journalists, White Media*. Stoke-on-Trent: Trentham Books.

Akomfrah, John (1983) 'Black Independent Filmmaking: A Statement by the Black Audio Film Collective', *Artrage: Inter-Cultural Arts Magazine*, 3/4, Summer.

Alexander, Karen (1989) 'Mothers, Lovers and Others'. *Monthly Film Bulletin*, 56, no. 669: 314–16.

Annan, Lord (1977) *Report of the Committee on the Future of Broadcasting*, Annan Committee on Broadcasting. London: HMSO, Cmnd 6753.

Anthias, Floya and Yuval-Davis, Nira (1992) *Racialized Boundaries: Race, Nation, Gender, Colour and Class and the Anti-Racist Struggle*. London and New York: Routledge.

Anwar, Muhammad (1978) *Who Tunes In To What?*, London: Commission for Racial Equality.

Anwar, Muhammad and Shang, Anthony (1982) *Television in a Multi-Racial Society: A Research Report*. London: Commission for Racial Equality.

Baehr, Helen and Dyer, Gillian (1987) *Boxed In: Women and Television*. London: Pandora.

Bailey, Ain (1994) 'New Imaginings' (Interview with Alrick Riley), *Black Film Bulletin*, 2(2) summer: 6–7.

Bailey, David A. and Hall, Stuart (1992) 'Critical Decade: An Introduction', and 'The Vertigo of Displacement: Shifts within Black Documentary Practices' in *Critical Decade: Black-British Photography in the 80s*. Ten-8 Photo Paperback, 20 (3), Spring: 4–7, 14–23.

Barker, Martin (1982) *The New Racism*. London: Junction Books.

Barnett, Steven, Seymour, Emily and Gaber, Ivor (July 2000) 'From Callaghan to Kosovo: Changing Trends in British Television News 1975–1999'. London: University of Westminster and Goldsmiths College.

Barthes, Roland (1990) *S/Z*, trans. Richard Miller. Oxford: Basil Blackwell.

Bennett, Tony (1981) *Poplar Culture: Themes and Issues 1*. Milton Keynes: Open University Press: 77–86.

Bennett, Tony (1986) 'Introduction: Popular Culture and the ' "Turn to Gramsci" ', in T. Bennett, C. Mercer and J. Woollacott (eds), *Popular Culture and Social Relations*. Milton Keynes: Open University Press.

Bennett, Tony, Boyd-Bowman, Susan, Mercer, Colin and Woollacott, Janet (1981) *Popular Television and Film*. London: BFI Publishing.

Bhabha, Homi K. (1983) 'The Other Question', *Screen*, 24 (6): 18–36.

Bhabha, Homi K. (1990) *Nation and Narration*. London: Routledge.

Bhabha, Homi K. (1994) *The Location of Culture*. London: Routledge.

Birt, John (1980) Press Release Launching London Weekend Television's London Minorities Unit. *Broadcast*, 1040, 14.1.80: 6.

Blanchard, Simon (ed.) (1982) *What's This Channel Four?* London: Comedia.

Bogle, Donald (1991) *Toms, Coons, Mammies, Mulattoes and Bucks: An Interpretative History of Blacks in American Films*. New York: Continuum.

Bourne, Stephen (1998) *Black in the British Frame: Black People in Film and Television 1896–1996*. London and New York: Cassell.

Brandt, George W. (1981) *British Television Drama*. Cambridge: Cambridge University Press.

Briggs, Adam and Cobley, Paul (1998) *The Media: An Introduction*. London and New York: Longman.

Briggs, Asa (1995) *History of Broadcasting in the Uniterd Kingdom Vols 1–5*. Oxford: Oxford University Press.

Broadcasting Research Unit (1985) *The Public Service Idea*. London: Broadcasting Research Unit.

Brown, Marina Salandy (ed.) (1983) *Black Media Workers Association Register*.

Bryant, Steve (1989) *The Television Heritage*. London: BFI Publishing.

CRE (1979) *Broadcasting in a multi-Racial Society*. London: Commission for Racial Equality.

Cashmore, Ernest and Troyna, Barry (1982) *Black Youth in Crisis*. London: George Allen & Unwin.

Central Office of Information (1997) *Aspects of Britain: Ethnic Minorities*. London: The Stationery Office.

Centre for Contemporary Cultural Studies (CCCS) (1982) *The Empire Strikes Back: Race and Racism in 70s Britain*. London: Hutchinson.

Cham, M.B and Andrade-Watkins, C. (eds) (1988) *Blackframes: Critical Perspectives on Black Independent Cinema*. Cambridge, MA: Celebration of Black Cinema, Inc. and MIT Press.

Chambers, Iain (1986) *The Metropolitan Experience*. London and New York: Methuen.

Chambers, Iain and Curti, Lidia (eds) (1996) *The Post-colonial Question: Common Skies, Divided Horizons*. London: Routledge.

Coakley, Jay J. (1994) *Sport in Society: Issues and Controversies*. St. Louis, MO: Mosby Publishing.

Cohen, P. and Bains, S. (eds) (1988) *Multi-Racist Britain*. Basingstoke: Macmillan.

Cohen, Philip and Gardner, Carl (eds) (1982) *It Ain't Half Racist, Mum: Fighting Racism in the Media*, Campaign Against Racism in the Media. London: Comedia.

Cohen, Stanley (1972) *Folk Devils and Moral Panics: The Creation of the Mods and Rockers*. London: MacGibbon and Kee.

Cohen, S. and Young, J. (eds) (1973) *The Manufacture of News*. London: Constable.

Collings, Rex (ed.) (1992) *Reflections: Selected Writings and Speeches of Enoch Powell*. London: Bellew Publishing.

Commission for Racial Equality (CRE) (1996) *Channels of Diversity*, Seminar Report.

Corner, John (ed.) (1991) *Popular Television in Britain: Studies in Cultural History*. London: British Film Institute.

Corner, John (1995) *Television Form and Public Address*. London: Edward Arnold.

Cottle, Simon (ed.) (2000) *Ethnic Minorities and the Media: Changing Cultural Boundaries*. Buckingham and Philadelphia: Open University Press.

Cripps, Thomas (1993) *Making Movies Black; the Hollywood Message: Movies from World War Two to the Civil Rights Era*. New York and Oxford: Oxford University Press.

Crusz, Robert (1985) 'Black Cinemas, Film Theory and Dependent Knowledge' *Screen*, 26 (3–4): 152–6.

Cumberbatch, Guy and Woods, Samantha (1996) *Portrayals of Minority Groups on BBC Television*. Key Research Findings 1 and 2 Communications Research Group, Aston University, Birmingham.

Cumberbatch, Guy, Gauntlett, Sally, Richards, Maxine and Littlejohns, Victoria (2000) *Top 10 TV: Ethnic Minority Group Representation on Popular Television*. The Communications Research Group for the Commission for Racial Equality.

Curran, James, Ecclestone, Jake, Oakley, Giles and Richardson, Alan (eds) (1986) *Bending Reality: The State of the Media*. London: Pluto Press.

Curran, James and Seaton, Jean (1988) *Power Without Responsibility: The Press and Broadcasting in Britain*. London and New York: Routledge.

Daniels, Therese and Gerson, Jane (eds) (1989) *The Colour Black: Black Images in British Television*. London: BFI Publishing.

De Nitto, D. (1985) *Film: Form and Feeling*. New York: Harper and Row.

Diawara, Manthia (1993) *Black American Cinema*. New York and London: Routledge, American Film Institute Readers Series.

Donald, James and Rattansi, Ali (eds) (1992) *'Race', Culture and Difference*. London: Sage Publications.

Dowmunt, Tony (ed.) (1993) *Channels of Resistance: Global Television and Local Empowerment*. London: BFI Publishing.

Dunant, Sarah (ed.) (1994) *The War of the Words: The Political Correctness Debate*. London: Virago.

Dyer, Richard (1987) *Heavenly Bodies: Film Stars and Society*. London: Macmillan.

Dyer, Richard (1993) *The Matter of Images: Essays on Representation*. London: Routledge.

Dyer, Richard (1995) 'The Colour of Entertainment' *Sight and Sound*, November: 28–31.

Dyer, Richard (1997) *White*. London and New York: Routledge.

Dyja, Eddie (ed.) (1997) *BFI Film and Television Handbook 1998*. London: BFI Publishing.

Eagleton, T. (1991) *Ideology: an Introduction*. London: Verso.

Ellis, John (1983) 'Channel 4: Working Notes', *Screen*, 24 (6): 37–51.

Elsaesser, Thomas (1984) 'Images For England (and Scotland, Ireland, Wales . . .). *Monthly Film Bulletin*, September.

Erlrich, Cherry (1986) *The Erlrich Report. London: BBC*.

Fanon, Frantz (1986) *Black Skin, White Masks*, trans. Charles Lam Markmann. London: Pluto Press (originally published in 1952).

Fiske, John (1982) *Introducing Communication Studies*. London: Methuen.

Foucault, Michel (1980) 'Truth and Power', in C. Gordon (ed.) *Power/Knowledge: Selected Interviews and Other Writings 1972–1977*. New York: Harvester.

Foucault, Michel (1982) 'The Subject and Power' in H.L. Dreyfus and P. Rabinow (eds), *Michel Foucault: Beyond Structuralism and Hermeneutics*. Brighton: Harvester.

Frachon, Claire and Vargaftig, Marion (eds) (1995) *European Television: Immigrants and Ethnic Minorities*. London: John Libbey.

Freud, Sigmund (1977*) On Sexuality: Three Essays on the Theory of Sexuality and Other Works*, Volume 7. Harmondsworth: Penguin.

Frith, Simon (ed.) (1988) *Facing The Music: Essays on Pop, Rock and Culture*. New York: Pantheon.

Frith, S., Goodwin, A. and Grossberg, L. (eds) (1993) *Sound and Vision: The Music Video Reader*. Routledege, London.

Fryer, Peter (1984) *Staying Power: The History of Black People in Britain*. London and Boulder, CO: Pluto Press.

Fusco, Coco (1988) *Young British and Black: A Monograph on the Work of the Sankofa Film/Video Collective and Black Audio Collective.* New York: Hallwalls/Contemporary Arts Center.

Gaines, Jane (1988) 'White Privilege and Looking Relations: Race and Gender in Feminist Film Theory', *Screen: The Last 'Special Issue' on Race?*, 29 (4), Autumn: 12–27.

Gardner, Carl (in collaboration with Margaret Henry) (1979) 'Racism: Anti-Racism and Access Television – The Making of ' "Open Door" ', *Screen Education,* Vol. 31, Summer.

Gardner, Carl (1984) 'Populism, Relativism and Left Strategy', *Screen,* 25 (1): 45–51.

Garnham, Nick (1983) 'Public Service Versus The Market', *Screen,* 24 (1): 6–27.

Ghani, Atif and Rashid, Ian (1994) 'Beyond Destination, Beyond Identity' *Fuse Magazine,* 18(1): Winter.

Giddens, A. (1990) *The Consequences of Modernity.* Cambridge: Polity Press.

Gillespie, Marie (1995) *Television, Ethnicity and Cultural Change.* London and New York: Routledge.

Gilman, Sander (1985) *Difference and Pathology: Stereotypes of Sexuality, Race and Madness.* Ithaca, NY: Cornell University Press.

Gilroy, Paul (1981–82) 'You can't fool the youths . . . Race and class formation in the 1980s', *Race and Class,* XXIII, 2–3, Autumn/Winter.

Gilroy, Paul (1983) 'C4 – Bridgehead or Bantustan?', *Screen,* 24 (4–5), Jul-Oct: 130–6.

Gilroy, Paul (1987) *There Ain't No Black in the Union Jack: The Cultural Politics of Race and Nation.* London: Hutchinson.

Gilroy, Paul (1993a) *The Black Atlantic: Modernity and Double Consciousness.* London and New York: Verso.

Gilroy, Paul (1993b) *Small Acts: Thoughts on the Politics of Black Cultures.* London: Serpent's Tail.

Gilroy, P (2000) *Between Camps: Nations, Cultures and the Allure of Race.* Harmondsworth: Allen Lane, The Penguin Press.

Gilroy, P., Grossberg, L. and McRobbie, A. (2000) *Without Guarantees: In Honour of Stuart Hall.* London and New York, Verso

Givanni, June (compiled by) (1987) *Black Film and Video List.* London: BFI Publishing.

Givanni, June (1994) 'Return to the Beloved Country'. *Black Film Bulletin,* 2(2) Summer: 3.

Givanni, June (ed.) (1995) *Remote Control: Dilemmas of Black Intervention in British Film and T.V.* London: BFI Publishing.

Gray, Herman (1995) *Watching Race: Television and the Struggle for 'Blackness'.* Minneapolis and London: University of Minnesota Press.

Greater London Council (GLC) (1986) *Third Eye: Struggle for Black and Third World Cinema.* London: Race Equality Unit, GLC.

Green, Geffrey, P. (1987) 'The High Society and Black Entertainers in the 1920s and 1930s', *New Community,* 13(3): Spring.

Grossberg, Lawrence, Nelson, Cary, Treichler, Paula A. (eds) (1992) *Cultural Studies.* London: Routledge.

Gutch, Robin (1984) 'Whose Telly Anyway?', *Screen,* 25 (4–5), Jul/Oct: 122–6.

Gutzmore, Cecil (1983) 'Capital, "black youth" and crime', *Race and Class,* Vol. XXV, 2: 13–30.

Hall, S. (1972) 'The social eye of Picture Post', *Working Papers in Cultural Studies,* 2. Birmingham: University of Birmingham: 71–120.

Hall, S (1973) 'Encoding and decoding in the media discourse', *Stencilled paper 7*. Birmingham: Centre For Contemporary Cultural Studies, University of Birmingham.

Hall, S. (1975) 'Television as a Medium and its Relation to Culture', *Media Series SP, 34*. Birmingham: Centre For Contemporary Cultural Studies, University of Birmingham.

Hall, S. and Jefferson, T. (eds) (1976) *Resistance through Rituals: Youth Subcultures in Post-war Britain*. London: Hutchinson.

Hall, S (1978) 'Racism and Reaction', in *Five Views of Multi-Racial Britain*. London: Commission of Racial Equality: 23–35.

Hall, S. (1980) 'Recent Developments in Theories of Language and Ideology: A Critical Note' in S. Hall, D. Hobson, D. Lowe and P. Willis (eds), *Culture, Media, Language: Working Papers in Cultural Studies (1972–1979)*. London: Hutchinson/CCCS: 157–62.

Hall, S. (1981) 'The Whites Of Their Eyes: Racist Ideologies and the Media', in George Bridges and Rosalind Brunt (eds), *Silver Linings: Some Strategies for the Eighties*. London: Lawrence and Wishart: 28–52.

Hall, S. (1982) 'The Rediscovery of Ideology: The Return of the Repressed in Media Study', in M. Gurevitch, J. Curran, T. Bennett and J. Woollacott (eds), *Culture, Society and the Media*. London: Methuen: 56–90.

Hall, S. (1983) 'The Great Moving Rights Show', in S. Hall and M. Jacques (eds), *The Politics of Thatcherism*. London: Lawrence and Wishart.

Hall, S. (1986) 'On Postmodernism and Articulation: An Interview with Stuart Hall', *Journal of Communication Inquiry*, 10 (2): 45–60.

Hall, S. (1990) 'Cultural Identity and Diaspora', in Jonathan Rutherford (ed.), *Identity: Community, Culture, Difference*. London: Lawrence and Wishart: 222–37.

Hall, S. (1991) 'The Local and The Global: Globalization and Ethnicity', in Anthony King (ed.), *Culture, Globalization and the World System*. London: Macmillan.

Hall, S. (1992) 'The Question of Cultural Identity', in S. Hall, D. Held and T. McGrew (eds), *Modernity and its Futures*. Cambridge: Polity Press: 274–316.

Hall, S. (1993) 'Culture, Community, Nation', *Cultural Studies*, 7 (3): 349–63.

Hall, S. (1995) 'The Local and the Global', *Vertigo*, 5, Autumn/Winter: 28–30.

Hall, S. (ed.) (1997) *Representation: Cultural Representations and Signifying Practices*. London, Thousand Oaks, New Delhi: Sage Publications in association with The Open University.

Hall, S., Critcher, C., Jefferson, T., Clarke, J. and Roberts, R. (1978) *Policing The Crisis: Mugging, the State and Law and Order*. London: Macmillan.

Halloran, James D., Bhatt, Arvind and Gray, Peggy (1996) *Ethnic Minorities and Television: A Study of Use, Reaction and Preferences: A Report for Channel Four*. Leicester: Centre for Mass Communication Research, University of Leicester.

Hardy, Forsyth (ed.) (1979) *Grierson on Documentary*. London: Faber and Faber.

Harris, Geoffrey (1990) *The Dark Side of Europe*. Edinburgh: Edinburgh University Press.

Hartmann, Paul and Husband, Charles (1974) *Racism and the Mass Media: A Study of the Role of the Mass Media in the Formation of White Beliefs and Attitudes in Britain*. London: Pavis Poynter.

Hebdige, Dick (1988) *Hiding in the Light: On Images and Things*. London: Routledge.

Henderson, Robert (1995) 'Is it in the blood?', *Wisden Cricket Monthly*, July, p. 9–10.

Higson, Andrew (ed.) (1996) *Dissolving Views: Key Writing on British Cinema*. London and New York: Cassell.

Hoare, Quintin and Nowell-Smith, Geoffrey (1971) *Antonio Gramsci: Selections from Prison Notebooks.* London: Lawrence and Wishart.

Hoggart, Richard (1957) *The Uses of Literacy.* Harmondsworth: Penguin Books.

Hood, Stuart (ed) (1994) *Behind The Screens: The Structure of British Television in The Nineties.* London: Lawrence and Wishart.

hooks, bell (1992) Black Looks: Race and Representation. London: Turnaround.

hooks, bell (1996) 'Talk Now, Pay Later' (Review of Girl 6), *Sight and Sound,* June: 18–22.

Horrox, Alan (1979) 'Our People', *Screen Education,* 31, Summer.

Houston, Penelope (1994) *Keepers of the Frame: The Film Archives.* London: BFI Publishing.

Husband, Charles (ed.) (1994*) A Richer Vision: The Development of Ethnic Minority Media in Western Democracies.* London/Paris: UNESCO.

Independent Television Commission (1994), *Television: The Public's View.* London: ITC Research Publication.

Independent Television Commission (1996) *Television: Ethnic Minorities' Views.* London: ITC Research Publication.

Institute of Race Relations (1979) 'Police against Black People', *Race and Class,* Pamphlet No. 6.

Institute of Race Relations (1981) *Southall: The Birth of a Black Community.* London: Campaign Against Racism and Fascism/Southall Rights.

Isaacs, Jeremy (1982) 'Channel Four – A different sort of television?', a lecture by the Chief Executive of Channel Four at the NFT, unpublished transcript, 19th January.

Jamal, Mahmood (1985) 'Dirty Linen', *Artrage,* Autumn: 17.

James, C.L.R. (1963) *Beyond a Boundary.* London: Hutchinson.

James, C.L.R. (1977) *The Future in the Present: Selected Writings.* London: Alison and Busby.

Jarvie, Grant (ed.) (1991) *Sport, Racism and Ethnicity.* London: The Falmer Press.

Jhally, Sut and Lewis, Justin (1992) *Enlightened Racism: The Cosby Show, Audiences and the Myth of the American Dream.* Boulder, CO and Oxford: Westview.

Julien, Isaac and MacCabe, Colin (1991) *Diary of a Young Soul Rebel.* London: BFI Publishing.

Kabbani, Rana (1986) *Europe's Myths Of Orient: Devise and Rule.* London: Macmillan.

Kershaw, H.V. (1981) *The Street Where I Live.* London: Book Club Associates.

Killam, G.D. (1977) *The Writings Of Chinua Achebe.* London: Heinemann.

Kohn, Marek (1995) *The Race Gallery: The Return of Racial Science.* London: Jonathan Cape.

Kovel, J. (1988) *White Racism: a Psychohistory.* London: Free Association Books.

Kureishi, Hanif (1988) *Sometime with Stephen: A Diary – Sammie and Rosie Get Laid.* Harmondsworth: Penguin.

Lambert, Stephen (1982) *Channel 4: Television With A Difference.* London: BFI Publishing.

Lukács, George (1963) *The Meaning of Contemporary Realism.* London: Merlin Press.

McLuhan, Marshall and Powers, Bruce (1989) *The Global Village: Transformations in World Life and Media in the 21st Century.* New York: Oxford University Press.

McNeill, William (1994) *Reasserting the Polyethnic Norm* in John Hutchinson and Anthony D.Smith (eds), *Nationalism.* Oxford and New York: Oxford University Press: 300–5.

McQuail, Denis (1994) *Mass Communication Theory: an Introduction*. London and New Delhi: Sage Publications.

McRobbie, Angela (ed.) (1989) *Zoot Suits and Second-Hand Dresses: An Anthology of Fashion and Music*. London: Macmillan.

MacMurraugh-Kavanagh, M.K. (1997) 'Drama' into "News": Strategies of Intervention in "The Wednesday Play" ', *Screen*, 38 (3), Autumn: 247–59.

MacShane, Denis (1979) 'Reporting Race', *Screen Education*, 31, Summer.

Macpherson, William (1999) *The Stephen Lawrence Inquiry: Report of an Inquiry by Sir William Macpherson of Cluny*, London: The Stationery Office, HMSO.

Majors, R. (1986) 'Cool Pose: The proud signature of Black survival', *Changing Men: Issues in Gender, Sex and Politics*, 17, Winter: 184–5.

Malik. Sarita (1995) 'The Perennial Search for Identity', *Black Film Bulletin*, Vol. 3(4): 13–4.

Malik, Sarita (1996) 'Beyond "The Cinema of Duty"? The Pleasures of Hybridity: Black-British Film of the 1980s and 1990s', in Andrew Higson (ed.) *Dissolving Views: Key Writing on British Cinema*. London and New York: Cassell: 202–215.

Malik, Sarita (1997) 'The New Multiculturalism' (interview with Yasmin Anwar) *Black Film Bulletin*, 5(2/3) Summer/ Autumn: 5–7.

Malik, Sarita (1998) 'The Construction of Black and Asian Ethnicities in British Film and Television', in Adam Briggs and Paul Cobley (eds), *The Media: An Introduction*. London: Longman: 308–21.

Manuel, Preethi (1986) 'The Representation of Blacks on British Television Drama 1984', Paper presented to the 1986 International Television Studies Conference in London.

Mead, C. (1985) *Champion Joe Louis: Black Hero in White America*. New York: Charles Scribner's Sons.

Mercer, Kobena (Guest Editor) (1988) *Black Film, British Cinema*, ICA Document 7. London: Institute of Contemporary Art.

Mercer, Kobena (1992) ' "1968": Periodizing Politics and Identity', in L. Grossberg, C. Nelson and P.A. Treichler (eds), *Cultural Studies*. London: Routledge: 424–49.

Mercer, Kobena (1994) *Welcome To The Jungle: Positions in Black Cultural Studies*. London: Routledge.

Mercer, Kobena and Julien, Isaac (1988) 'Race, Sexual Politics and Black Masculinity: A Dossier', in R. Chapman and J. Rutherford (eds), *Male Order: Unwrapping Masculinity*. London: Lawrence and Wishart.

Montgomery, M., Durant, A., Fabb, N., Furniss, T. and Mills, S. (1992) *Ways of Reading*. London: Routledge.

Morley, David (1992) *Television Audiences and Cultural Studies*. London and New York, Routledge.

Morley, David and Brunsdon, Charlotte (1978) *Everyday Television: 'Nationwide'*. London: BFI Publishing.

Morley, David and Chen, Kuan-Hsing (eds) (1996) *Stuart Hall: Critical Dialogues in Cultural Studies*. London and New York, Routledge.

Mulvey, Laura (1975) 'Visual Pleasure and Narrative Cinema', *Screen*, 16 (3), Autumn: 206–15.

Neale, Steve (1979–80) 'The Same Old Story: Stereotypes and Difference', *Screen Education*, 32–3: 33–7.

Neale, Steve (1981) *Genre*. London: BFI Publishing.

Newcomb, Horace (ed.) (1997) *Encyclopedia of Television*. Chicago, IL: Museum of Broadcast Communications.

Nichols, B. (ed.) (1976) *Movies and Methods*. Berkeley: University of California Press (originally published in 1969).

Nichols, Bill (1990–91) 'Embodied Knowledge and the Politics of Location', *Cineaction*, 23, Winter: 14–21.

Owusu, K. (1986) *The Struggle for Black Arts in Britain: What Can We Consider Better Than Freedom?* London: Comedia.

Owusu, K. (1988) *Storms of the Heart: an Anthology of Black Arts and Culture*. London: Camden Press.

Owusu, K. (2000) *Black British Culture and Society: A Text Reader*. London and New York: Routledge.

Parekh, Bhikhu (1989) 'The Rushdie Affair and the British Press', *Social Studies Review*, November.

Parekh, Bhikhu and Bhabha, Homi (1989) 'Identities on Parade', *Marxism Today*, June.

Park, James (1982/3) 'Four Films', *Sight and Sound*, 52 (1): 8–12.

Patterson, Sheila (1969) *Immigration and Race Relations in Britain, 1960–67*. London: Open University Press for IRR.

Peach, Ceri (1969) *West Indian Migration to Britain: A Social Geography*. London: Open University Press for IRR.

Perkins, T.E. (1979) 'Rethinking Stereotypes', in M. Barrett, P. Corrigan, A. Kuhn and J. Wolff (eds), *Ideology and Cultural Production*. London: Croom Helm.

Petley, Julian (1989) 'Possessed by Memory' (Interview with Black Audio Film Collective), *Monthly Film Bulletin*, 56 (668) September: 260–1.

Philips, Caryl (2000) Interview in *Black Film Bulletin*, 8(1): 1–2.

Phillips, Mike and Phillips, Trevor (1998) *Windrush: The Irresistible Rise of Multi-Racial Britain*. London: HarperCollins Publishers.

Pieterse, Jan Nederveen (1992) *White On Black: Images of Africa and Blacks in Western Popular Culture*. New Haven, CT and London: Yale University Press.

Pines, Jim (1975) *Blacks in Film: A Survey of Racial Themes and Images in American Film*. London: Studio Vista.

Pines, Jim (1988) 'The Cultural Context of Black-British Cinema', in Mbye B.Cham and Andrade-Watkins, C. (eds), *Blackframes: Critical Perspectives on Black Independent Cinema*. Cambridge, MA: Celebration of Black Cinema Inc: The MIT Press: 26–36.

Pines, Jim (ed.) (1992) *Black and White in Colour: Black People in British Television Since 1936*. London: BFI Publishing.

Pines, Jim (1997) 'British Cinema and Black Representation' in Robert Murphy (ed.), *The British Cinema Book*. London: BFI Publishing: 207–16.

Pines, Jim and Willemen, Paul (eds) (1989) *Questions of Third Cinema*. London: BFI Publishing.

Powell, Enoch (1969) *Freedom and Reality*. Farnham: Elliot Right Way Books.

Rai, Alok (1992) 'Black Skin, Black Masks', *Framework* 38/39: 74–86.

Ramdin, Ron (1999) *Reimaging Britain: 500 Years of Black and Asian History*. London and Sterling, VA: Pluto Press.

Reid, Robert (1960) 'An Experiment in Television Reporting', *The Listener*, 1 December: 980–2.

Renov, Michael (1993) *Theorizing Documentary*. London and New York: AFI Film Readers, Routledge.

Richards, Michael and French, David (1996) 'From Global Development to Global Culture?', in D. French and M. Richards (eds), *Contemporary Television: Eastern Perspectives*. New Delhi and London: Sage Publication: 22–48.

Robins, Kevin, (1991) 'Tradition and Translation: National Culture in its Global Context', in J. Corner and S. Harvey (eds), *Enterprise and Heritage: Crosscurrents of National Culture*. London: Routledge: 28–41.

Robinson, Andrew (1985–86) 'Boys from the Currystuff' (an interview with Farrukh Dhondy), *Sight and Sound*, Winter: 14–18.

Romney, Jonathan and Wootton, Adrian (eds) (1995) *Celluloid Jukebox: Popular Music and the Movies since the 1950s*. London: BFI Publishing.

Rose, E.J.B. (1969) *Colour and Citizenship: A Report on British Race Relations*. London: Oxford University Press.

Ross, Karen (1996) *Black and White Media: Black Images in Popular Film and Television*. Oxford: Polity Press.

Runnymede Trust (2000) *The Future of Multi-Ethnic Britain: The Parekh Report*. London: Profile Books.

Rushdie, Salman (1988) 'Minority Literatures in a Multi-Cultural Society', in Kirtsen Holst Peterson and Anna Rutherford (eds), *Displaced Persons*. Sydney: Dangaroo Press: 32–42.

Rushdie, Salman (1991) *Imaginary Homelands*. London: Granta.

Rutherford, Jonathan (ed.) (1990) *Identity: Community, Culture, Difference*. London: Lawrence and Wishart.

Said, Edward (1993) *Culture and Imperialism*. London: Vintage.

Scannell, Paddy (1979) 'The Social Eye of Television 1946–55' in *Media, Culture and Society*, 1 (1), January: 97–106.

Scannell, Paddy and Cardiff, David (1991) *A Social History of British Broadcasting*, Vol. One *1922–1939*. Oxford: Basil Blackwell.

Scarman, Lord (1981) *The Brixton Disorders 10–12 April 1981*. London: HMSO, Cmnd. 8427.

Scarman, Lord (1983) *The Scarman Report: The Brixton Disorders*, 10–12 April, 1981. Harmondsworth: Penguin.

Schlesinger, P. (1991) *Media, State and Nation: Political Violence and Collective Identities*. London: Sage Publications.

Searle, Chris (1990) 'Race before Wicket: Cricket, Empire and the White Rose', in *Race and Class*, 31 (3), January–March: 31–60.

Self, David (1984) *Television Drama: An Introduction*. Basingstoke: Macmillan.

Seymour-Ure, Colin (1974) *The Political Impact of the Mass Media*. London: Constable.

Sharma, Sanjay, Hutnyk, John and Sharma, Ashwani (eds) (1996) *Dis-Orienting Rhythms: The Politics of the New Asian Dance Music*. London: Zed Books.

Shohat, Ella (1991) 'Gender and Culture of Empire: Towards a Feminist Ethnography of the Cinema', *Quarterly Review of Film and Video*, 13 (1–3): 45–84.

Sivanandan, A. (1976) *Race and Class*, Vol. XVII, no. 4: Spring.

Sivanandan, A. (1982) *A Different Hunger: Writings on Race and Resistance*. London: Pluto.

Sivanandan, A. (ed.) (1983) 'British Racism: The Road to 1984', *Race and Class*, Vol. 25 (2), Autumn.

Smith, Celina (ed.) (1996) *Transmission Impossible! – Serving Ethnic Minority Audiences Into the 21st Century*. Edinburgh International Television Festival, 1996: Session Report, November.

Snead, James (1994) *White Screens, Black Images –Hollywood From the Dark Side – James Snead*, (ed. Colin MacCabe and Cornel West). London and New York: Routledge.

Solomos, John (1989) *Race & Racism in Contemporary Britain*. Basingstoke: Macmillan Education.

Sreberny-Mohammadi, Annabelle and Ross, Karen (1996) *Black Minority Viewers and Television,* Key Research Findings 3. Leicester: Centre for Mass Communication Research, Leicester University.

Stern, Lesley (1982) 'The Body as Evidence', *Screen*, 23 (5), November–December: 38–60.

Stevens, P. and Willis, C. (1979) 'Race, Crime and Arrests'. *Home Office Research Study, no. 58.* London: HSMO.

Steward, Sue and Sheryl Garratt (1984) *Signed Sealed and Delivered: True Life Stories of Women In Pop.* London and Sydney: Pluto Press.

Strinati, D. (1995) *An Introduction to Theories of Popular Culture.* London: Routledge.

Swallow, Norman (1966) *Factual Television.* London: Focal Press.

Troyna, Barry (1981) *Public Awareness and the Media: A Study of Reporting on Race.* London: Commission for Racial Equality.

Tumber, Howard (1982) *Television and the Riots.* London: British Film Institute/Broadcasting Unit.

Twitchin, John (ed.) (1988) *The Black and White Media Book.* Stoke-on-Trent: Trentham Books.

Van Loon, Joost (1995) 'Televising Black Youth: Myth, Race and Violence in Urban Riots', unpublished paper, University of Wales College of Cardiff.

Vahimagi, Tise (1994) *British Television.* Oxford and New York: Oxford University Press.

Waites, Bernard, Tony Bennett and Graham Martin (eds) (1981) *Popular Culture.* London and New York, Routledge.

Wallace, Michele and Dent, Gina (eds) (1992) *Black Popular Culture.* Seattle, OR: Bay Press.

Walmsley, A. (1992) *The Caribbean Artists Movement 1966–72: A Literary and Cultural History.* London: New Beacon Press.

Wambu, Onyekachi and Kevin Arnold (1999) *A Fuller Picture: The Commercial Impact of Six British Films with Black Themes in the 1990s.* London: Black Film Bulletin and British Film Institute

Werbner, Prina and Anwar, Muhammad (eds) (1991) *Black and Ethnic Leaderships: The Cultural Dimensions of Political Action.* London and New York: Routledge.

West, Cornel (1990) 'The New Cultural Politics of Difference', in Russell Ferguson, Martha Gever, Trinh T. Minh-ha and Cornel West (eds), *Out There: Marginalization and Contemporary Cultures.* Cambridge, MA: MIT Press in association with the New Museum of Contemporary Art: 19–36.

White, Hayden (1972) 'The Forms of Wildness: Archeology of an Idea', in E. Dudley and M.E. Novak (eds), *The Wild Man Within: An Image in Western Thought from the Renaissance to Romanticism.* Pittsburgh, PA: University of Pittsburgh Press 3–38.

Williams, Raymond (1958) *Culture and Society 1780–1950.* Harmondworth: Penguin Books.

Williams, Raymond (1974) *Television, Technology and Cultural Form.* London: Fontana.

Williams, Raymond (1976) *Keywords: A Vocabulary of Culture and Society.* London: Fontana.

Williams, Raymond (1977) 'A Lecture on Realism', *Screen*, 18 (1), Spring.

Wilson, Amrit (1978) *Finding A Voice: Asian Women in Britain.* London: Virago.

Woffinden, Bob (1988) 'Blacking Up, Blacking Down', *The Listener,* 119 (3069), 30 June: 10–11.

Young, Lola (1996) *Fear of the Dark: 'Race', Gender and Sexuality in the Cinema.* London and New York: Routledge.

Index

Note: Illustrations are indicated by page references in *italics*.